THE
GANGSTER'S
COUSIN

GROWING UP IN THE LUCIANO FAMILY

SALVATORE "SAL" LUCANIA

WILDBLUE
PRESS

WildBluePress.com

THE GANGSTER'S COUSIN published by:

WILDBLUE PRESS
P.O. Box 102440
Denver, Colorado 80250

WILDBLUE PRESS is registered at the U.S. Patent and Trademark Offices.

ISBN 978-1-948239-27-1   Trade Paperback
ISBN 978-1-948239-26-4   eBook

Editing by Cynthia Kellogg

Interior Formatting/Book Cover Design by Elijah Toten
www.totencreative.com

THE
GANGSTER'S
COUSIN

TABLE OF CONTENTS

FOREWORD

I was ten years old when I first found out I was the cousin and namesake of the infamous Charles "Lucky" Luciano, whose real name was Salvatore Charles Lucania, like mine. I didn't really know what that meant at the time, but from the respectful way people spoke about him, I remember thinking, *I want that.* He had power, money, and was fiercely smart. By all personal accounts, he was a soft-spoken, charismatic, generous man who knew how to deal with life. He made his money outside the law, so he was an outlaw. Yet contrary to all public accounts, he never harmed anyone.

I'm now seventy-six years old, and looking back, I can see how our lives were similar in many ways—I think I've been the lucky one.

PROLOGUE

I didn't realize as a child that my life was vastly different from the lives of most people. I spent a lifetime looking for a thread that would help me make sense of it all. Here's what I came up with:

There are four classes that make up all societies. These societies are governed by laws created by the wealthy few who neither intended to, nor have ever had to live under them. Those few are referred to as our leaders, or the *ruling class*, if you will. Politicians are not the leaders; they are the paid help. The real leaders pay the politicians to do their work for them.

The next class is the *law-abiding citizens*. They live under these laws because they are indoctrinated at a very early age to obey them. They mistakenly believe that laws are somehow rooted in moral principles rather than the resolve of the ruling class to protect their power and wealth, and, most importantly, to maintain control of the citizens who actually generate that wealth.

Only a small segment of the population truly understands the intent of these laws and the nature of those who create them. This segment has two sub-classes: the "criminals" and the "outlaws."

The criminal class survives by taking from others, by any means, what does not belong to them (not so different from the ruling class).

Then there are the outlaws. Outlaws see through the game. They see very clearly the life of the lower class to which they and their families are relegated, and they are having none of it.

Outlaws are different from criminals. For a criminal to make money, someone has to lose money. This is immoral. No one loses anything when the outlaw makes money. There is a difference between robbing someone at gunpoint and being a bookie or growing pot. Making book and growing pot may cross legal lines created by the elite ruling class, but neither is inherently immoral.

I was born an outlaw in outlaw culture. I refused to be forced into the powerless class of the ordinary, law-abiding citizen. I always saw things from outside the box because I was born outside the box, so I was free to think for myself. This does not mean I did illegal things my whole life. I did not. Whatever I did through the years to make a living, I kept one rule: *Do no harm.*

I am seventy-five years old now. I've lived through almost eight decades. I turned sixteen in October of 1959. Two months later the sixties arrived, and with it, a new decade of huge cultural change and experimentation.

Self-betterment groups like *est* and Scientology sprang up all over the country, followed by widespread inner exploration through various religions and gurus. I spent years involved in these "spiritual" adventures trying to find the answer to the question, *Who am I?* Only to realize after years of disappointment that I was asking the wrong question. If you want to know who you are, find out what made you who you are now. That will tell you everything you need to know.

I was born Salvatore Charles Lucania, a second-generation Sicilian in East Harlem, on October 19, 1942. I had an older cousin, also named Salvatore Charles Lucania, who became the infamous Lucky Luciano. I'm sure this had something to do with my outlaw view of life.

My early mentor was my father's cousin Carl Lucania. He was Lucky's nephew and my father's closest friend. It is always difficult for a young person to step out into the world on their own for the first time. My own entrance into the world was a little more complicated owing to the fact I was married at sixteen and had three children by the time I was twenty.

My life was a lot of things, but one thing it was not, was *boring*. When I first decided to write this book some twenty years after I left New York, it was in response to a question I was often asked here in California: "What was it like to grow up in East Harlem in the forties, fifties, and sixties?" I didn't originally intend to write an autobiography, but rather a day-in-the life kind of read with all its colorful characters.

Be that as it may, this book is the end result. Come along for the ride. If nothing else, I think you will be entertained.

CHAPTER 1

THE PERFUME BUSINESS

I started bootlegging Chanel No. 5 perfume in 1959, when I was sixteen. I got into the business through my cousin Carl, who first introduced me to Cue Ball Kelly that same year. Kelly owned the 7-11 pool hall in Midtown Manhattan. He was also the ref for Brunswick's TV Pool Tournaments.

Kelly was short, Friar Tuck bald, stocky, and fiftyish, His complexion, like his hair, was cadaver gray. Besides running the pool hall, Kelly was in the bootleg perfume business, the subject of our meeting that day. Arranged by my cousin Carl, a member of the Gambino Family, this meeting was to kick off my "business career." Kelly had only one line of perfume, Chanel No. 5, which at the time sold for twenty-five dollars an ounce.

I was excited but nervous. It was highly unusual for someone my age to be given this opportunity. This was my way out of the limitations of Harlem. These men were high rollers to a boy like me.

The two-landing walk up was dimly lit by a nineteenth-century alabaster light that hung from a long, dirt-encrusted chain. *It must have been gaslight,* I thought to myself. The wooden stairs creaked, and the stairwell smelled like an abandoned warehouse.

It was strangely quiet as I approached the swinging green doors of my destination, the loft. I stepped through into a fog of cigarette smoke with scant patches of light. When my eyes adjusted, I was surprised how crowded and large the hall was.

About twenty ornately carved walnut pool tables with a Mark Twain-era look about them were placed throughout the area. Six were in action, but action was what this joint was all about. There were at least thirty guys in the hall watching different games. You could tell by the seriousness of the spectators that this was a high-stakes place. *The Hustler* should have been filmed here.

"Hey Butch," Carl called out. "Over here!"

I loved Carl. He was my father's first cousin, thirty years my senior. Out of respect, I always called him Uncle, as I did with all my older relatives. His charm was his self-assured attitude. "Know what to say, who to say it to, and you can get anything you want done," Carl would say. He was right, except for one detail. You also needed access, but Carl always had access.

"Kelly, this is my nephew Butch," he proudly introduced me.

"How are you, Butch?" Kelly smiled warmly as he shook my hand with both of his, his eyes searching mine. I never looked away, maybe because it was natural for me or maybe I was doing the same thing he was doing. He seemed pleased by it.

Kelly got right down to business, which I liked.

"Sit down, Butch." He gestured to the curly, wire-backed chair. "Your uncle has spoken well of you. He's asked me to help set you up in my business. What do you know about perfume?"

"Nothing," I declared candidly. "Why don't you give me a crash course?"

Kelly looked at Carl across the white marble table and smiled, "I like him already."

As Kelly began to give me the rundown on the perfume business, he placed two little white boxes with black print on the table.

"This is Chanel No. 5 perfume, Butch. It is one of the most expensive perfumes on the market. It retails for twenty-five dollars an ounce. I can supply you with as many bottles as you can sell." He said it as if he were awarding me the first MacDonald's franchise.

"How good is it? How much does it come to me for? How much inventory do you have? What can you supply on a monthly basis, and what are the discounts for quantities," I asked, almost in one breath.

Carl and Kelly glanced at one another and started laughing. Kelly looked directly into my eyes, his blue ones lighting up, and said, "Butch, you will never be poor. Poor is a state of mind, a state you will never visit." Carl nodded his agreement.

"The quality is the same as the legit stuff. I import the bottles from France." Proudly, he opened the package and showed me the bottom of the bottle, with *France* molded into the base. "I sell it by the gross, that's 144 bottles to the case. I want five dollars a bottle; you can sell it for ten. If you give me ten days' notice, I can deliver ten to fifteen cases at a clip."

My mind was racing in two directions as he spoke. I was doing calculations in my head, trying to figure out how to sell those quantities.

After that first meeting, I grabbed a cab back to East Harlem, where I was born and raised. I met with Vinnie and Tom-Tom, my two partners, in the back of Joe's bar on the corner of 106th and Third Avenue.

Joe's was the classic Italian restaurant—little white octagon floor tiles, a long, old mahogany bar and checkered tablecloths. It was our main hangout. We could drink there even though we weren't eighteen. The three of us were all connected by blood to various "Mafia families," but were by no means *members* of those families. We were relatives, still in our teens.

I explained the perfume deal to them. I knew Vinnie's cousin ran a fencing operation out of a large printing plant in Jersey. I believe they printed *The New York Daily Mirror*. They would print the paper at night for the morning edition and use the facility during the day to unload hijacked trucks and distribute goods.

As I was showing them the bottles, Vinnie leaned forward, "I think the first thing we ought to do is buy the real stuff and see if it's as good as Kelly says it is. If it is, we can dump it in those quantities to the guys in Jersey."

"Yeah, but not at those prices," Tom-Tom chimed in.

"He's right, Butch, goods that sell out of the trunks of cars go for one third of the stores' retail prices. That would be about eight dollars a bottle. The fences won't pay more than ten to fifteen percent of that. That puts it between $2.50 and $3.50 for each bottle. We would have to get it for half that price to make any money."

"There go our careers in the perfume business," Tom-Tom laughed.

"Butch, let me check with Jersey, I wanna see what they will pay and what kind of quantities they can handle. You check with your cousin and see what you can do with the price."

"Okay, I will."

"Are you going to tell them it's bootleg stuff?" Tom-Tom asked.

"No, not yet. If it's as good as Kelly says it is, they won't know—or care for that matter." Vinnie casually leaned back in his chair as he spoke.

Vinnie was seventeen, a year older than me. He lived in Yonkers, where you could get a driver's license at sixteen, something you couldn't do in New York City. He drove a 1957, metallic-gray Ninety-Eight Oldsmobile Coupe. I loved that car. Standing at about five foot seven, with a round face capped by a sandy brown crew cut, he was always neatly dressed in slacks and a starched shirt.

Tom-Tom, on the other hand, was tall for a Sicilian, about five-eleven, an inch or so taller than me. He had honey-blonde, short-cropped hair and smooth white skin that tanned easily. His eyes, like mine, were more green than brown, and he spoke with a deliberate stutter, which was why we called him Tom-Tom.

I called Carl the next day to set up a meeting. We met at the Roman Gardens restaurant in Whitestone that Carl used as his "office." He and his "friends" would eat there every day, but never received a bill.

Always curious, that day I finally asked, "Uncle Carl, why doesn't Joe ever give you a bill?"

Carl smiled. "Because we're his draw. His customers come to see the gangsters. Joe's business has tripled since we started hanging out here. So tell me, what's up."

"Okay," I jumped straight into it, "so I am fairly sure I can move large quantities of the stuff, but the prices need to come way down."

"How far down is way down?" he asked, clearly enjoying the moment.

"Between $1.50 and $2 a bottle, but we would move quantities quickly and take five gross to start." I felt like I had just asked the impossible.

"Butch, Kelly would have to turn over his sources for you to get it at that price," he looked amused.

"Yeah, that's what I thought." I felt the wind coming out of my sails.

"But, let me see what I can do."

He smiled warmly at me. Carl had an olive complexion, nappy salt and pepper hair, a flat nose, and dark circles under his hazel eyes. He spoke in short, quick sentences, and was heavy for his five feet, ten inches, about 240 pounds, yet still tall for a Sicilian. Except for my father, we were all tall on that side of the family.

I didn't think Carl could do anything about the price, but he had a knack for making things happen. I liked watching him handle things. One day, a young girl from the Whitestone neighborhood came into the restaurant very upset. Carl and I were having lunch when Joe Abbondola, the owner, approached us and said, "Carl, do you have a minute."

"Sure Joe, what's up?"

"The girl I was just talking to, she's pregnant, but wants an abortion. She's a nice kid from a good Sicilian family. Do you know anyone that can do it?" Abortions were illegal in those days. He met with the girl and her parents later that evening and made a deal with them.

Carl, who was childless, set her up in an apartment and covered all her living and medical expenses. The night the child was born, he went to the hospital and gave his name as the father. A week later, he picked up the mother and her baby, a little girl whom he named Sophie, after his mother, and took her home. He and his wife raised that girl into a fine woman. It was classic Carl.

I was always amazed how Carl moved through life. He always made money but lived modestly. Once in a conversation about money he said to me, "Butch, most people don't understand money. It's not about cars, homes, and fancy things. Ultimately, money is about freedom, freedom to do what you want when you want. It's about the freedom of time to enjoy life."

"About time or life, I don't get it," I asked, perplexed.

"Listen, from the time we are born, until the day we die, all we have is time."

"Right."

"So, in that sense, the only real thing we have to spend in life is our time. Money gives us the freedom of time. How we spend that time, where and who we spend it with, determines how good our life will be.

"It's very important that you understand money is about freedom, because when someone takes your money without giving you something in return, they are robbing you of your freedom, your very life."

"You mean like taxes?" I laughed.

"Bingo!" Carl laughed too.

He called the very next day. "Meet me at Angelo's on Mulberry Street at 2:30."

When I walked into Angelo's, I saw Carl, Kelly and two other men I didn't know sitting at a large red leather booth in the back of the restaurant. They had just finished lunch and were having espresso.

I casually walked over to the table, leaned over and kissed Carl as I always did. The two men immediately stood up and shook my hand as Kelly introduced them.

"Butch, this is Fred Clark my chemist, and this is Abe Flick my printer and bottle supplier. They will supply you with all the materials you need. Between the bottles and packaging you've got fifty-one cents in the deal. The perfume comes by the gallon and works out to twenty-five cents an ounce. You will have to supply your own labor. Here is a list of what you will need to assemble the package," he explained, handing me a yellow sheet of paper. "Fred's and Abe's phone numbers are on the list. They will help you set up."

I was stunned. "Kelly, I appreciate what you are doing. I don't know what to say I…"

"Please, there is no need to thank me. This is the first time I've had the opportunity to return one of the many favors your Uncle has done for me over the years." Kelly was beaming. He looked like Saint Patrick. "Besides, you and I are the only ones doing this in the country. There is plenty of room for the both of us," he said graciously.

Kelly, Fred, and Abe got up from the table, shook my hand, wished me luck, said goodbye, and left. I sat there for a moment, reading the yellow sheet of paper: candle wax, syringe, black twine....

I looked up at Carl, "Why is he doing this?"

"He told you why. He is the kind of man who doesn't forget favors. He's the only kind of man worth doing a favor for. I've helped Kelly throughout the years. I never asked for or accepted money for what I did, but that's what makes it a favor. You will find out that being successful in life is a matter of how you handle relationships.

"Helping others is like putting money in the bank. It's rare in life when people do favors like that, but it's precisely because it's rare that it's not forgotten, unless, of course, you are dealing with a five-dollar man."

"What do you mean, a *five-dollar man?*"

"I mean, never give a five-dollar man, ten dollars. Kelly is a ten-dollar man. Had he been a five-dollar man, he'd see me as a chump. Instead, he showed gratitude. A five-dollar man will never show you gratitude or loyalty. He will never acknowledge that you had anything to do with his success. It's his way of getting something for nothing. That's what makes him a five-dollar man. So just remember, never give a five-dollar man, ten dollars."

"But, how will I know if someone is a five-dollar man?"

"You won't. That's a chance you'll have to take. People who want something from you will appear humble at first. They will tell you what you want to hear. It's after they get what they want that you'll begin to see the change in them. The first sign is the humility disappears. Later on they'll start acting arrogant. It's my experience that arrogance and stupidity are two sides of the same coin. Whenever I see one, I always see the other. The moment you notice that change, distance them, cut off any help and never have anything to do with them again," he warned.

"Just like that."

"Yes, just like that." He got louder as he spoke, "You see, arrogant people think they know it all, but no one knows it all. That's how you know they're stupid. Stupid people are dangerous. They're unpredictable. A dummy will break you quicker than a thief. I would rather deal with a smart thief. At least he's predictable; a dummy isn't. They're losers, short-term thinkers. Get them out of your life as fast as possible."

I got up from the table and gave Carl a long hug, then kissed him goodbye. He held my face in both of his thick hands, looked at me with great affection, and said, "Butch, be careful out there. Things are rarely what they seem to be."

I walked out of Angelo's a foot or two off the ground. Mulberry Street was alive with children, music, and the aromas of Italian home cooking. The redbrick buildings were not so different from the ones in Harlem, but there were many more storefront social clubs down this way. The summer brought everyone out. The men from the social clubs played cards and conducted their "business" outside, while the women sat looking out their front windows, keeping an eye on the children, watching for strangers and cops. It's what a neighborhood is about, everyone watching out for one another.

With Carl's advice bouncing around in my head, I grabbed a cab back to my neighborhood, knowing the deal would work. I also knew that what Carl just said to me was worth more than the deal itself.

"You're shittin' me. I don't believe it!" Tom-Tom said when I told him what Carl had done. "What's his cut?" he asked, as we stood on the corner in front of Joe's bar, waiting for Vinnie to pick us up.

"It's a favor," I said. "If Carl wanted a cut, he would have asked for one. We owe him a favor."

"I'll say. Wait 'til Vinnie hears this! I hope he worked out the other end."

"We'll know soon enough. Here he comes now."

Vinnie pulled up to the curb. I opened the door and jumped into the back seat. When I saw Vinnie's eyes, I knew he had scored, but he was silent. He waited for Tom-Tom to get into the front seat, then reached over him, grabbed two bottles of Chanel No. 5 out of the glove compartment, handed them to Tom-Tom and said, "One of the bottles is ours. The other is legit. See if you guys can tell the difference."

Tom-Tom and I tested the bottles. Neither of us could note any difference whatsoever.

"You'd have to be an expert to tell the difference," I said.

"Right, and that's who I gave it to," Vinnie laughed.

"Who d-d-do you know that's an expert, Vinnie?" Tom-Tom stuttered.

"My Mother. She's been using Chanel for years. Not only couldn't she tell the difference, but also, she said it lasted just as long as, if not longer than the real thing." Vinnie's eyes were dancing.

"God…God… bless your Mother, Vinnie." Tom-Tom made the sign of the cross with great authority over Vinnie's head, and then, turning to me, continued his gracious benediction.

Vinnie looked at me, then at Tom-Tom, then back at me, and broke into more laughter, "Has he been drinking that fuckin' Holy Water again?"

"Tell 'em Butch… Tell…Tell…"

I leaned over the front seat and put my hand over Tom-Tom's mouth. "Tom-Tom, if you don't calm down, you're going to have a heart attack."

I told Vinnie what Carl had done for us.

"It's seventy-six cents to us, plus labor, but I don't know what's involved with labor. We need to pick up the materials and assemble thirty or forty bottles to see how long it takes."

"Then what?" Tom-Tom asked.

"Well, I was thinking that my mother makes dresses on an assembly line. That's probably what we are going to need—an assembly line. Anyway, she does piece work and gets a set price for each specific piece of the garment she completes. That way the manufacturing costs are fixed. If we could get the packaging done for twenty-five or thirty cents a bottle, we could make a killing."

We drove to Rao's on 114th Street to have lunch and figure out how to get the packaging done. Rao's had only about six or seven tables, but it was home cooking. On the way, Vinnie broke the news.

"How about $3.50 a bottle for the first ten cases, and $3.25 for the second? That's per week."

There was silence in the car for about twenty seconds.

"That's about three grand a week," I said.

"Thirty-six hundred," Vinnie shot back.

This time Tom-Tom was speechless. He remained that way until after we ordered lunch. "Tom-Tom, what's going on in that head of yours? I can smell the wood burning from here."

"I think I have the solution to our labor problem. My cousin Joanne does piece work, too, but she does it with jewelry. She, her three daughters, and her two sisters put in sixty man-hours a week, and they make less than $50 each. Our project is perfect for them. Just give me a couple days to work it out."

Two days later, Tom-Tom had the deal worked out. Four weeks later, we shipped our first ten cases. We made $3,600. That's more than my mother made in a year. Joanne made $360, almost half her husband's monthly salary. She paid her sisters $200 and stopped working at her other job. Everyone was happy, especially our customers.

I called Carl the day I got my first "paycheck" of $1,200. "Uncle Carl, I just got my first paycheck. I wanna take you to dinner. You name the place."

"Patsy's on 118th. I haven't been there in years."

Patsy's was an old Sicilian restaurant. It looked very much like the restaurant in *The Godfather* where Michael kills the cop. Octagon tiles on the floor and embossed tin ceilings, with a nineteenth-century bar and nineteenth-century waiters. The music was always Italian. This part of Harlem was virtually unknown to outsiders.

Whenever Harlem is mentioned, generally people think of Black Harlem or Spanish Harlem. Black Harlem is West Harlem. East Harlem, later to become Spanish Harlem, was not just Italian, but mostly Sicilian. In those days it was referred to as the *other Little Italy*.

There's a big difference between Italians and Sicilians, both in language and mentality. Italians cannot speak or understand the Sicilian language, which is largely rooted in Greek and Arabic, rather than Latin. Sicily suffered three thousand years of occupation. The citizens survived these occupations by creating and living by their own rules. The so-called Mafia, or Black Hand, as it was called in those days, was a political organization that functioned as liaison between the occupied and the occupiers. A kind of shadow government, if you will. Not much different from our own political parties today. Hence, the Sicilian mentality, which could be summed up as, "There is no authority higher than our own." An attitude that suited me perfectly.

East Harlem was twenty-two blocks long, running north from 103rd Street to 125th, and eight blocks wide, beginning at the East River and running west to Madison Avenue. It was the domain of the Luciano/Genovese family, the destination of the French Connection, and the financial center for the gambling business—both east and west.

"Pasta con sarde," Carl said to the waiter—spaghetti and sardines with fennel, browned breadcrumbs and pine nuts. It's a Sicilian dish, and Patsy's was one of the few places in the city that still made it. I ordered rolled stuffed veal.

"What are you going to do with your money?" Carl asked.

"I really haven't had a chance to think much about it yet."

"You know, Butch, making money and keeping money are not the same thing. If you want to keep it, don't flaunt it. If you do, people will find ways to take it from you. Also, people can be very jealous, and jealous people will do things that you and I wouldn't think of doing.

"Keep a low profile, save enough money to live for a year without an income. That way, you'll always have the time to put another deal together. Do you understand?"

"Yes, I do."

"Good, let's eat."

"By the way, my partners send their regards and gratitude. They wanted you to know, we owe you a favor."

"That's a good sign," he said, smiling.

CHAPTER 2

NO ONE GETS OUT OF CHILDHOOD SANE

It was about 8:30 p.m. and still light outside when we walked out of Patsy's.

"Do you want me to drop you off?" Carl asked.

"No thanks. It's a nice night. I'm gonna walk. Thanks again for all the help." I meant it. I had a lot to think about now. It was still early summer. The hot, muggy nights were still weeks away. I had about a thirteen-block walk ahead of me.

The smell of the moist evening air, along with the different neighborhoods I remembered from childhood, turned out to be a walk down memory lane.

I walked south along First Avenue, going downtown towards my neighborhood. I passed Benjamin Franklin High School on 116th Street, a virtual war zone after the Puerto Ricans started attending. At one point, the cops had to be stationed on every floor. It was a beautiful redbrick building, three stories high with round white pillars. The architecture was Ben Franklin Philadelphia.

I passed Jefferson Park and Pool on 113th where I learned to swim and where an Italian gang had beat a Cuban refugee to death two years earlier. The Cuban was sitting with his girl on a park bench, unaware there were turfs where "his kind" was not allowed.

A dozen guys attacked one man who couldn't speak English while his girlfriend looked on in horror. They ripped the wooden slats off the park benches and beat this poor young man to death. Italians were very territorial and were not racially tolerant. I never understood it.

Three or four weeks prior to the incident, the same punks had tried to kill me. They were out "spic hunting"—their idea of fun—and proving how tough they were. They roamed the streets looking for Puerto Ricans or blacks they could beat senseless. A bunch of them cornered me one night. I was with Chino and Lefty, two of my Puerto Rican friends.

"What are you doing with these spics, you spic-loving motherfucker?" they demanded. Without another word, they went to work on me with stickball bats (sawed off broomsticks). Just as I was hit from behind, I grabbed the loudmouth in front of me by the throat and went down on top of him. I was going unconscious and remembered little after that.

Later, Lefty told me what happened. "Your hands were on this guy's throat like a vice. You were choking him to death and wouldn't let go."

A blast had gone off inside my head. Fear, survival instinct, and massive infusions of adrenalin kept me semiconscious, but the light of the world had begun to dim.

Lefty went on to explain, "When I saw that motherfucker point that piece at the back of your head, I closed my eyes and waited for the shot I knew was coming. I couldn't watch, Butch. Once the shot went off, I couldn't believe you were still alive."

When I regained full consciousness, I was bleeding all over my face and head. I assumed one of those wounds was a bullet grazing my head. It was hard to tell. As soon as the shot was fired, they all ran. I was livid. The adrenalin was pumping through my body like high octane.

I ran to Jimmy's candy store where Jimmy was having a private party. I ran into the hallway and banged on the backdoor of the store until Jimmy opened it, looked at me and said, "What the fuck happened to you?" I didn't answer him but went straight for his closet where he kept a shotgun.

"Butch, tell me what's going on."

I still didn't answer. I started out the door just as Chino and Lefty were coming in.

"Hey! Where the fuck are you going? You can't go out there with that fuckin' rifle!" Lefty shouted as I ducked past him.

All I could think about was killing those low-life bastards. I ran two blocks looking for them. I started getting nauseated and feeling faint. Jimmy, Lefty, and Chino pulled up in Jimmy's car and grabbed me just as I was passing out.

They drove me to Flower Fifth Avenue Hospital on 106th Street and Fifth. A year before, I had been in this same hospital with a stab wound. Puerto Ricans had stabbed me for being Italian. Now I was shot and beaten by Italians for having Puerto Rican friends.

When I got home, my mother didn't recognize me. She called my father and told him what happened. "We have to do something about this, Carl. He's going after them."

I spent the next week going to different neighborhoods asking about these guys. I knew it wouldn't be long before I found out who they were. Shit like that never stayed quiet. Two weeks later, I was standing in front of Joe's bar when my father pulled up in his 1953 brown Packard.

"Get in. I got a meeting with the Salerno brothers." My father was never long on words, so I didn't ask any questions.

The Salerno brothers, Mike and Adam, were bookies and Shylocks working out of their parking lot on 110th Street and 1st Avenue. They were "made men," that is, *real members* in the Genovese/Luciano family. My father parked the car in the lot and went into the office to talk to them. I waited outside. I had no idea what the meeting was about or why I was there.

While I was waiting, I spotted two of the guys who had attacked me. They were walking up the street in my direction but didn't see me. I grabbed a stickball bat that was leaning against the office wall and waited. I was trembling with fear and anger. I came out of the lot swinging. I caught the first one across the face. The blood poured out through his fingers and covered his face. The second one started running. I let him go and went to work on the prick I had on the ground. He curled up into a ball to protect himself, so I started jamming the end of the bat into his ribs, cracking them. Mike and Adam ran out of the office yelling at me. Mike grabbed my arms and took the bat from me.

"What the fuck do you think you're doing? We called these guys here to straighten this shit out."

I was foaming at the mouth. I looked at my father and yelled, "Why didn't you tell me about this?"

He said, "Look, Butch, Big John arranged this meeting, and as long as he's involved, you can't do this." Big John Ormento was my cousin on my mother's side of the family and the Underboss of the Genovese/Luciano family.

"These guys tried to kill me, and you want me to *talk* to them?"

"Out of respect for John, you better do this. Now let's go in the office and hear what they have to say," my father replied.

"I don't give a fuck about what they have to say."

Adam brought the other guy back to the office. The guy I nailed was sitting on the ground outside the office crying like a baby.

"Sit down, Butch," Mike motioned to a chair.

"No thanks, I'll stand."

The kid, trying to defend himself, blurted out quickly, "It was a mistake. We thought he was someone else. Monty just slapped him. He went down and hit his head on the sidewalk." I stood there looking at him, stunned by his bullshit. I picked up a large heavy glass ashtray sitting in the middle of the table and smashed it into his face.

"You mean like this?"

Mike grabbed my arm and held it tight.

"Get your fuckin' hands off me," I demanded. He let go immediately.

He looked at my father and said, "Is he crazy?"

"I'm gonna kill every fuckin' one of you. No one is going to save you from me." I stormed out of the office and started walking back to the neighborhood.

My father caught up with me. "Do you have any idea what you just did? This should not have happened."

"You're right! You should've told me about this meeting and let me kill those two bastards. I'll bet you if it was Big John's son, those two pricks would be dead already."

My father saw it was useless trying to talk to me and left me alone. Shortly afterwards, the same guys killed the Cuban in the park. They were arrested, convicted and sentenced to twenty years. As far as I was concerned, they got off easy.

After leaving my father that night, I walked passed Saint Anne's on 108th where my girlfriend Louise went to school and where I had watched them film some of *West Side Story*.

My mother and father were born and raised on 107th Street. Against all the laws of probability, they were both born Sicilian, of immigrant parents, in the same building, in the same month, the same year and with the same first name—Carmella and Carmelo.

My grandparents on my mother's side, John and Teresa Forte, never learned to speak English. They both worked full time in the garment business and later as dress manufactures. They had three children—two boys and my mother Carmella, whom they called Millie. My grandparents on my father's side, Salvatore and Suzanne Lucania, had seven children— six girls and my father Carmelo, whom they called Carl.

My grandfather Sal, who died when I was two years old, owned a barbershop on 108th Street. Unlike my mother's father, this grandfather spoke English and used his shop as a classroom to help people become citizens. He was very proud of being an American. He tried for years, unsuccessfully, to convince my mother's father to become a citizen.

My mother made dresses for forty years. She was five foot nothing, with dark brown hair and eyes. My father was five foot seven with sandy hair and blue eyes. His skin was scarred from acne as a boy, and for whatever reason, he became addicted to gambling, which kept us broke most of the time. Oddly enough, he was very talented. He could fix cars, play different instruments without lessons or experience, and invent things, but he never had a business mind.

In 1930, his cousin, the infamous Charles "Lucky" Luciano, took my father to a warehouse downtown. It was full of new equipment. Charlie told my father, "Someday this will be a big business," and offered to give him half the business to run it for him. My father turned Charlie down. The new equipment was a set of the first vending machines.

When I reached 106th and First Avenue, I turned right and started walking west, towards Second. This block and the next three blocks, Third, Lexington, and Park Avenue, is where I spent my entire youth. These four blocks and the experiences that occurred within them shaped my life forever.

My earliest memory of 106th Street between First and Second avenues was my grandmother taking me to the poultry store. I was about two or three. The chickens were alive in their cages. My grandmother would choose one and the butcher would pull it out of the cage by its legs and hold it upside down so she could inspect it. Upon her approval, he would grab the chicken by the neck, swing it around like a softball pitcher and chop its head off.

I was too small to see the rest of the process, but I could smell feathers burning. The fish store was next door. The fish were fresh, laid out on ice. The crabs were live in season, but the store always kept live eel for some reason. Those were the days when food was always fresh.

We lived in a cold-water flat on the third floor of a red brick tenement building. The arrangement was known as "railroad rooms." It was made up of four consecutive rooms: a kitchen, living room, and two bedrooms. You had to walk through each room to get to the next. There was not enough room for two beds where my older sister and I slept, so I had a fold up bed until I was able to move out on my own.

From 1944 to about 1950, there was no heat or refrigeration in our apartment. In 1950, the landlord, who also lived in the building, decided to put in steam heat, but could not afford to do it on the $29-a-month rent everyone was paying. One day, he came to each apartment and asked if he could raise the rent to pay for the heating project. The tenants agreed, and some were willing to pay a little more to make up the difference for those who could not afford the increase. Our rent went up to $45 a month.

Until that time, for heat we had a two-burner, brown enamel kerosene stove without ventilation. In the winter, my mother cut orange peels and placed them on top of the stove to cover the smell of fumes. Every winter morning, I'd wake up to the aroma of burnt orange peels and kerosene.

My mother did laundry on Saturdays with a washboard in a grey metal washtub. We had an icebox for refrigeration, which we had to drain a few times a day. Every Saturday during the summer, Tony the iceman would deliver two large blocks of ice. The ice was supposed to last all week but didn't.

Summer nights my sister and I slept on the fire escape facing the backyard. The red bricks and black-iron fire escape radiated the heat that had been absorbed all day. Then the humidity kept the heat in place like an invisible dome. It wasn't much relief, but it was social. All the other kids did the same thing.

The evening entertainment was provided by the eight bocce ball games played on the courts located in the back of Belvedere Bar in the building next to ours. The arguments among the *Ginzos*—Italian men who spoke little or no English—were the highlight of the evening. I learned almost all my Italian/Sicilian curse words from those games, as well as the Italian sign language to go along with them. I am convinced that if you tied an Italian's hands, he would be unable to speak. I've often thought about publishing an illustrated book of Italian hand and facial expressions.

My mother dried the laundry on a clothesline attached to a telephone pole in the backyard. The backyards of the four-story buildings formed a courtyard. Hanging laundry out the back window was a social event for my mother since she worked all week. My mother also kept a long clothesline with a canvas bag tied at the end. Two or three times a week, Franco, the vegetable man, would arrive with his horse-drawn wagon. He would stand on his wagon and sing out, in what he thought was English, "veg-a-ta-bulls!" My mother put money and her order in the bag and lowered her line out the front window, three floors down to the street. Franco filled the bag with her order and her change. It was actual window-shopping.

Franco gave me my first job. I was eleven years old. Every Saturday, I'd ride with him into different neighborhoods and guard his wagon, so no one could steal from it while he was doing business. I got $1.25 a day.

I created a second job for myself on Sundays—an entrepreneur at a very young age. Every Sunday, a tall, teenage Irish kid named Huey would go into the neighborhood backyards and sing Irish folk songs. It was an odd thing to do in an Italian neighborhood. I think the neighbors felt sorry for him, but they admired his spirit.

People threw change out the window for him, and I noticed he couldn't sing and pick up change at the same time. One day, after he left our yard, I went down and found about eighty cents he had missed. The following week, when Huey returned, I gave him the eighty cents. "I found this after you left last week," I explained.

He looked at the money, surprised. "How come you didn't keep it?"

"Because it doesn't belong to me. It belongs to you," I said. He looked down at me, smiled and handed me a quarter.

"What's your name, little guy?"

"They call me Butch, but my real name is Sal."

"My name is Huey. How would you like to go around with me on Sundays and pick up the money for me? I will pay you ten percent of what I make."

I was thrilled. "You got a deal, Huey." We shook hands and that was it. I ran upstairs all excited and told my mother about it.

"I don't want you to do it," she told me.

"Why?"

"I don't want people to think my son has to go around picking up change in yards." Somehow, in her mind, she would lose face. My mother was always concerned about what people thought. I did it anyway. It only lasted until the weather got cold, but I earned a few extra bucks.

A year later, I wanted her to buy a shoeshine box. I was going to go into business. I had it all worked out. Capello's Drugstore was on the corner of 105th Street and Second Avenue, about a hundred yards from where I lived. Capello's had five or six telephone booths. They functioned as the business office for the local mafia types. They were always impeccably dressed in silk or gabardine suits and cashmere topcoats, with beautiful hats and shoes.

They let the older kids wash their cars and always gave huge tips. I knew I would do well shining their shoes, but my mother wouldn't hear of it. It was too public. Later in my life and for the rest my life, when she saw I was getting into illegal ventures, she would say, "I should have let you shine shoes."

My best memory of 106th Street was the Feast of San Eugenia, which took place in early September. It brought everyone together: wise guys, neighborhood men and women, kids, shopkeepers, old and young, everybody and anybody who lived in the neighborhood—even the people who had moved out of the neighborhood for a better life returned for the event.

The food was made by the people who lived in the redbrick tenements. They cooked their homemade specialties, like handmade ravioli covered in a meat sauce that had simmered for five hours. There were grills eight feet long and two feet deep piled high with homemade Sicilian sausage on one side, onions and peppers sizzling on the other side.

My favorite spot was the zepella stand. Zepella is fried dough dusted with powdered sugar. The stand, always crowded with customers, had three large washtubs, two filled with hot oil, sitting on open fires. The other tub, filled with freshly made pizza dough, sat between the hot oil tubs. Men would pinch off pieces of dough the size of golf balls and toss them into the hot oil. The dough puffed up in seconds. Then with a hand strainer, they would scoop out six pieces at once, put them in a bag, and sprinkle them with powdered sugar. They sold for twenty-five cents a bag. I burnt my hands and mouth eating them, but it was worth it.

The highlight of the feast was the dancing saint. A large platform was constructed, upon which a five-story, pyramid-like structure was built. Starting at the bottom, large paper-mâché sculptures of saints were placed one on top of the other, each about eight feet high and nailed to the wooden frame. Each sculpture, painted in beautiful blues, reds, purples, and golds, was different. At the top stood San Eugenia.

It's difficult to imagine, but the platform holding this tower was large enough to hold a ten-piece band. Extending out from under the platform were four-by-four-inch wooden beams. Each side of the platform had two fifteen-foot extensions, eight in all. When the band started to play, some eighty men, ten on each beam, would lift this huge structure and dance down the street with it while the crowd danced around it.

The music was happy, *um-pa-pa* music, and old. It was considered an honor to be one of the men chosen to make the saint dance. They wore white T-shirts, white caps, black pants and red neckerchiefs, reminiscent of how men dressed in Italy years ago in similar festivals. This block gave me my happiest memories.

CHAPTER 3

THE DARK AGE

I spent eleven of the darkest years of my life on 106th Street between Second and Third Avenue. My mother always worked to make ends meet. Working mothers were rare in 1944. I was two when my mother put me in a Catholic Protectorate. It was the medieval version of daycare.

Franciscan nuns ran it. They were an Order started by Saint Frances of Assisi, who dressed them in brown robes, tied at the waist with a white-knotted rope hanging to their ankles on one side. Their hair and faces were encased in a white plastic hat, with a five-inch crown at the top, draped with a black veil. The sight of them scared me. I was only two and didn't know what to make of them. I wasn't sure they were women.

They were sexually suppressed women, dominated by sexually suppressed men. I can tell you from firsthand experience, those conditions do not produce spiritual, loving human beings.

The building where we were housed was joined at the rear to the grammar school I would later attend. Both buildings shared the same basement, which was converted into an auditorium. As a result, I was moved back and forth between the two for ten years, rarely seeing the light of day.

There were three other cultic "Orders" that dominated my life: The Sisters of Mercy (who had none), the Irish Christian Brothers (who were anything but brotherly), and the Jesuits (who, with help of the conquistadors, spread Christianity throughout the world by killing anyone who wouldn't be converted or subjugated by them).

The Jesuits were the scholars of the church, the gatekeepers of knowledge, language and Heaven. The church, as far as I'm concerned, was and is the model for organized crime as it exists everywhere in the world today—home of the true criminal. I have a healthy, well-earned disgust for organized religion.

I broke away from those institutions when I ended my first year at Rice High School on 124th and Lenox, just a few blocks from the Apollo Theater. This blessed event took place at the yearly dance at Power Memorial High, located in Midtown Manhattan.

The dance was held in the huge gymnasium. Some three hundred people would attend. Those in attendance were a mix of priests, nuns, and brothers of various Catholic orders, along with lay teachers that staffed the schools in the archdioceses. The rest were students and parents from all over the city.

I was sitting at a table with some friends, drinking a spiked Coke, when suddenly, I was lifted out of my chair by my left arm. I turned, looked up and there he was: Brother Duffy, my last teacher in grammar school.

He was a skinny, five foot ten, one-hundred-forty-pound, poor excuse of a man. He was pale, freckle-faced, and thin-lipped, and wore round wired-rimmed glasses. His thinning light brown hair sat on his head like a cheap wig. He wore the usual "Prince of Darkness" garb—long black robe and white collar. The shoulders of his robe were always covered with dandruff, and he smelled awful.

Duffy would spend entire days ranting about God instead of covering the six subjects a day he was there to teach. Then, he would assign the lessons as homework and expect us to pass a ten-question quiz the next day. Anyone who failed was subjected to "the strap."

The strap was two flat, three-inch wide, eighteen-inch long, one-quarter inch thick pieces of shoemaker rubber soles tied together at both ends with thin wire. If he wasn't angry, he would have you bend over his desk, situated in front of the class, and would walk back about twenty feet before running at you full speed and, *crack,* like a rifle shot, hit you as hard as he could on the buttocks. The blood would rush to your face, creating heat. The sting was unbearable; the humiliation worse. If he was angry, which was most of the time, he would take you out into the hall where no one could see and beat you mercilessly. The screams from the hallway echoed through the whole floor, terrorizing the other children.

He was a perfect model of "brotherly" love and forgiveness for a thirteen-year-old boy. Like most celibates, he had a mean streak in him a mile long.

"I am taking you home to your parents right now," he screamed in my face at the top of his lungs. I could smell the booze on his breath and see the hatred in his eyes.

I dropped the spiked Coke out of my right hand as he pulled me out of my chair by the arm. I came up with a punch from the floor and caught him between the eyes. He spun around and crashed head first into a decorated folding table full of drinks and surrounded by adults and students.

The three seconds of silence that followed seemed like an eternity to me. Then all hell broke loose. The crowd turned ugly, and like good, God-loving Irish Christians, they wanted my blood. It was like a wave of red hair and freckles falling over one another to get to me. Three of my friends formed a circle around me and got me out a side exit into the dark schoolyard.

Tony, a friend since first grade, was in a state of shock and couldn't believe what he just saw.

"Butch," Tony whispered, "Brother Duffy is on his way out here. He says he wants to talk. Do you want to do that?"

"Yeah," I heard my voice say.

The only light in the schoolyard came from the open gym door, where Duffy was making his entrance into the yard. All I could see was his silhouette. Time was suspended and everything moved into a silent slow motion. I felt like I was in a silent movie as I cracked my swollen fist into Duffy's already bloody face. It was revenge and justice for all the years of abuse, and it felt great. I remember thinking, *I'm never going to see heaven now.*

I expected to feel terrified, but didn't. Instead, I felt like a yoke was removed from my soul. I never wanted to see another one of those fucking spiritual vampires again. I was free, on my own. God, as I understood Him for years, was now relegated to the same category as Santa Claus, the Easter Bunny, and the Tooth Fairy. AMEN!

My name was being announced over the PA system when I arrived at school that Monday morning. I was to report immediately to the principal's office. Brother Sinnon, the principal, was a six-foot four inches black-haired Irishman. He was Tom Selleck handsome, with a similar demeanor.

"You've done enough to get yourself kicked out of school and put in jail," he said in a stoic voice.

"It was self-defense as I see it," I shot back without a second thought. I realized, in that moment, that he and everything he represented, no longer had any power over me. It was truly liberating.

"I'll tell you what I'm willing to do," he reasoned. "If you apologize publicly to Brother Duffy and Brother Galway," (the principal of my former grammar school) "they will not press charges, and I will find an alternate punishment other than expelling you." The word *punishment* started my blood boiling.

"Brother Galway! What's he got to do with it?"

"You attacked him while he was helping Brother Duffy off the ground," he said, looking at me and seeing that I had no memory of it at all.

"Punishment," I said, remembering all the humiliating beatings. "Here's the deal," I said, trying to control my temper, "I'll tell my parents that I want to change schools. You say nothing, and I'm out of here. In return, you have my word I won't kick Duffy's teeth in every time I see him, which is every day, since he has to pass through my block to get to work."

Losing my patience for the conversation, I asked, "Do we have a deal or not?"

"Yes," he said, realizing I was dead serious. I never looked back. I stepped out onto the streets of Harlem feeling very different. Everything looked different, too, like going from black and white to color.

CHAPTER 4

COMMUNITY

When I reached Third Avenue, I started walking toward Lexington, where my present life was playing itself out.

"Hey, Butch," Clancy yelled from his new unmarked car. Clancy had been a beat cop in the neighborhood for years and had just made detective. In those days, uniformed cops were on foot and stationed in the same neighborhood for twenty years. In fact, you couldn't be a cop in New York City unless you lived in New York City. Clancy had known me and most of my friends since we were kids. He was part of the neighborhood.

They had good police policies in those days. If Clancy or any beat cop caught a neighborhood kid doing something wrong, he wouldn't think of arresting him. Instead, he would take him to his father, who would give the son two good smacks: one for breaking the law, the other for getting caught. Kids were more afraid of their fathers than they were of jail.

"Hi, Clancy, what's up," I said warmly.

I liked Clancy. He was cheerful, funny, and had earned the respect of the neighborhood.

"I need a favor, Butch."

"Sure, what can I do for you?"

"City Hall has put a lot of heat on us to stop the blood baths that go on up here," he said, earnestly. The Italians, Puerto Ricans, Irish, and blacks had been going at it. There wasn't a day without gang violence exploding somewhere in the city.

"They've come up with a plan to deal with the gang problem. They want to open Youth Centers around the city, like the Union Settlement." These were community centers for all ages. He went on, "There's a large, vacant, double storefront right next door to Jimmy's candy store, where you and the boys hang out. They want to rent that space."

"You need to talk to the landlord, Clancy, not me."

"I know, Butch, but we need help with this project."

"Who are *we*, Clancy, cops?"

"No, Butch, they're social workers."

"What's a social worker?" I had never heard of a social worker. I'm not even sure there were social workers in 1959. These may have been the first.

"Do they have badges and answer to the captain?" I asked respectfully,

"No, they're hired by the Youth Board. It's a new department, operating directly out of the mayor's office. The mayor's idea is to get the gangs to sit down and talk to one another. Maybe even get them to play baseball or basketball against each other. The empty store, with the playground forty feet away, is ideal." Clancy knew my father and how things worked. I knew he wouldn't be here talking to me if he hadn't run it past the local "authorities," meaning mafia types.

"Okay, Clancy, so what do you want from me? You have everything you need." Remembering Carl's, *never give a five-dollar man, ten dollars*, I wanted to test it out.

"Not everything. We need a neutral turf and the trust of the gangs, or it won't work. You and the boys have both."

I must have looked doubtful because he went on to explain, "You guys are like the League of Nations. A lot of the guys are ex-gang members, some were the leaders. They have the respect of these gangs, which would go a long way in helping us gain their trust."

I started to think about all the possibilities of this situation. "I see, but, what's in it for us?" I said it as if I were joking, but I wasn't.

"A neighborhood that's safe and peaceful, Butch." Clancy smiled, lighting up his bright red face.

"It's already safe and peaceful, Clancy. You'll have to do better than that." Jimmy and I wanted to start our own numbers business. If we could do it without paying the cops, it would be a score. Without missing a beat, I asked, "How about you guys declare this block a safe zone?"

"What do you mean?" He half-smiled suspiciously.

"I mean no foot cops or patrol cars come into this block, unless we call them. Since, as you say, the block will be safe and peaceful, you won't need to waste the manpower."

"I can't make that call. This comes out of the mayor's office."

"Then talk to the mayor. I'll talk to the guys." I started slowly walking away.

"Okay, I'll give it a try. But I wouldn't get my hopes up. I'll get back to you," he said, shaking his head in disbelief.

When I walked into the candy store, I saw the usual gang. I nodded at my friend Andy, who was my age, but I was surprised to see him with his older brother Steve and his best friend Charlie. Steve and Charlie were about twenty-six. Steve had just finished a four-year hitch with the Marines and had started hanging out in the neighborhood again.

He was six foot four, with blond Marine-cut hair, blue eyes and thin lips. He worked as a laborer on construction. Married with three children, he was a tough guy and made sure everybody knew it. I knew he hadn't known Jimmy long, and I wondered why he was suddenly interested in hanging out with us since we were ten years younger. My life was oddly connected with Steve's, but neither of us knew it at the time.

When I walked into the candy store, Jimmy asked me, "What the fuck do those donkeys want?" He growled around the cigar he always had in his mouth. "Donkeys" was how he referred to the Irish, like Clancy.

Jimmy was about forty-five. Like most Sicilians, he was short, with blue eyes, thick brown hair, and deep smile lines around his eyes and mouth. He was a big influence in my life. I liked him. He was funny.

"They want us to help them with the gang problem."

"Yeah, tell 'em for ten grand a head we'll kill 'em all," Jimmy said laughing.

"That's not exactly what he had in mind." I laughed. I told Jimmy about the Youth Board and what role they saw us playing. Jimmy's reaction was not good at first. The storefront the city wanted to rent was ten feet from his store. The idea of a bunch of gangs meeting ten feet away did not appeal to him.

"First of all, who wants all those fucking assholes around here, and why would we want to help them?" he asked in one breath.

"Exactly, that's what I said. I told Clancy I would talk it over with everyone. I also told him, if we agreed to help, we had something comin'."

"Yeah, what are they going to do, give us free tickets to the policemen's ball," Steve said sarcastically.

"No, I told them we wanted the block declared neutral, meaning no foot cops or patrol cars in the block unless we called them."

Charlie chimed in, "You're kidding!? You actually said that?" Charlie Conroy was Steve's best friend. Half Irish and half Spanish, with the most beautiful teeth I have ever seen. His smile and laugh were contagious. He, Steve, and Steve's wife Annie all grew up together. He was Steve's best friend and best man at his wedding, as well as godfather to all his children.

While Steve did his four years in the Marines, Charlie watched over Steve's family and got a degree from Cornell

University, a rare occurrence in my neighborhood. He wanted to be a lawyer but couldn't afford law school.

Jimmy saw I wasn't kidding.

"What did he say?" Jimmy asked, removing the cigar from his mouth.

"He said he would talk to the Mayor's office about it, then get back to me."

Jimmy motioned me to the back of the store where we sat at one of his new red Formica tables. He had just fixed up the store. The first twenty feet of the space was narrow. It consisted of a soda fountain, with no room for counter stools, followed by an extensive glass candy case, which doubled as a bar. The other thirty feet had six red Formica tables, a jukebox, and a large soda cooler, with cherry-stained tongue-and-groove knotty pine walls.

There was also a 20 x 20 foot room in the back where Jimmy slept most of the time. He was married and had an apartment on the top floor in the same building, but didn't spend any time there.

"This could be very good, Butch," he said. "We could start our own numbers business. Do you really think they'll go for it?"

I could see he was looking at me with different eyes now. He knew nothing about my perfume business, and I saw no reason to tell him. He had no children of his own and enjoyed mentoring me. I was still very young, and, therefore, not to be taken too seriously as far as business was concerned. That was about to change.

"I think the mayor's office will go for it. It's the police commissioner and the precinct Captain that might try to kill it. First, because they will take the heat if anything goes wrong, and second, they won't be on the payroll, but let them work that out amongst themselves."

Jimmy knew my family pedigree but not too much about my present connections. I had told him about my blood connections early on in our relationship. He was impressed, which is what I wanted. I needed him to trust me. He advised me not to mention it to anyone else. I never did.

"Even if the cops went along, Butch, how are we going to get all those guys to work together and help?" Jimmy was a little out of touch with what went on in the park bordering his store. The so-called "gangs" were really ball clubs that originally competed along ethnic lines. The Puerto Rican clubs played other Puerto Rican clubs. The same was true of the black clubs in west Harlem and Italians in upper east Harlem, as well as the Irish from Hell's Kitchen, somewhere between 50th Street and 11th Avenue. It was also true that belonging to a club gave you status and protection.

Now, the members of the ball clubs were older—getting jobs and getting married. The sports they once played for fun they now played for money. The teams were organized around skill rather than ethnic lines, and the park was the place for high-stakes games. It was the beginning of integration and new friendships.

I responded to his earlier question, "Money, Jimmy, it's all about money now. We need three things to start the business: a numbers bank to handle our bets, protection from the cops, and as many runners (bookies) as we can hire to take the bets. We'll hire all these guys. Give them a living and I guarantee you, we will never have a gang problem in this block."

"I always knew you were smart, Butch, but this is a hell of an idea. Don't forget, we still need an okay from the *authorities*."

"Don't worry about that, Jimmy. It will come with the bank." I knew I could put that in place.

The numbers bank for Harlem, both east and west, belonged to my cousin, Big John. I was sure I could put the bank in place. Big John ran the bank operation out of my parent's apartment.

I was eight when I was first exposed to the so-called Mafia through Big John's operation. I had just had my appendix removed and was home from school. The guys who were running the operation in our apartment bought a television so they could watch the Kefauver hearings on organized crime, but I wanted to watch Howdy Doody, so I made a deal with them. For three weeks, I let them watch the hearings in return for my first bike, a brand-new English Racer. I would say that was my first successful business deal.

As a result, I watched the hearings for three weeks while I was home from school. Later in the evening, after watching the hearings, I would see some of the same men I saw on TV at my house, and they were pissed off. I wasn't old enough to really understand what was going on. I viewed them as celebrities, and the reason I had my first bike. It was later, when I was about ten or eleven, that I found out Salvatore Charles Lucania (a.k.a. Lucky Luciano) was my cousin and we had the same name.

CHAPTER 5

BUMPY JOHNSON, DUTCH SHULTZ,
LUCKY LUCIANO, THOMAS DEWEY,
WORLD WAR II, THE MAFIA CONNECTION,
AND WHAT MY FATHER TOLD ME.

As I left the candy store, I could hear the harmonizing coming from the playground. I loved singing. It was my passion. I saw my guys in the usual corner of the playground that bordered Jimmy's store. I walked over and joined them.

We were an interracial group: two Puerto Ricans, two Italians, and one black guy. Daddy-o, Lefty, Paulie, Snooky, and I had been singing together for two years. Three nights a week, we would practice at one another's houses. Our mothers would cook and leave us the best ethnic foods you can imagine. Lefty and Daddy-o's houses were my favorites: a roasted pig marinated and basted with garlic and black pepper, with red kidney beans, and yellow saffron rice. Every week it would be something different.

Snooky's house was the most fun. He came from a very religious and musical family. He lived on 136th and Lenox in the heart of black Harlem. Both his brothers were opera singers. His mother played piano; his father the drums. Sunday nights we would stand outside the storefront "Hallelujah" churches, as we called them, waiting for Snooky and his family. I loved the singing that came from those storefront churches.

When the services were over, we would all go over to Snooky's house and eat. It was always a feast: ham roast, ribs, black eyed peas, cornbread, sweet potatoes, and mama's home baked pies. After supper, we would go to the music room. Snooky lived in a huge eight-room flat, with fourteen, foot high ceilings and large sliding doors that separated the living room from the parlor. It was the first time I had ever seen two living rooms.

Snooky's father, Clifford, would say, "okay let's hear whacha got," and we would do renditions of "Stormy Weather," "Over the Rainbow," and other songs from the forties and fifties. Clifford was an avid Jazz and Blues buff. He had a record collection that was stacked two feet high and ran the length of the room. He knew exactly where everything was without a catalog.

We were treated like family, warm hugs, and Christmas gifts. I could never understand the racial conflicts in New York.

Clifford would say, "Here, try this!" and would sing "Stormy Weather" in a progressive jazz style, something like Manhattan Transfer would do. It was a complete departure from the simple three-chord harmony of Little Anthony, Frankie Lymon and other groups of the day. Snooky's family would fall into perfect harmony, crossing over one another's notes in different octaves. It was mesmerizing.

After practice we would hit the subway stations where the sound of our harmony was amplified. People would gather 'round us and applaud. The playground was where we would try out our new material. It wasn't long before other groups came to the playground from all over the city on weekends to show their stuff.

The playground was the first and only real melting pot in the city. The city to me was Manhattan. The other four boroughs were considered foreign countries requiring passports. Every nationality came and competed. During the day it was basketball and handball; at night it was singing.

Every Sunday we went to the Apollo on 125th Street. We saw ten live acts for $1.25. Every Wednesday was amateur night. Many of the famous groups got their start on that night. It wasn't unusual to run into Sherman, the bass singer for Frankie Lymon, or some of the Miracles from Smokey Robinson's group. Amateur night was a blast.

Jocko was the disc jockey for the Harlem rock and roll station that everyone listened to. It wasn't the same music that was played nationwide. It was black rock and roll, more rhythm and blues. The Apollo decided to hire Jocko as their new Emcee. Previously, if you didn't do well, you were pulled off the stage with a long hook. When Jocko took over the show, he would fly above the stage in an airplane hung by wires, then shoot you off the stage as he flew past you. They were a rough audience to please. You had to be better than good to make it there.

I spent a lot of time in black Harlem. I never had a problem with black people. I loved the culture and enjoyed their company. I was one of the very few whites that could move around Harlem without getting into trouble. There were good reasons for this free pass. First of all, I went to high school there. Secondly, I sang up there, but the most important reason was that I would transport thousands of dollars in bet payoffs to the black number offices.

My relationship to all this, goes back to a time before I was born. I have heard and read a lot of stories about my cousin Charlie, many of which were accurate, and many were not. But the reason I was trusted was because of Charlie's relationship to Bumpy Johnson.

A black woman from Harlem controlled the "numbers business back then. I believe she was called Queenie. When Dutch Shultz tried to take over the business by force, Bumpy Johnson, a close friend of Queenie's went to war with Shultz. Shultz was doing a lot of killing and was bringing down a lot of heat. Charlie warned Shultz to stop the killing. When

Thomas Dewey, the New York Attorney General, went after Shultz, Shultz decided to have Dewey killed.

In a meeting with Shultz, Charlie warned Shultz not to make that kind of a move. Shultz argued with Charlie and said. "You mark my words, Charlie, after me he's coming for you." The irony is that Shultz was right.

Charlie knew Shultz wasn't going to listen, and he also knew if you killed a district attorney, that all hell would break loose. The "Commission" or the "Combination," which is what Charlie called his organization (not Cosa Nostra) back then, had a rule that you didn't kill "citizens," meaning, anyone that was not a "member" and never a cop or public official. So Charlie had Shultz killed, which, unknown to Dewey, saved Dewey's life. There is a saying that "no good deed goes unpunished." This was a perfect example of that.

Dewey was a political animal. He was fiercely ambitious and wanted to be Governor and then run for the presidency. Prosecuting my cousin Charlie would be his ticket to fame. There was no way he could get near Charlie and charge him with anything, so he had Charlie framed for "White Slavery," i.e., prostitution, in other words, for being a pimp.

Imagine, the man in charge of an organization that took in more money than the federal income tax indicted for being a pimp, a charge that would have gotten the average pimp a fine and probation or maybe a year in jail. Charlie got fifty years.

Dewey paid off some prostitutes to testify that Charlie indirectly was their boss. Dewey went on to become Governor of New York.

Charlie, as "Lucky" Luciano was called by friends and family, formed an alliance with Bumpy Johnson. The deal was that Bumpy would keep his own bank and oversee all the other operations in Harlem for Charlie. Bumpy was given a cut on all the black operations for his services. Even though

Bumpy and Charlie spent many years in prison and had not seen each other since 1936, the alliance between Charlie's organization in East Harlem and Bumpy's organization in West Harlem, still existed. When the ethnic turf wars began in the late fifties, it became dangerous for Bumpy's men to come to East Harlem. It was equally as dangerous for Charlie's men to go to West Harlem.

When the payoffs were small, the money was given to little old ladies (bag ladies) who could move around unnoticed. When large payoffs had to be delivered, I was asked occasionally to make them, which was sometimes as much as $25,000. That was a great deal of money in the late fifties. I was the most protected white boy in black Harlem. I had Bumpy's money.

Those deliveries brought me into the nightclubs in Harlem. I would arrive in the early evening about 8 p.m., a couple of hours before show time. I got to meet guys like Muddy Waters, Louie Armstrong, and other great musicians. I didn't really know who most of them were at the time, but I enjoyed listening to them jam.

I didn't meet Bumpy until 1963, after he got out of prison. He knew who I was and was very gracious to me. He had a reputation for being hard and ruthless, yet he seemed just the opposite to me. He told me stories about the old days and what Charlie was like. I enjoyed hearing those stories since I had never met Charlie. He was already in jail by the time I was born.

Two days after I had talked with Clancy, he walked into Joe's where Andy and I were having lunch. He pulled a chair up from another table and sat down between us. "You got a lot of balls, Butch. I'll give you that," he said.

"What's wrong, Clancy?"

"You got a deal," he said with a begrudging smile.

"Great! How come you're not happy, Clancy?" I asked.

"I am and I am not, Butch. If anything goes wrong in the block, it's going to be my ass. You know that, don't you?" he asked sternly.

"Relax, Clancy. Nothing is going to happen. Even if something went down that was out of our control, you have my word we will cover your ass. Okay? Now let's have a drink and go over some of the details."

Two months later the new center called The Youth Board opened. It was a surprising success. I was introduced to the six "social workers" who staffed the center about a month before it opened. An interesting lot, I must say.

They asked me to introduce them to anyone who could give them an insight into the reasons for the gang wars. They also wanted to know if I would or could bring these factions to the table. I told them it was a tall order, but I would do my best.

It was a tall order. I reached out to the most influential ex-gang members I knew. Some were ex-presidents, but, more importantly, some were ex-war councilors, the ones who actually called the shots if there was to be a gang conflict. Some were friends of mine. Others I knew from the high stakes handball and basketball games.

I explained to them that they would be our numbers runners and would collect 10 percent of all the bets they collected, which the going rate for numbers runners. They loved it. As controllers, Jimmy and I got 15 percent from the bets. We paid the runners 10 percent and kept the 5 percent override.

I set up the meeting between the social workers and these neighborhood leaders on a Saturday evening after the games were over. I brought six of the leaders with me. Together they represented six clubs, each consisting of somewhere between fifty and two hundred members: the Chaplains (Black) with six chapters in different parts of the city; the Red Wings (Italian) from East Harlem; the Dragons (Puerto

Rican) with four chapters, and the Senecas and the Pumas (Puerto Rican), both from East Harlem.

Clancy introduced the social workers then left. The social workers were surprised and a bit overwhelmed by the size of the "gangs" and how well they were organized. We set up the ground rules and lines of communication.

A month later we had a Grand Opening. My guys showed up with about thirty high-ranking members from various gangs. Clancy and the precinct captain were there along with some dignitaries from the mayor's office. *El Dario* and *El Tiempo,* the only Spanish newspapers in the city, showed up along with *The Daily News.* Most of the kids that were in the park joined the festivities. It was a crowd of about a hundred people. The gang members loved the attention from the press and the Mayor's office. The press took pictures of the dignitaries, the police captain, and even rival gang members shaking hands. They gave interviews to reporters pledging their support and cooperation. I believe that one event did more to curb the violence than anything else up to that time. The gang members felt important, and they were important.

I stepped outside the center to pat myself on the back. I stood there looking at what I had accomplished. Carl was right, I thought to myself, *Just know what to say and who to say it to, and you can get anything done."*

Jimmy came staggering out of the candy store, as drunk as I have ever seen him. He threw his arms around me. "You did it. You fuckin did it!" he whispered in my ear.

Clancy approached us. "Butch, I want to thank you for doing this. I am proud of you. I am really proud of you," he said with great sincerity.

I was glad to be acknowledged by these two men. They made me feel important and good about myself. Jimmy hated cops, no matter how nice they might be, but I couldn't resist the moment.

"Jimmy, have you met Detective Clancy?"

Clancy grabbed Jimmy's hand, "I'm really glad to meet you, Jimmy," he said in a very respectful manner.

Jimmy was caught off guard and was smart enough to be gracious. I found it amusing that both these men were thanking me for very different reasons. You couldn't miss the irony of it all. Because of the center, Jimmy's business went through the roof. The jukebox alone made so much money that his half of the proceeds from it paid for his entire overhead.

It was a hot August day when the center opened. The muggy weather was upon us. The party went on into the evening. The center closed at 10 p.m., and the party moved over to Jimmy's store. It was 2:00 a.m. when Steve, Charlie and two of the girls at the party, decided to go to Orchard Beach for a swim.

"Hey you guys, what about us?" Andy shouted to his brother.

"There's not enough room," Steve yelled out the window as they pulled away.

Andy was determined to go. Jimmy was passed out on his cot in the back room of the store. Andy grabbed the keys to Jimmy's car.

"Come on Butch, let's go!"

"Andy, they're with the two girls. They don't want us with them."

"Who cares? I want to go swimming!"

We got to the beach, parked the car and got up on the boardwalk.

"Come on. Butch, let's go in," Andy said as he started taking off his clothes.

"Your nuts. This is jellyfish season. I am not going in that water. I'm gonna go down the boardwalk and see if I can find these guys and let them know we're here."

"Okay, I'll meet you here."

The full moon made it easy to spot them. They were about a hundred yards away. I told them where we were and headed back. When I got back, Andy was being busted for disrobing on a public beach. I saw the cops handcuffing Andy and ran back to tell Steve and Charlie, both very drunk.

"If those bastards touch my brother, I'll break their fuckin' heads," Steve yelled.

"Take it easy, Steve. They're cops, with guns." I warned.

"I don't give a fuck who they are, Butch. Do me a favor and drive the girls home. The last thing I need is my wife hearing about them.

"Right," I said.

The next day, the headlines in the Spanish papers read. VODKA PARTY AT ORCHARD BEACH, THREE POLICE HOSPITALIZED. The centerfold had pictures of Charlie, Steve, and Andy in night court. Charlie and Steve had on only shirts, Fruit of the Loom underwear, and French-toes dress shoes.

The next day, I asked Andy, "What the fuck happened?"

He said, "I was running down to the water bare ass. All of a sudden, I had flashlights shining on me. At first, I thought it was my brother fucking around with me. Then I hear, 'Stop, you're under arrest.' I turned around and saw these two assholes coming at me with their guns pointed, 'Put your hands on your head,' one of them says. 'You got to be kidding me,' 'I said, 'What's this about?'

"'It's about indecent exposure,' the prick says to me.

"So I said, 'You guys are real crime stoppers.' That's when he smacked me across the face with his flashlight. They handcuffed me, grabbed my clothes, marched me to the station about fifty yards away, and hand cuffed me to the chair naked.

"When my brother walked in with Charlie and saw me handcuffed, naked and bleeding, he went nuts. He hit the first cop that was closest to him and knocked him cold. Charlie kept yelling that he was an attorney and was going to have their asses. They clubbed him. I kept telling him to shut up. The other two cops rushed my brother. He hit one of them and broke his jaw. The other one pulled his gun and threatened to kill him. While trying to handcuff him from behind, Steve grabbed the cop's wrist and I heard it snap. These cops didn't know what hit them. They were shaking.

Charlie kept sighting all the laws they were breaking, and they kept clubbing him with blackjacks. They broke his eardrum."

Because Andy was a minor, the cops had a problem. Both sides dropped the charges. A small "donation" was also made to the cops who were hurt.

This story made Steve the neighborhood hero. He and Jimmy became friends after the story broke. Shortly after, Jimmy approached me. He wanted to bring Steve into our numbers business.

"Why?" I asked.

"He can put the numbers bank in place,"

Jimmy was impressed with Steve's balls, his size, and good looks. I didn't like what I was hearing. I thought Steve was reckless. He could have gotten everyone killed that night.

"We don't need him to do that, Jimmy. He's a wild card as far as I am concerned, but, if you want him in, let him buy me out."

"Butch, I don't want you out of the deal or pissed off."

"It's okay, Jimmy, I'm not pissed off. After you're up and running, give me a grand a month. When you reach ten grand, we are done. Fair enough?"

"That's more than fair, Butch, but I'd rather you stayed in the deal."

"I understand, but my gut tells me Steve is a disaster waiting to happen. He wants to be top dog, Jimmy, and I don't want to be anybody's dog. You know what I mean? Be careful, OK?"

My cousin Charlie Luciano sold booze and booked gambling operations. His business didn't hurt anyone. He was an outlaw, and I saw myself in the same category. Steve was reckless and violent. He was a criminal.

"Sure, Butch, "Jimmy said. "I hope there are no hard feelings?"

"No, Jimmy. Don't worry about that. We're friends. This is just business."

I was making plenty of money in the perfume business, and I didn't want any problems. Little did I know, that my problems were about to begin.

CHAPTER 6

LIFE HAS ITS OWN AGENDA

"I just heard on the radio that Kelly got busted. Get a hold of Tom-Tom and meet me at Joe's in an hour," Vinnie told me over the phone. I passed the word to Tom-Tom and picked up the newspaper to see if I could find more details. I found a small item on the third page "Perfume Bootlegger Arrested." I read the article to see if anyone else was mentioned. Kelly was the only one. It did say they expected more arrests.

I called Carl. "Carl, do you know Kelly has been busted?"

"No, where did you hear this?"

"It's in the papers," I said nervously.

"Okay, Butch, you have nothing to worry about. Don't talk to anyone about it, and I'll get back to you before the day is over."

"Okay,"

I did a few errands and headed over to Joe's. When I got there, Vinnie and Tom-Tom were drinking and smoking. It was 11 a.m.

"It's a little early for that, don't you think?" I said.

"Maybe," Vinnie said. "We got problems with our customers."

"What's their problem? They're not the ones busted. Are they afraid someone is going to rat them out?" I asked

"No, Butch, they know better than that. They said they're stuck for $18 grand because now they can't sell the stuff and want us to make good for it."

"What! That's bullshit. First of all, I don't believe they're stuck for anything. Secondly, that's not the way the game is played, and they know it. When a bust comes down, everybody takes their own losses; something smells here. The first thing you need to do is go take their inventory, Vinnie." Otherwise, how would we know they hadn't already sold the stuff and want to collect twice.

Tom-Tom said. "Right, I agree with Butch. It doesn't sound right to me either. I also think they could easily unload the inventory at cost if they had to."

Vinnie said, "I already told them that. They told me, that since Kelly's arrest hit the papers, everyone knows its bootleg, and they can't get rid of it."

I asked, "How do they know, have they tried? The bust is only twelve fuckin' hours old for Christ sake. Right now, we need to make sure this thing doesn't spill all over us. That's the first order of business. I already called Carl; he said he'll get back to me before the day's out."

Carl got back to me sooner than I expected, "Meet me at my house tonight at seven. Don't eat. Rose is making dinner," Carl said in his usual confident manner.

After dinner we went into Carl's beautiful rosewood paneled study. Rose brought us a pot of black coffee and left us alone. Men in Carl's world never talked business in front of their wives; not because they didn't trust them, but to protect them. "You want them to be able to take lie detector tests and pass," he once said to me.

"How is Kelly doing?" I asked.

"He's fine. Nothing's going to come of this," Carl said chuckling.

"What makes you so sure, Uncle Carl?"

"Well, the D.A. doesn't know it yet, but they fucked up. They charged Kelly with fraud and avoiding import tariffs. The tariff charge is in conflict with the fraud charge. If he bootlegged it, there is no import tax. As far as the fraud charge is concerned, how are they going to prove it's not Chanel?" Carl laughed.

"What do you mean?"

"The formula for Chanel is in a safe in Paris. It's a trade secret. They're not going to disclose it to anyone. Even if the D.A. found a way to check it against Chanel's formula and it's a match. There goes the fraud case and a good chunk of Chanel's business with it."

"What do you mean?"

"If the public finds out they've been paying $25 bucks for something that Kelly made for less than a buck, what do you think would happen?" Carl laughed.

"Yeah, but what happens, if it isn't a match?"

Carl looked into my eyes and said, "Butch, it's never going to get that far. It's all about money. Chanel will squash this case, but if it makes you feel better, it is Chanel's formula."

"Are you serious?" I said excited.

"Yes, don't tell anyone, including your partners, ok?" he said, smiling warmly.

"Sure Carl. I feel bad about Kelly. He's good people. Give him my best and tell him if there is anything I can do, let me know."

"I will. I am sure he will appreciate that."

"Carl, I also have a problem with the customers, these guys from Jersey." I explained the situation to Carl.

"Who are these guys? Are they made or connected?"

"I don't really know. One of them is my partner Vinnie's cousin, a guy name Cosmo. Do you know Joe Googs?"

"Yeah sure. He works for Big John's numbers office with your father. Is he involved in this?"

"No, he's Vinnie's father. In that sense, Vinnie's cousin is connected like I am."

"Not necessarily, Butch. This situation could get very complicated. If these guys are "made men," they had to have permission to do this business. They also had to send a third of their profits up to their bosses. If they did everything according to the rules, they could call for a "sit down." Then the powers that be will make the decision."

A sit-down was like a mini court for the mafia families. Each person in a dispute went to a meeting with a "made man" to represent them. After each side laid out its position, a higher up in one of the families would make a judgment. His word was the last word.

I had another worry. I said, "I don't want my old man finding out about all this"

"Neither do I."

"I'm sure Vinnie and Tom-Tom feel the same way. I especially don't want Big John to know."

"I understand. I don't need the problem either. The cleanest way to deal with this is to check the fence's inventory, pay them, and sell the inventory to recoup."

"I agree. Thanks, Uncle Carl."

I said my goodbyes and headed back to the city. It was close to midnight when I sat down with my partners. I told them, "I got good news and bad news. The good news is, Kelly will walk and nothing will spill over here. Carl said Chanel will squash the case because they won't disclose the formula."

"That's great; unbelievable," Tom-Tom laughed.

"What's the bad news?" Vinnie asked.

I ran it down to them. "It's also a big problem for Carl. He didn't tell me what it was, but I know it could be that if he gets pulled into it, his boss is going to want his cut," I said.

"But Carl didn't get a cut," Tom-Tom objected.

"Right, but who is going to believe that?" I said.

"Carl is right; the cleanest way is to pay these guys off," Vinnie said.

I said, "Maybe, but it is still bullshit. They know the score. We shouldn't have to eat this whole thing. When are you going to check the inventory, Vinnie?

"Tomorrow."

"Ask them to give us the inventory and let us sell it, and then we'll pay them. That's the least they can do." I said.

"Yeah, if they don't want to do that, tell them to go fuck themselves," Tom-Tom said.

The next day I got a call from Vinnie. "It's no go," he told me. "They want the dough up front and they want it now."

"Or what; what are they going to do? Who the fuck do they think they are? This guy is your cousin?" I asked.

"It's not my cousin that's causing all the problems. It's his partner. I know who he is, and he's a real prick. I'll tell you more when I see you. Let's meet at Rao's tonight."

"Okay, I'll tell Tom-Tom."

"This is just what I needed," I thought to myself. I backed out of the numbers business, I lost my income from the perfume business, and now I owe $6,000, my share of the $18,000. *What's next?* I wondered.

Louise was my girlfriend of two years, and I loved her. We already agreed that we would marry when we were old enough. We were both 16 years old. She was a junior in high school, and I was... well, I was doing, what I was doing.

"Butch, I need to talk to you right away. Can you meet me later?" Louise asked.

"Sure Louise, what's wrong?"

"I can't talk now. Meet me at three by Tina's building, okay?" she said and then hung up.

"I'm pregnant," she said with tears in her eyes.

"Are you sure? How do you know?"

"I just got the results."

"Did you tell your Mother?"

"No, she told me."

"What do you mean she told you?"

"She does the laundry and noticed there was no blood on my underwear for the last two months. She confronted me about it, and I had to admit that we were having sex. It went over like a lead balloon, then she slapped me and..."

"She what?" I went off like a bomb.

"Please, Butch, don't make it worse."

I could see she was getting more upset, so I got a hold of myself and hugged her. "I love you, Louise, and I promise everything is going to be all right."

"I don't think so. You know she hates you already, and now she's got a reason to go on a war path."

"You let me worry about that. I need some time to think. I'll call you tomorrow, and we'll go for a walk by the river, ok?"

I hardly knew her mother, and she hated me. It seems Louise's CYO or Catholic Youth Organization friends talked a lot about me, none of it good. I came from the wrong side of the tracks. I would be slandered like that all of my life because of my family. My head was spinning. I knew I had to focus on one thing, so I turned my thoughts on that night's meeting.

When we met at Rao's, I asked Vinnie. "So, who's this prick?"

"His name is Sonny Osso. He's looking for a button to become a made guy in your cousin's John's Family and guess who's sponsoring him."

"I'm afraid to ask." I said.

"Angelo "Puggie" Logicono."

Puggie was one of Big John's lieutenants, who oversaw all of Big John's gambling and loan shark operations. He also controlled his own Local in the Plaster's Union.

Vinnie and I knew him very well. We used to see him when Big John had parties for his crew and their families, and he would come to my house often to pick up the cash from the numbers operation. Puggie was married and had three children. He also had a mistress and had two children with her. I saw him every other day coming out of a building right across the street from Jimmy's store. I always thought he had some business running out of there.

All of a sudden it hit me. Puggie's mistress was Steve's sister. I knew Steve's sister had two kids, no husband and lived in that building, but I never put it together. Now I knew how Steve was going to put the bank in place. What a small fuckin world. I drifted off into a maze of thoughts.

"Butch, where the fuck are you?" Tom-Tom asked.

"Sorry, I got a lot on my mind. What does Sonny do for Puggie?" I asked.

"He works the crap games, loans money to the losers, and collects. That's where he gets his reputation as a prick, He's merciless," Vinnie said.

"How did he get involved with this deal?" I asked.

"My cousin Cosmo borrowed the money from him to do the deal. That's why there's so much pressure."

"*Oh fuck!*" I was about to say, *could things get any worse?* But I thought better of it.

"Does he know any of us?" I asked.

"Well, he knows me and that I have two partners, but he doesn't know who you and Tom-Tom are."

"That's good," I said.

"How do you want to handle this, Butch?" Vinnie asked.

"Carefully," I laughed.

"Will he take a check?" Tom-Tom laughed.

"It comes down to this: if there's a sit down and Sonny was a partner, then he and your cousin will have to eat it. If he just loaned your cousin the money, then your cousin is on the hook for the dough. Either way, we're not responsible according to the rules. Wait a minute; you said that Sonny was your cousin's partner. Then you said he borrowed the money, which is it?"

"I really don't know, Butch"

"What difference does it make? If it goes to a sit down, our families are going to find out, and Carl might get pulled into it. It could go anywhere." Tom-Tom said.

"Tom-Tom's right Butch, and Carl's right. Let's pay them off, and then see if we can recoup."

"Well, then we have two problems: where are we going to get $18,000 and how are we going to recoup it? We'll be on social security by time we dump those quantities." I said.

"Oh shit, I don't believe it." Vinnie said.

"What's wrong, Vinnie?" I asked.

"That prick Sonny Osso just walked in the door, and he's coming right towards us."

Osso was in his late thirties, about five foot, ten inches, one hundred-ninety pounds, dark brown curly hair and pockmarks all over his face. He had the same look and attitude as those assholes that tried to kill me. I hated him already.

"Hey, Vinnie, just the guy I wanna see. You got a minute? I'd like to talk to you outside," Osso said with an arrogant smirk on his face.

"I'm sorry, Sonny, but I am in the middle of a meeting right now," said Vinnie, putting Sonny in his place. Sonny didn't like it at all. The line was drawn right then and there. Vinnie had handled it perfectly.

"Are these your partners?" Sonny asked.

I knew that question would set Tom-Tom off. Tom-Tom was a scrapper. He loved a good fight and the adrenalin that fear and danger generated.

"Who we are, is none of your fuckin' business," Tom-Tom fired back. The tension filled the room.

"Do you know who I am? I'm Sonny Osso," he said, as if he were the Pontiff himself.

Tom-Tom stood up from his chair. "Yeah, so fuckin what? Why don't you go tell somebody who gives a fuck?"

Just then, Louie "Lump, Lump" Barone walked over to the table. Louie was five foot, seven inches of fearless muscle and a short fuse. He had brown wavy hair, blue eyes and high cheekbones. He tended to favor his left side when he walked, talked, and smiled because of early childhood polio, I had heard.

Louie lived a block away from Rao's on 115th Street. This was my father's turf; 114th Street was the 'executive offices' for the Luciano Family, which was now run by Genovese and his right-hand man, my cousin Big John Ormento.

Louie knew my father, but I didn't know what he knew about me. I also didn't know if he knew Sonny personally.

I did know that, everyone knew who Louie was. He had a reputation for being dangerous. Don't get me wrong, he was charming, respectful, and well liked; very much a gentleman, but he could snap. The word was that he did some "work" for the Genovese Family and wanted to be brought into the family, but he was too volatile. They called him Louie Lump Lump for his ability to take and give his lumps and never go down. It was said if you wanted Louie to go down, you had to hit him with a truck.

"What's the trouble, Butch?" Louie asked, with his hand placed affectionately on the back of my neck. Louie knew exactly what he was doing.

"Hello Lou. It's okay. Just a misunderstanding," I said, grabbing Tom-Tom's arm and sitting him back down.

Sonny's entire demeanor changed in an instant. I wanted to check out Sonny and Lou's relationship, so I said, "Lou, do you know Sonny Osso?"

"No, I don't." Louie smiled warmly and shook Sonny's hand. "It's my pleasure."

It was clear to me that Sonny knew who Louie was.

"It's a pleasure to meet you, Lou. You know, we know a lot of the same people. Can I buy you a drink?" Sonny asked as if he were in the presence of a celebrity.

"No, thanks, Sonny, but I'll take a rain check."

"Okay, Lou, any time." Sonny said his humble goodbyes and left.

"Butch, I don't know what you're doing with that guy, Sonny, but he's bad news; stay away from him," Louie said in a fatherly manner. I introduced Tom-Tom and Vinnie to Louie and asked if he wanted to join us for dinner.

"No thanks, Butch. I got a meeting to go to. Say hello to your old man for me," he said as he was walking away.

"Ok, Lou, I will and thanks."

Lou smiled knowingly and left.

I often wondered what happened to Louie. One day I picked up a copy of the *New Yorker* magazine and there was a picture of Louie in handcuffs. The story said that Louie shot and killed a young "wise guy" from Jersey in Rao's. Louie was sitting at the bar listening to some woman singing Italian songs. The "young Turk" complained very loudly that he didn't want to hear her anymore. Louie told him, "You don't act like that around here, pal."

The Turk said something like, "Who the fuck are you?" or "Who's going to stop me?" Without another word, Louie pulled his gun and shot him dead right then and there, in full view of a packed restaurant.

Relieved, Vinnie said, "It's a good thing Lou stepped in when he did."

"Did you see Sonny's face when Louie came over? He shit his pants," Tom-Tom laughed.

I said, "Yeah I know, I can tell you lots of Louie Lump Lump stories when we have more time, but I'll tell you a short one right now. Louie hangs out with a guy name Clemmy. This guy is two hundred-forty pounds, forty of which is solid balls. They both love Latin women and Latin music. They go to the Palladium when Tito Puente plays there, which is often. I ran into them there a few times. One night I walked in and there is Louie on one side of a large round table and Clemmy on the other. Sitting at the table are twelve to fifteen Latin guys. Louie is smiling out of the side of his mouth, his eyes wild and laughing. He yells to Clemmy, "We got 'em surrounded Clemmy." I turned around and walked right out.

Tom-Tom and Vinnie laughed. They got a real kick out of the story, and they also got the point.

"Do you think Louie can straighten Sonny out?" Vinnie asked.

"If it was just Sonny, yes, but we aren't dealing with Sonny alone. I don't believe Sonny had that kind of money himself. It's probably Puggie's money that Sonny puts out on the street for him. Do you know where the crap games are?" I asked Vinnie

"What crap games?"

"The ones that Sonny runs for Puggie."

"No. I don't. Why do you want to know?"

"Are you thinking what I think you're thinking, Butch?" Tom-Tom asked.

"I don't know. What do you think I am thinking?"

"You want to knock off the crap game, right? Am I right? I love it. It's perfect. Butch. It's real justice." Tom-Tom couldn't stop laughing.

Vinnie lost his usual calm demeanor. "Are you both out of your fuckin' minds? Do you want to get us all killed?"

"Take it easy, Vinnie. It's just a thought. I don't know where I can put my hands on eighteen grand, do you? If you got a better idea, let's hear it"

"I don't right now, but that's not an idea. It's an act of suicide," Vinnie said, shaking his head back and forth in disbelief.

"Maybe, maybe not, but think about it, what could really happen if they found out it was us? Do you think Big John or Puggie would hurt you or me? They wouldn't touch Tom-Tom either, because of Tom-Tom's old man. The women in our families would go on the warpath. They wouldn't get laid for the next ten years." I said laughing.

"He's right, Vinnie. Not only that, but that fuckin prick Sonny will have to answer for it. I love it, Butch; it's a stroke genius. Talk about killing two birds with one stone."

Vinnie was exasperated "That's it," he said. "Now I know I am hanging out with two fuckin lunatics. You guys are nuts. No one would believe this."

"That's right, Vinnie. No one would, and that's exactly why we can get away with it," I said.

Tom-Tom, sitting next to me, reached over grabbed my head then started kissing me all over my face. "I love you, Butch! I love you."

I said, "Think it over, Vinnie. Lou just put the brakes on Sonny for a while, so we have some time to think it through. Call your cousin Cosmo and find out if Sonny loaned him the money or if he banked the deal. I have a feeling that he's got it working both ways."

"What do you mean both ways? "Vinnie asked.

"I mean if the deal works, Sonny gets half. If something goes wrong, like what just happened, he sticks your cousin with the tab. Ask Cosmo if that's what happened. I'm curious. In the meantime, think it over. Okay?"

Tom-Tom said, "You know, Vinnie, we've made about twenty-five grand in the last two months. Those guys made at least that much, so where's their fuckin loss?"

"Tom-Tom's right, I didn't even think of that," I said. "Maybe that's what smells about all this. If that's what's going on, that prick deserves his ass handed to him in spades."

"Okay, Butch, I'll talk to Cosmo and get back to you."

"I've decided to have the baby and give it up for adoption," Louise said.

"You've decided? You mean your mother decided. What about me? Don't you think I should have something to say about this?" We were walking across the Ward's Island Bridge that connected Manhattan to Ward's Island at 102th street and East River Drive. It was our hideaway. There were no cars and very few people.

We spent hours walking and talking that day. It was a clear beautiful summer day. A soft breeze was coming off the river, and the air was moist and sweet smelling from last night's rain. It seemed surreal to me that the day was so beautiful, and we were so gloomy.

I knew my life was going to change no matter what decision was made. I was trying to sort out all of my emotions. I loved Louise. I couldn't imagine being without her. I felt sad and angry, and I knew if she went away and gave the baby up, our relationship would be over. Her mother would make sure of that. I felt devastated at the thought of losing her. I was also troubled by the feeling of having my child somewhere out there without me to protect it.

Louise was sitting on a bench facing the river. I was standing on the rocks at the river's bank with my back to her. I turned and looked at her. She was beautiful. Her large brown almond shaped eyes were full of tears. Her face and features were like Sophia Lauren's. She was five foot, three, one hundred-twenty pounds earthy and vivacious, always happy and ready to laugh. She was the only real joy in my life. My throat curled up into a knot. The tears fell from my eyes uncontrollably. All I ever wanted was to make her happy. I wanted to be her hero. Instead, look what I had done. It was more than I could bare.

I walked over to her, took both her hands, drew her up to me and put my arms around her, my words and tears falling from me, "Louise, I am so very sorry for what I've done."

She tilted her head up and looked at me, her eyes, scared and innocent. "Butch, don't blame yourself. You didn't do this alone. I am just as responsible as you are," she said trying to ease some of my pain, but I didn't feel any better.

"Listen, Louise, we need to put everyone else's feelings aside. We need to decide what is best for all of us. It's not just you and me. It's the baby, too. I've never been good at knowing what I want, but I know what I don't want. I don't want to lose you, and I don't want to wonder what happened to our baby. I can't speak for you, but I know I would regret it for the rest of my life," I said, feeling the worst pain I had ever felt in my life. It was the first hint I had of what a parent feels for their child.

"I know, Butch, I thought a lot about that, but you know I have always been afraid of how you make your living. You don't say much about your family, but my family knows who they are. It worries them and it worries me. I don't want to live that kind of life, and I wouldn't want a child raised in that kind of life," she said.

I really didn't know what to say. Given the mess I was in the middle of, what could I say?

"I understand, Louise. Is that the real problem here?"

"No Butch, you quit school. I still have two years to go just to finish high school. How and where are we going to live? You're not even old enough to get a job. I'm scared." She said, starting to cry again.

I thought, *A job! The last thing I need or want is a fuckin job.*

"Louise, I have money saved." I had about $5,000, but I didn't want her to start asking me questions. "It's enough for us to get an apartment, furniture, and live for about six months. I am sure my family will give us a bunch of envelopes." Italian families were always generous at weddings with the traditional gifts of envelopes of cash.

"There is nothing to worry about," I assured her. "I can get a construction job. I am sure someone in my family can get me a union book." The thought of working with my hands in twenty-degree weather was very depressing.

"I'm sure they could, Butch. The question is will you do it?" she asked staring at me through her tears.

I needed time to think. "If I do it, will you marry me and have the baby?"

"I don't know," she said, surprised at her own answer.

"Well, I don't know either, but I don't like the options, do you?"

"No, of course not. I just wish it didn't happen." she said frustrated.

"Me too, but we're not going to be able to wish our way out of this, Louise" I said gently.

"I know, Butch. I'm tired. Let's go home," she whispered.

"Sure, we need to let things settle down a bit. Take some time and get some rest. We can talk in a few days, okay?"

She didn't answer. She took my hand and started walking. Neither one of us said anything during the six-block walk home.

I woke up the next morning feeling like a piece of shattered glass. I had so much to deal with that I didn't know where to start. I couldn't think. Every time I put my attention on the matters at hand, my emotions sucked the thoughts out of my head and into my stomach. Without Louise I felt lost. I had known how much I loved her, but I didn't realize how much I needed her.

CHAPTER 7

THE WORLD KEEPS GOING AROUND

When I got home the phone rang. It was Lefty.

"Guess who's at the Apollo?" he said laughing. I had forgotten it was Sunday, the day we always went to the Apollo's matinee. "Clay Cole is filling in for Jocko. He's featuring Danny and the Juniors and Louie Lymon and the Teenchords" Louie Lymon was Frankie Lymon's brother. He had one hit called "I'm So Happy" and faded after that.

Clay Cole was a white boy who had a local TV dance show a la Dick Clark. He got his start in radio when Allen Freed got into his problems with "payola." He played white teenybopper rock and roll. In Harlem he was considered a joke. Danny and The Juniors, to us, were an even bigger joke. They had a hit record "At the Hop." They were not the best singers, and they were probably scared to death to play the Apollo.

"I don't know, Lefty. I am not feeling too good." I moaned.

Lefty knew me very well. "What's wrong, Butch, you sound really down."

I told Lefty about Louise and what was going on. It felt good to talk to someone. It took some of the weight off me.

"God, Butch, I am sorry. I know how you feel." he said gently. He too was having problems with his girlfriend's parents. He was Puerto Rican and she was Italian. In those days, that could have gotten you killed.

"Listen, Butch, you need to get your mind off this for a while. Take it from Dr. Hector." Hector was Lefty's real name. "This show is going to be a riot. It will clear your head out."

He was right. It did clear my head out with its damn near riot. I don't know what Clay Cole was thinking or if he was thinking at all. The place was half empty and not surprisingly we were the only whites in the audience. After all, what white suburban parents would let their kids go to Harlem? If it were not for Louie Lymon and the Teenchords we might have been the only ones in the audience.

The theater went dark. Out of the darkness came a voice: "And now ladies and gentleman, the Apollo Theater is proud to present the Clay Cole show! Let's have a warm welcome for our Master of Ceremonies, Clay Cole!" Without the orchestra, you could have heard a mouse walking across the stage.

Cole came running out on to the stage dressed like Pat Boone, right down to the white buck shoes. "Thank You! Thank you, Ladies and gentleman for your warm welcome!" I felt bad for him.

He brought Louie Lymon on first, next came Danny and The Juniors. They went right into their hit song. First the baritone: "Ahhhhh', the second tenor: "ahhhh, they were off key. They tried again. They were off again. The audience started to heckle them. "Get those turkeys off the stage" and finally booed them off.

Clay came out on the stage pleading with the audience to give them a chance. The crowd started booing and throwing whatever they could find at Clay, but Clay kept trying to continue the show. Finally, management came out and escorted Clay off the stage.

Needless to say, it was a short show. My group had a couple of opportunities to play the Apollo, but there was no way I would take the chance at being humiliated like that.

As we left the theater I turned to Lefty and said, "Well, what do we do now/'" feeling the dark clouds returning.

Paulie said, "You know, Butch, Louie Farina, The Scorp, is fighting a four rounder at the Garden later. A bunch of guys from the neighborhood are going. Why don't we go?"

"That sounds good to me," I said. Madison Square Garden was the big time for any amateur boxer. The Garden put on four, six, and nine rounder fights before the main events.

Louie Farina, a highly decorated tail gunner in the Korean War, was about 26 years old, six feet tall and one hundred-eighty pounds of muscle. The eldest of the three Farina brothers, he looked more Spanish than Italian though he was both.

We got to the Garden early to get good seats. Benny Lip and Vinnie Mule, Louie's two younger brothers, had already taken twenty empty seats in the front row that belonged to other ticket holders, who wouldn't show up for the early fights.

Louie was fighting a huge Samoan in the first match. This guy, tall with a long reach, had at least fifty pounds on Louie. He looked more like a Sumo wrestler than a boxer.

I asked Benny, "Where did they find this gorilla?"

"I don't know, Butch, but Louie will make gorilla steaks out of him." Benny laughed.

The bell rang and Louie came out of his corner dancing like Ali. The Samoan walked, and I mean walked, to the center of the ring and stood there with his left arm extended and his right arm cocked. As Louie danced around him looking for an opening, the Samoan merely turned in the center of the ring. He was making Louie look real bad.

Louie finally ducked under his arm and laid in three devastating punches to his stomach. You could see Louie's body reverberate, like he was hitting a brick wall. The Samoan smiled at him and Louie went nuts. He started swinging wild punches and fell on the mat twice. The Samoan stood there holding Louie at bay, like an adult would do to an angry child.

The fight went to the Samoan. Benny was furious at the mismatch. "Come on Vinnie," Benny said to his brother.

"Where are we going, Benny?" Vinnie yelled over the crowd.

"We are gonna make sure that elephant never gets in a ring again."

They waited for the Samoan at the back door of the Garden. They put the Samoan and his manager in the hospital, and the Samoan quit the business.

We all went back to Jimmy's store to talk about the fight and wait for Louie. When Louie walked in, Jimmy started breaking his balls for losing. He was merciless. "I could've kicked that turkey's ass with one hand behind my back, you pineapple. Maybe the next time, they'll let you use a baseball bat."

We were hysterical. When Jimmy got on a roll, he could keep you laughing all night. Louie took it very well. He knew he blew it by getting mad. Jimmy broke out a couple of bottles of Seagram's and started pouring shots for everyone. We played the jukebox, ordered a half a dozen large pizzas and got blind drunk. It was just what Dr. Hector ordered. It was two in the morning by time I got home.

Louise called me the next day. I found out that my parents and her parents spent the whole day discussing our situation.

"Where have you been? You had me worried," she said.

"What's the matter?"

"Our parents decided to sign the papers and let us get married," she said excitedly.

The ceremony was to take place at Saint Cecilia's Church, the one I attended six days a week for eight years. Because Louise was pregnant, they wouldn't let us get married on the altar.

I hate those self-righteous, condescending, mean spirited pricks; they'd kill a wet dream; on whose fuckin authority did they become the gatekeepers of heaven, I thought to myself.

They also made an issue of Louise wearing a white wedding dress. I personally couldn't have cared less, but her mother wanted her to wear white. I think she didn't want people to know that Louise was pregnant, as if no one was going to find that out.

So a week before the wedding, I paid a visit to the head gatekeeper, Father Driscol, the alcoholic "shepherd" of the flock. I reminded him that I had served as his altar boy for three years and that it meant a lot to both our families if he would forgive Louise and me for "our sin" and bless our union by allowing her to wear white and then handed him three $100 bills as a "special donation." Needless to say, Louise got to wear her dress.

A few years later when my cousin Charlie Lucky died, the church refused to place him in his own mausoleum, for which he paid $20,000 in 1930's money and where his mother and father were laid to rest. They said he was a gangster and, therefore, could not be buried in 'sacred ground.' That problem was solved with a $5,000 donation.

The church had a long history of these practices. In Medieval times, they sold places in heaven to the rich. The more you paid the closer you would be to The Man Himself.

We were married on September 13, 1959, just five weeks before my seventeenth birthday. Apart from Louise being an hour or so late, a habit she kept for some thirty years, the wedding went off without a hitch. I often told Louise that she would be late for her own funeral.

We took a small, furnished apartment in her mother's building. The rent was $45 a month. The envelopes we received as gifts helped pay it. My sister was married just three weeks before me. She had some 150 guests and collected enough envelopes to spend three months in Europe and furnish her new apartment. She also got to meet our cousin Charlie (Lucky) in Naples, who was in the middle of dictating his memoirs at the time. We, on the other hand, had about thirty people with some drinks and pastries in my mother-in-law's 800-square foot apartment. After all, Louise was pregnant. How shameful!!! Still, our families were very generous. I was glad to get the whole thing behind us.

CHAPTER 8

SMART IS YOUR ABILITY TO ACQUIRE KNOWLEDGE; INTELLIGENCE IS YOUR ABILITY TO APPLY IT.

Later Tom-Tom called me. "Butch, I just got a call from Vinnie. You were right. That prick Sonny had it both ways. He grabbed Cosmo and slapped him around in public, right in front of Cosmo's son. Vinnie's on his way down from Yonkers. He's ripping mad. I think we got our crap game. He should be at Joe's in an hour. Can you make it?"

"I'll be there," I said and hung up.

Tom-Tom was at the bar drinking boilermakers when I walked in.

"What are you going to have, Butch?"

"A double scotch and two aspirins," I said laughing.

I wasn't there two minutes when Vinnie stormed into the bar like a hurricane yelling, "That low life mother fucker slapped him. Can you believe it!? He slapped him! Right in front of his son, no less."

I'd never seen Vinnie that pissed off, but I knew why. In our culture when you slap another man it's a humiliation. You're saying he's less than a man. Sonny would have been better off if he had hit Cosmo with a baseball bat. It was an insult, not just to Cosmo, but to us as well.

Vinnie was foaming at the mouth. He could barely speak. I handed him my drink. "Here drink this and calm down. What else did he say?"

"I don't know. I couldn't get passed the slap. What's more, I don't give a rat fuck about what that prick has to say. I want to cut his eyes right out of his fuckin' head," he said still steaming.

"I should've cracked is head open that night at Rao's," Tom-Tom said angrily.

"How is Cosmo doing?" I asked.

"What do you think? Sonny humiliated him. He lost face in front of his son. He's mad enough to kill 'em."

"Is he mad enough to help us take the crap game down?" I asked.

"I don't know, Butch. I never mentioned it to him, but at this point I wouldn't be surprised if he came with us."

"Good, then let's get the show on the road."

It was Tuesday, late September. I had been married a whole week. We had a few more drinks and waited for the lunch crowd to clear out of Joe's. Then we sat down to eat and started to make plans.

"What do you know about these games, Vinnie?" I asked.

"I don't know any of the logistics. Time, day, location, things like that. Cosmo can find out all of that for us. What I do know is that they have different levels of action." Vinnie said, returning to his normal understated demeanor.

"Good, that's exactly what I was getting to. If we're going to do this, we've got to make sure we hit the right game at the right time."

"Right, we got to score big enough to pay the eighteen grand and have some change left over for us. I can't wait to see that prick's face when we walk in there," Tom-Tom said excited.

"When can we get together with Cosmo, Vinnie? I want to get this thing done as soon as possible," I said.

"He works swing shift at the plant, four in the afternoon to midnight. I'll call him tonight and set it up for tomorrow."

"Good, but let's meet at Angelo's on Mulberry Street. I don't want to take the chance of Sonny walking in on us while we are meeting with Cosmo."

"Good thinking Butch! I can't fuckin wait!" Tom-Tom said, and then began his benediction, blessing us with the sign of the cross.

Vinnie started laughing and said "Tom-Tom, you should've been a fuckin' priest."

"I gave that idea some very serious thought, Vinnie, but I just couldn't see myself dressed in black. It's not my color," Tom-Tom said deadpan, making Vinnie laugh even harder.

"A very wise and well thought out decision, Tom-Tom," Vinnie countered. We all laughed, hugged one another, and left.

I went home to my new bride and new apartment. I liked my new life and the sense of independence it gave me.

"Butch, have you given any thought to what we are going to do for money?" Louise asked, still concerned.

"Yes," I said, "as a matter of fact, I spent the whole afternoon with Vinnie and Tom-Tom-Tom doing just that. Vinnie and Tom-Tom are going to talk to their people to see what they can come up with"

"Good "she said.

"Are you hungry?"

"Only for you baby" I said, chasing her into the bedroom

At the meeting, Cosmo explained in a high nervous voice, "Every couple of months Puggie brings in high rollers from all over. They come from Philly, Miami, and Pittsburgh. It's a big deal. Sonny hires drivers to pick the players up at the airport, take them to their hotel and then to the game. He calls it an escort service. The players are usually here for the weekend. If there's a big winner from out of town, Sonny will send one of the escorts home with the guy to make sure no one robs him -- that's the game to hit"

Cosmo was bald, skinny, and fortyish, with the demeanor of a third-grade school teacher. He was a printer by trade.

How he got into this business was beyond me. He continued, "The next game is two weeks away. Sonny is gearing up for it right now."

"Where is it going to be?" I asked Cosmo

"Do you know where the Democratic Club is on 103rd Street?"

"Yeah, but that's a few doors down from the 23rd Precinct. Why the fuck is he holding it there. Are the cops in on this?" I asked.

"No, I asked Sonny about that once. He said if they knew how big it was, they'd shake him down for a big cut. Besides, he said, the best place to hide from the fox is under his nose. I told him that foxes had a great sense of smell, but so far, he hasn't had any problems," Cosmo said, shrugging his shoulders.

"Okay," I said, "but why the Democratic Club? It's a street level storefront. It doesn't make sense."

"Yes it does, Butch, because the game is in the basement, underneath the club. The players come in the front door and go down a back staircase to the basement," Cosmo said.

"Is there another way into the basement?" Tom-Tom asked.

"Yeah, there's a fire exit that goes into the backyard. You can get into the yard from any of the buildings that have open cellars. There must be at least a dozen buildings like that on the next block," Cosmo said.

I could see Tom-Tom's mind working. "Cosmo, when the drivers bring in the players, how do they get in the club?"

"They all have keys, so no one has to go upstairs to let them in," Cosmo said.

"I see."

Tom-Tom was the only one who had any experience with stick-ups. I could see things clicking into place for him. He was asking the right questions. He signaled me to end the meeting. "Cosmo, its 2:30. Don't you have to be at work by 4:00?"

"Oh shit, I got to go. Thanks for lunch. It was nice meeting you guys. If you need me again, just call me."

"Cosmo, you understand how dangerous this is, don't you?" Vinnie warned.

"Yes, I do Vince," Cosmo acknowledged.

"Okay, thanks, Cosmo."

"This is even worse than I thought, Butch!" Vinnie said, losing his calm.

"What's wrong Vinnie?" Tom-Tom asked.

"What's wrong? Are you kidding? Let's start with how we're going to get in the front door." Vinnie said in a little higher voice.

"We could knock," Tom-Tom said laughing. He loved to tease Vinnie.

"And how are we going to stop from being recognized? I could just see us with stockings over our heads, standing outside the club door, twenty feet from the station house. How do you get around that? You fuckin' nut!"

"Well," Tom-Tom pressed on, "it's very close to Halloween, maybe we could go as Batman and Robin. Or better yet, how about Robin Hood and his merry men?"

I couldn't help but laugh. "You know, Tom-Tom, you might be on to something."

"You mean you wanna go as Robin Hood and his merry men?" Tom-Tom laughed.

"No but, what about Friar Tuck?" I laughed.

"I can't believe you guys are having this conversation!" Vinnie said exasperated.

"Friar Tuck? Oh! I get it! Brilliant, absolutely brilliant, Butch." Tom-Tom said excitedly.

"What the fuck are you guys talking about?" Vinnie asked.

"A priest. Vinnie a fuckin' priest. Who else could stand out in front of the club and the station house without being suspicious? Who would question it? Perfect. It's perfect." Tom-Tom was elated.

"How does that get us in the front door, Butch? Somebody still has to open that door for us," Vinnie asked.

"The drivers who bring in the high rollers will open the door for us, Vinnie. Didn't you hear Cosmo say they had their own key?"

"Yeah but…"

"Listen Vinnie," Tom-Tom interrupted, "I know this is not your thing, and I understand why you're nervous about it, but, believe me, this is a piece of cake. All you have to do is park your car on the next block and wait for Butch and me. Leave the rest to us, okay? Me and Butch will work out the details. We'll call you when we have it all worked out. In the meantime, find out as much as you can from Cosmo. Like when is the best time to hit the game; after 10 or after midnight? Should we go on Friday night or Saturday night?"

Vinnie left. Tom-Tom and I stayed at Angelo's and ordered drinks. Then Tom-Tom started to run down his plan. "We're going to need a small handgun, a sawed-off shotgun, two ski masks, and a priest's costume. I'll buy a black suit and hat. Can you get the white collar and vest?"

"I'll find a way. Don't worry about it," I said, having no idea how I was going to do it.

"I'll wait for the driver to open the door to the club. I'll move in behind them and, while their backs are to me, I'll put on my mask. You need to be waiting in the back yard right by the back door. I'll open the door and you move in with the shotgun. We're also going to need a laundry bag to put the money in." Tom-Tom was on a roll.

"Tom-Tom, we have to assume someone is going to be packing. The last thing we need is a standoff,"

"Yeah, I thought about that. We also don't want anyone following us either. Got any ideas?" Tom-Tom asked.

All of a sudden, I got this picture in my mind of all these guys standing around without their pants. I started laughing.

"What are you thinking about, Butch?" Tom-Tom asked suspiciously.

"Well, if we made them take off their pants and took the pants with us, they wouldn't be able to follow us or have guns in their belts." I laughed.

Tom-Tom started to howl. "What a picture that would make, all those guys standing around in their draws. I love it Butch! That definitely will solve the problem."

"One more thing, Tom-Tom, my old man goes to a lot of crap games. I remember overhearing him and his friends talking about what to do if a game got hit. They would take the money out of their pockets and drop it on the floor, then pull their pockets inside out to show they didn't have any more money. So we should move these guys from one side of the room to the other just before we leave."

"God bless your old man, Butch. I sure hope he's not at that game." Tom-Tom started laughing.

"That would be just my luck."

"Let's meet next week at my house. My mother and father will be gone for the weekend. You bring the collar; I'll take care of the rest. We can go over everything with Vinnie and see if he has any more information from Cosmo."

"Okay, Tom-Tom, I'll get a hold of Vinnie and let him know." We walked out of Angelo's at about 4 p.m. You could smell the fall weather even though we were still in Indian summer. We lost our ride when Vinnie left. I called a cab.

"C'mon Tom-Tom, I'll drop you off."

"No thanks, Butch, I gotta see a man about a horse," Tom-Tom winked and smiled as he walked away.

I figured Tom-Tom was going to pick up some things for the score. I started laughing to myself on the way home. I kept seeing Tom-Tom dressed as a priest. I had the cab drop me in front of Saint Cecilia's, my old church.

The church was hundred years old and Gothic in its architecture. The outside was done in a red brick with stone steps leading up to the arch and columned entryway. You entered a vestibule and then walked through large swinging doors that were open when there were no services. The church was open 24 hours a day. There was always someone in there, praying or lighting candles. There were three altars. The main altar in the center was done in carved white marble. The tabernacle doors, crosses and candelabras were gold. The side altars were also white marble, with large life-sized, hand carved marble statues of the Blessed Virgin and other patron saints.

The forty-foot ceilings were arched and supported by large round columns. The ceilings were painted with beautiful Fresno of angels and various saints, done in blues, golds, tans and reds. The Stations of the Cross that ran down the walls of the side isles were done in tiny. beautifully colored ceramic tiles. They looked like oil paintings until you got up close to them. Before the church got electricity, candles lit it. There were about twenty large round chandeliers with room for twenty-five candles on each. During special holidays the chandeliers were lowered by a hand rope-and-pulley system and all the candles were lit. Now they were electric. Entering Saint Cecilia's was like stepping into the fifteenth century.

The smell of incense, candles and flowers moved me back to my youth when I walked in. It was a strange feeling, since I no longer believed in any of this anymore, and yet I felt safe and protected as I did when I was a boy. The tabernacle, where the priests were always bowing and praying, was always a mystery to me. I thought that somehow God was in there. One Sunday after I became an altar boy, I decided to see for myself.

There were six masses on Sunday. Showtime was the 9 am. Mass -- that mass had the largest attendance. Since I could never get the Latin down right and was always responding at the wrong time, I was given the 12 o'clock Mass, which had the least attendance. After mass it was my job to clean up. When mass ended at 1p.m., everyone left for the day. I shut the lights out and walked over to the little gold doors where I thought God might be sleeping.

I was about 9 years old. My hands were shaking as I opened the double gold doors. I saw two gold chalices and a stack of large round white wafers or hosts as they were called, but to my disappointment, no one was in there.

Suddenly, a thunderous voice reverberated through the church: *Get off that altar.* I got so scared I wet my pants and ran into the dressing chamber. Father Driscol cornered me. "What were you doing up there?" All I could do was cry. I was terrified.

"Don't you ever do that again," he admonished. I thought he was going to beat me, but he just let me go.

There were a few women kneeling at the side altars saying their rosary when I walked in. I walked straight up the aisle and then into the dressing chambers where the priests changed into their God costumes. I found two collars of different sizes. I grabbed both of them and left through the side doors. I felt like that little boy again, I even felt like peeing. It was very strange.

I stopped by Jimmy's store, a block away, put the collars in a brown bag and gave the bag to Jimmy. I didn't want Louise to see it.

"Jimmy, hold this for me. I'll pick it up next week."

"What the fuck are doing with this?" he asked laughing.

"I'm thinking about a career change." I said laughing. He didn't ask any more questions.

On my walk home, I started thinking about the crap game and what we were about to do. And, more importantly, who we were going to do it to.

Big John Ormento, who was married to my mother's first cousin, started his career as a member of the "107th Street Gang" and later became the head of that gang. The alumni of that gang read like a who's who in the mafia world: Thomas Lucchese, Vito Genovese, Johnny (Dio) Dioguardi just to name a few. Years later, around 1955, Big John got into the heroine business. He brought in Vito Genovese, Vincent Gigante, Natale Evola, of the Lucchese Family, and Rocco Mazzie, of the Anastasia Family.

According to federal records, Big John ran a $300 million-a-year heroin business in East Harlem; 116th Street was his base. Vincent Rao's restaurant on Pleasant Avenue was his hangout. Rao was also a member. This was the destination of the French Connection. These were heavy-duty men. That's why Vinnie was so worried. But in the scheme of things, our little crap game score would be the equivalent of robbing a pay phone of AT&T. I knew if we got caught, money would not be the issue. It would just be embarrassing. At least that's what I thought.

When I got home I called Vinnie. "We are going to meet at Tom-Tom's house at ten Saturday morning. We have everything worked out."

"Did you also make funeral arrangements for us in case you don't have it worked out?" Vinnie said half joking.

"No, but I'm sure we will have a great send off. I'll see you Saturday."

Tom-Tom lived around the corner from me on 106th Street between First and Second Avenue. He didn't know many of my friends who hung out on 106th Street between Third and Lexington Avenue. It was not unusual for guys in one neighborhood not to know guys who lived two blocks away. Each block was like a different town. If you lived in the Bronx or Queens, you were considered a foreigner from another country. Except for the fiesta of San Eugenia, I rarely went into this block.

It was Saturday morning and the block was humming with life. The kids were playing stickball, the older guys were washing their cars and the women were shopping and getting their hair done. The sun was shining, and the air was crisp and clean. I could feel all the eyes on me as I approached Tom-Tom's building.

"Hello, can I help you?" a young woman asked said as she stepped in front of Tom-Tom's doorway. She was beautiful.

"I'm here to see Tom-Tom. Is this the right building?"

"You must be Butch." she smiled.

"Yes"

"I'm Tom's sister, Mary. He asked me to watch for you. He's upstairs, top floor, first apartment on the left," she said, then rang the doorbell for me.

"Thanks, Mary," I didn't know Tom-Tom had a sister.

I scaled the marble steps three at a time, as I did in my building. When I got to the top floor, there was Father Thomas in full dress, except for the collar and vest. At the top of the stairs I dropped to my knees and held the vest and collar above my bowed head and said, "Bless me, Father, for I have sinned."

Tom-Tom took my stolen gift and said, "Rise my son. All is forgiven."

"I hope one of them fits," I laughed.

"C'mon in and help me put it on before Vinnie gets here."

I walked into Tom-Tom's kitchen. The walls had yellow embossed "conga wall," a linoleum made to look like four-inch square ceramic tiles with black trim. There was a large, green Formica table with matching vinyl chairs up against the wall. The living room had very expensive white and gold Italian Provincial furniture covered with clear plastic. A large crucifix hung above the couch.

I snapped the collar in place and tied the bib-like vest from behind.

"Boy, Tom-Tom, if your mother could see you now."

"Should I wear the straw hat or the felt one?" Tom-Tom asked laughing.

"Since it will be nighttime, I don't think the sun hat will play very well," I said laughing.

The doorbell rang. "That's Vinnie. Ring 'em in, Butch"

I sat at the kitchen table where I had a clear view of Tom-Tom and the door. The door opened and in walked Mary.

She stood there looking at Tom-Tom with her mouth open. Tom-Tom didn't miss a beat.

"What do you think, Sis? Did I miss my calling?" he asked.

Mary was speechless as she made the sign of the cross. The doorbell rang. I thought, *This is the stuff for a sitcom.*

"What are you doing in those clothes, Thomas?" she asked shocked.

"It's my Halloween costume. Don't you like it?"

"That's a sacrilege, Thomas," she said making the sign of the cross again.

By this time Vinnie had climbed the five flights of stairs and knocked on the door. Mary opened the door. She and Vinnie stood there speechless for a moment.

Then Mary said, "Hello Vincent. You're just in time to take Thomas to Bellevue," the well-known hospital for the insane. This was an idea, I am sure, that had crossed Vinnie's mind before.

Vinnie stepped through the door, took one look at Tom-Tom and began to laugh uncontrollably. It was contagious. Tom-Tom and I began to laugh and finally Mary couldn't help herself. She laughed so hard she had to run to the bathroom to pee.

Mary came out of the bathroom, looked at all of us and said; "I don't want to know," and left. We made some coffee and then got down to business. Vinnie really did his homework. He unrolled a large piece of printing paper that Cosmo had given him. It was a detailed layout of the club upstairs on one side and the basement on the other.

"Cosmo said the best time to go in is 11p.m. Saturday night; that's an hour before the shift change at the precinct. He also said that we should assume that Sonny will be packing. That's the bad news. The good news is that no one else will be."

"How does he know that for sure?" Tom-Tom asked.

"Because Sonny doesn't want any drunken losers with a gun," Vinnie answered.

"That makes sense. He's not as stupid as he looks." I said.

"Far from it. I had three four-hour meetings with Cosmo this week. I spent most of the time learning about Sonny. He has a memory like a steel trap. Based on what I learned, I recommend you guys say as little as possible, nothing at all if possible." Vinnie kept looking at Tom-Tom then said, "Tom-Tom will you get out of those fuckin clothes?"

"Why?" Tom-Tom asked.

"Because, there's something very strange about planning a robbery with a priest. I can't concentrate."

Tom-Tom changed and came back to the table.

"Butch, I think you should do the talking when you get in the basement. Sonny might recognize Tom-Tom's voice, given the way Tom-Tom went off on him at Rao's"

"Maybe we should bring cue cards." Tom-Tom laughed.

Vinnie was right. I was surprised at his attention to detail. Even Tom-Tom was impressed.

"Just two more points: neither of you should wear cologne. Butch, I bought you a pair of overalls to wear over your street clothes. Tom-Tom, before I leave here, I want you to give me your priest costume, except for your pants. When I pick you up, wear one of your sport jackets, a white shirt and tie. You can change in the cab,"

"In the cab? What cab?" Tom-Tom laughed, "We are going to have a cab driver as our getaway man? Are you nuts, Vinnie?"

"No, I have a friend who drives a cab. He's giving me the cab for the night. I am giving him 100 bucks. That's three times what he would make if he drove it all night."

"I'm impressed, Vinnie. You seemed to have covered everything," I said.

"Not everything, Butch. I'm still worried about Sonny following you guys through the backyard. He may not worry about having no pants since he won't be in public."

"I wouldn't worry about that, Vinnie. If he's as smart as you say he is, he won't take the chance of getting killed. We just have to make sure we get his gun," Tom-Tom said.

"I think Tom-Tom's right, Vinnie. That would be a really stupid move,"

"Well, that's one of the reasons I got the cab. I didn't want to give Sonny any chance to see my car," Vinnie said.

"Good thinking. I think you covered all the bases. There's just one more thing: where are we going to go right after the score? We need to count the money and stash the guns. I can't go home with all that stuff. My wife will see it," I said.

"I can't either," Vinnie said.

"How about your cousin Joanne's house, Tom-Tom?" I asked.

"Yeah, that's good idea; I'll give her a call. Well, I guess that's it."

"Just one more thing, Vinnie, I want Cosmo to pay Sonny and pick up the inventory, but he shouldn't give him all the money at once. That would tip Sonny off. Tell Cosmo to make a payment plan. Give Sonny $2,500 and take $2,500 in inventory each time. That way he'll think we are selling the inventory to pay him." I said.

"Good thinking, Butch, I think that covers everything." Tom-Tom said.

"I'll pick you guys up here Saturday at ten forty-five downstairs," Vinnie said. We hugged one another and left.

I stepped out on to the sunny street. I loved October weather. The temperature was about 75 degrees. The sun warmed my face and gave me a sense of calmness. I took a deep breath. The air had a cleanliness to it that swept all thoughts from my mind for a moment. I lost any sense of time and with it any sense of myself. It was not an unfamiliar feeling; I wanted to feel this way all the time.

I was going to Jimmy's to see who was around, but without thinking I headed for the East River a block away. I walked along the river past the older Italian men who fished for eel every weekend. They seemed so happy, like their thoughts, too, were being washed away by the same October light and air. I wondered: do you get happier as you get older?

I sat on one of the many green wooden benches that the city provided all along the riverbank. I let the warm sun do its magic. The reflections of the sun off the moving river put me into a trance-like state. I felt safe in this state, but why? Is feeling safe the same as being happy? I wondered. What is being happy? If I don't know that, how will I know when I've become happy?

I tried to think of the last time I really felt happy; the last time the air and sun washed away thoughts and time. I felt myself drifting upwards, above the quiet buildings and rooftops. So this is what it's like to float on the wind like those seagulls. I knew I was asleep, but how could I know I was asleep?

"How strange and delicious this is," I thought, enjoying the conversation with myself. "Hey, there's Frankie Lipman and me, flying pigeons on the blue roof."

I suddenly felt happy. Frankie and I were 12 years old when Johnny Hearn's brother Tom asked us to take care of his birds, while he went to jail for a couple of years. The coup was on the roof of Frankie's building on 108th Street and Park Avenue.

It was called the blue roof because Tom had painted the coup blue. Tom, who was always afraid of being robbed, put a 2-foot by 2-foot metal door on the coup so no adult could get into it, not even Tom. Frankie, who was small, even for a 12-year-old, could easily get in to clean it.

We had about forty-five tiplets. Unlike the blue-gray homing pigeons that were trained to race home from different parts of the country, tiplets, colorful birds of many varieties, were trained to fly into other flocks from neighboring rooftops and bring home as many of those birds as they could to our coup.

All the coup owners had a catch price (ransom) painted on their coup. If you wanted your bird back, you would have to pay anywhere from 50 cents to $1.50 per bird, unless you were at war with the other owners. In that case, it was "catch/kill." Your bird was either hung off a T.V. antenna or sold to local Latin families for dinner.

Having the birds was very exciting for me. Our coup was a six-foot cube, with an eight-foot cube cage attached to it. It had a transom you could open to let the birds back into the coup.

Frankie lived in the building and fed the birds' daily. Every Saturday morning before the neighborhood was awake; Frankie and I let the birds out. Frankie would climb through the small metal door and clean the coup. When he was done, I would clean the cage. We had a ten-foot long bamboo pole that we used to "poke" the birds into the sky. As long as we moved that pole, they would stay in the air circling a square block and moving into different flocks.

To bring the birds down, we threw bird feed on top of the cage roof. I loved watching them land on the coup. Every owner had a "chico," a very well-trained bird that could fly solo into a flock and instead of being absorbed by the flock, would bring back a few birds. I was fascinated by that ability. I wanted to be a "Chico."

We had two Chicos we named Heckle and Jeckel, after the cartoon characters we watched on television. We cheered them on as they flew into different flocks. At lunchtime, if we made any money, we ran to the hot dog stand and bought six hot dogs at seven cents apiece. If we got real lucky, we bought two Yoo-hoo chocolate sodas each.

The blue roof was my sanctuary in the sky where I could forget the black robed vampires that spiritually molested me during the week.

I came to, smiling and wanting a Yoo-hoo soda. I looked at my watch and was surprised that two hours had passed. I felt refreshed and ready for the rest of the day.

I started the four-block walk to Jimmy's. I didn't get one block.

"Butch!" Beans called out from his new black Caddy. Beans was a friend of my father's and a "made guy" I hadn't seen him around for a long time. He just got out of jail and already had a new car. He was in his mid-forty's, short, and stocky, with a husky barroom voice. He always wore dark glasses, even at night.

"Hey Beans! Long time no see. How the hell are you?" I smiled, genuinely lad to see him.

"I am fine. Butch. Congratulations, your dad told me you got married."

"Yeah, thanks, Beans."

"You got a few minutes, Butch? I got a problem. Maybe you can help. Hop in," he said.

"Sure Beans, whatever I can do," I agreed, flattered, that he would ask for my help.

"It's about this kid John Forte. You know who I mean?"

"Yes. I do. It's a shame; he's really strung out on that junk (heroin)."

"Yeah, I know. Do you know Jake the Jew, who owns the pharmacy on Second Avenue?"

"Yeah, I know who he is."

"Well, this kid robbed him so many times, he's going to go out of business, if it doesn't stop," Beans started to laugh. "It's not funny, but it got to the point that when John walked into the store, Jake emptied the register and got the money ready for him." We both laughed.

"I want you to give John a message for me. Tell him if he robs Jake again, it will be his last day on earth. You think you could get that across to him?" Beans asked seriously.

"Yeah, I'm sure he will take me very seriously. I just hope I see him before he does it again."

"Me too; Thanks, Butch. Can I drop you somewhere?"

"Yeah, drop me off by Jimmy's store. I'll put the word out right now," thinking, *There's never a dull moment around here.*

I walked into Jimmy's candy store and right into a "Boss and Under Boss" game.

"You're just in time, Butch. Get your ass over here," Jimmy yelled through his cigar. Boss and Under Boss was the neighborhood's version of group therapy long before there was group therapy. It was a fun way of clearing up gripes and hostilities between friends before they got out of hand.

The game involved any number of participants and anyone could call for a game. There were seven guys involved with this one. The boys were gathered around Jimmy's glass candy case, which subbed as a bar. There were three quarts of Scotch sitting on the bar. The game started with Anthony, the guy who called the game, but excluded him from being Boss or Under Boss.

A number was pulled out of the air, 10 in this case. Each man was counted until the numbers ran out. The next two men, after the numbers ran out, were declared Boss and Under Boss. It was the job of the Under Boss to suggest to the Boss, who was worthy of having a drink. Then the guys around the bar would give all the reasons why that guy should or shouldn't get a drink. The Boss, like a judge, after hearing the arguments, would decide if the guy should get a drink or not.

But his real job was to get everyone drunk enough to loosen up and clear the air, a practice, I think, that would be effective in today's therapy.

In this game Jimmy was Boss and I was the Under Boss. Today's game was called around a failed robbery of a supermarket's Friday receipts that were being taken to the bank early Saturday morning. Since the banks were closed on Saturday, the money was put into a drop box provided by the bank.

The story goes like this: Antonio, who worked at the supermarket, accompanied the manager to the bank, which was just across the street from the market on 15th Street and Second Avenue. The money, cash, checks, and excess coins, was put into a bank canvas lock bag, then into a brown paper shopping bag to conceal the bank bag.

When the manager reached the drop box, he would hand the bag to Antonio while he got his key out to open the box. Then, holding the box open, Antonio dropped the money into the box. It was a score Antonio couldn't pass up. Antonio asked Marcy, Little Louie and Blue Eyes to do the score. None of them were over 23 years old.

That morning, Marcy and Little Louie waited a half block away, while Blue Eyes waited around the corner in his car. When Antonio and the manager left the store to cross the street, Marcy and Little Louie started walking towards the drop. When the manager handed the bag to Antonio, Marcy and Louie open their jackets, put their hands on their guns and Marcy said, "This is a stick-up. Hand over the bag and no one will get hurt."

Suddenly, out of nowhere, a white car with two plain-clothes private armed security guards screeched to a stop in front of the bank. Marcy, thinking the two men was also there to rob the bank, yelled at Antonio: "Hand over the bag asshole." Antonio froze and wouldn't hand the bag over.

"Get the fuckin bag," Marcy yelled to Louie as the two security guys drew their guns and took cover behind their car. Louie tried to pull the paper bag out of Antonio's frozen grip. The paper bag broke, dropping the canvas bag to the ground. One of the security guys yelled, "Police. Get your hands up where I can see them." Marcy pulled his .38 automatic and emptied it on the car.

Marcy, laughing as he recounted this part of the story, said, "These guys watched too many cop shows. When I opened up on them, the guy on the passenger side using the open door as cover, dove into the back seat of the car. The other guy on the driver's side tried to dive under the car but couldn't fit. I think he's still there. We run around the corner where Blue Eyes is waiting for us, and this fuckin asshole is getting a ticket for double parking."

"What the fuck did you want me to do, tell the cop I am in the middle of a robbery, come back later?" Blue Eyes shot back.

"Give that man a drink, Jimmy," I said laughing and thinking, *This is going to be a good one.*

Jimmy poured a double for Blue Eyes and said. "You know Blue Eyes, if you'd a slipped that cop ten bucks, he'd a driven the car for you."

Everyone laughed. "What happened when the cop heard the shots?" I asked Blue Eyes.

"Nothing, he didn't know what to think. If Marcy and Louie hadn't come running around the corner and then run the other way when they saw him, he probably would have finished writing the ticket and left."

"You mean you never got the ticket? Give him another drink, Boss," I said. Everyone cheered.

Blue Eyes continued, "The cop ran to the corner and looked left in the direction of the bank; then looked right, in the direction that Louie and Marcy were running and decided to go to the bank."

Marcy, looking at Antonio says, "...and you, you fuckin idiot, why didn't you give us the money?"

"I was scared, I couldn't move."

It looked like Marcy was going to hit Antonio, so I said. "Boss, give Marcy a double for not killing Antonio." Everybody cheered and Marcy broke into a smile, a very small smile.

Antonio wasn't out of the woods yet. The best was yet to come. Sammy, Antonio's cousin said, with typical neighborhood humor, "I think Antonio deserves a drink for coming away with the $500 reward money for saving the company fifteen grand."

Marcy exploded as we all roared.

"Reward, what reward? Fifteen grand? There was fifteen grand in that bag?"

"Yeah," Sammy pressed on, "and he got promoted to assistant manager too."

Jimmy started filling everyone's glass, giving Marcy a triple. "I propose a toast to Antonio for being the best stick-up tipster this side of the street."

Everyone cheered and then drained their glass. Jimmy quickly refilled them and said, "I propose another toast, to Little Louie for leaving the cash on the ground. After all, Antonio would have never gotten a promotion if it weren't for Louie."

We all cheered and drained our glasses. Jimmy was on a roll, and we were getting bombed . "Another toast to Blue Eyes, the only getaway driver who couldn't get away."

By this time, even Marcy was laughing at the absurdity of it all, but Jimmy wasn't finished. "Raise your glasses guys. To Marcy, the biggest dummy, for going on a score with all these other dummies"

Marcy raised his glass, understanding what Jimmy was driving at, then said with a genuine smile and free of his anger, "I'll drink to that."

We all drained our glasses, hugged one another, thinking the game was over. Then Jimmy said, "Hey! Where are you guys going? We got one more toast. Here's to the smartest guy of the whole lot: the cop who had the good sense to walk in the direction that would keep him out of trouble, no small feat for a cop."

CHAPTER 9

THE SCORE

I got to Tom-Tom's house at 10:40 p.m. He was already waiting in front of his building. My stomach felt like I ate a plate of jumping beans.

"Well, are you ready?" Tom-Tom asked looking excited.

"Yeah, I'm ready, but my stomach is having a nervous breakdown."

Tom-Tom laughed at me. "That's natural, Butch. It's your adrenalin starting to rev up."

"Oh, is that what it is? It feels like I'm scared shitless."

"Yeah I know. It's always that way before a score, but as soon as you step into that basement, that fear will turn to pure adrenalin."

"Where are the guns, Tom-Tom?"

"They're in the laundry bag in back of the hallway." I looked at my watch. It was 5 to 11. "Where the fuck is Vinnie? He's ten minutes late."

"Do you want me to call Sonny and tell him we're going to be late?" Tom-Tom asked laughing.

"Here he is now. Let's get this thing done. Don't forget the guns, Tom-Tom. Vinnie pulled up in the cab dressed like a cabby. Tom-Tom and I changed in the car.

"Butch, I don't know how long it will take for one of the drivers to show up. It could take an hour or ten minutes. Just stay in the yard and wait until I open the basement door. I'll make sure I get Sonny's gun before I open the door. The shotgun is in the laundry bag. Keep it there until I open the door. I also put a flashlight in the bag. It will be very dark in the yard," Tom-Tom said calmly.

"Don't forget these," Vinnie said, as he threw the ski masks into the back seat.

We dropped Tom-Tom off a block away and drove around the corner to the yard entrance. I said to Vinnie as I got out of the cab. "Make sure you don't get a parking ticket while you're waiting for us."

"What?"

"Never mind, I'll tell you later." Vinnie didn't know anything about the robbery.

I descended into the open cellar on 105th Street. The gray stonewalls on either side of me looked like something out of a Dickens's novel. When I got to the bottom of the stairs there was a forty-foot long stone or should I say rock tunnel that ran under the length of the building into the back yard. The rear of all the buildings on the square block faced this yard, forming a large courtyard. Apart from the yellowish glow coming from a few of the rear apartment windows, there was no light at all.

I moved slowly across the yard toward the back door of the club, but I didn't really know where the back door to the club was, and I didn't want to use the flashlight. I was starting to panic. *Fuck, I should've checked this yard out a couple of days ago and gotten the layout,* I said to myself.

I heard some voices just to my right. I turned my head and saw a light coming from the bottom of a door about thirty feet away. *That must be it,* I thought nervously.

I moved quickly towards the door and fell head-on into a bunch of full garbage cans. It was a good thing they were full. Otherwise, they would have sounded loud like a tin drum.

I broke out into a cold sweat and lay perfectly still with my face in a pile of shelled clams, mussels, and spaghetti. *So much for the smell of cologne,* I thought. I waited and listened to see if anyone was alerted. Now I had to pee and thought, *I hope this doesn't turn out to be a Marcy fiasco.*

I was feeling around in the dark, trying to find the laundry bag, which not only had the shotgun and flashlight in it but also my ski mask. My eyes started to adjust to the darkness; I spotted the laundry bag a few feet away. Still lying on the ground, I crawled over the garbage to the bag. I reached in, grabbed the flashlight and mask, leaving the shotgun in the bag. I put the mask on and turned on the flashlight for two or three seconds to make sure I had a clear path to the door.

I made it to the back door, took a piss, and waited. I could hear the excitement of the game coming through the door. I smelled of fish and other things I didn't recognize. A half hour passed. Suddenly everything went silent. My heart started pounding rapidly. My stomach was filled with fear. I reached into the bag and grabbed the shotgun. I heard a metal-to-metal sound and realized I still had my ring on. I took my ring off to put it in my pocket, but my gas station jump suit didn't have any pockets. I threw the ring into the bag and pulled out the double-barreled sawed-off shotgun.

The door swung open, but I couldn't see a fuckin thing. I was blinded by the sudden burst of light. When my eyes adjusted to the light, I stepped into the smoke-filled room. The players were around the crap table with their hands on top of their heads. I didn't see Tom-Tom or Sonny until the door shut behind me. Tom-Tom had Sonny face down on the floor with his foot on Sonny's back. He had one gun pointed at Sonny's head and Sonny's gun pointed at the players.

Suddenly I was calm. Everything shifted into slow motion. "Put everything in your pockets on the table and leave your pockets inside out." I said calmly.

There were about a dozen players in the room. "Now back away from the table."

I put the bag on the table, pointed to the bartender. "Put the money in the bag and don't forget the money on the floor."

I could hear groans when I said that. I recognized two of the players from the neighborhood. "Now put the bag on the table and back away."

I pointed my gun at Sonny. "You, get against the wall"

Tom-Tom let Sonny up off the floor and pushed him hard towards the wall. I knew Tom-Tom wanted to hurt Sonny but hoped he wouldn't do it. I could tell who the out of town guys were by the fear in their eyes. I could see and feel Sonny's anger. He was going to be out for blood.

"Now everyone take off your pants. Leave them on the floor and step away."

The men looked at one another as if they weren't sure what they were hearing. I raised my voice and my shotgun. "You heard me. Do it now!" I pointed to the bartender, "Pick them up and put them on the table."

I handed Tom-Tom the bag of money and my gun and scooped up all the pants with both hands and walked backwards to the door and said, "If you stick your head out the door, I'll blow it off."

"Let me go out first, leave the door open, so we could see where we are going." I whispered to Tom-Tom as I passed him.

"Follow me." We ran across the yard into the long tunnel and up the stairs. I dropped the pants at the top of the stairs, and then Tom-Tom and I jumped into the cab.

"Where to, gentlemen?" Vinnie laughed as he turned on the meter and speed off.

"What the fuck is that smell?" Tom-Tom asked.

"Spaghetti and clams," I said laughing.

We changed into our street clothes and drove the three blocks to the house of Tom-Tom's cousin Joann.

"Take everything out of the cab. I'm going to pick up my car and I'll meet you guys back here in about ten minutes," said Vinnie.

Joanne was watching for us out her window. She rang us in and was waiting for us at the top of the stairs. "C'mon in. I made a little something in case you guys are hungry."

"Where are the kids?" I asked.

"They're upstairs at my sister's, sleeping." Joanne had a table full of food: meatballs, sausage, macaroni, salami, provolone cheese, and a gallon of homemade wine.

"I'm starving," Tom-Tom said as he sat down and jabbed a fork into a sausage.

"I can use a real drink. Got any scotch, Joanne?"

"Sure, Butch. There's a bottle in that cabinet behind you. Help yourself."

"Thanks, Joanne. You shouldn't have gone through all this trouble."

"It's no trouble, Butch. Where's Vinnie?"

"He'll be here in ten minutes," Tom-Tom answered.

"What's that smell?" Joanne asked.

"It's a long story, Joanne." I said laughing, "I tell you about it sometime."

"I'd love to hear it. I know you guys have business to take care of, so help yourself to whatever you want. I'll be upstairs at my sister's. Call me when you're ready to leave."

"Thanks, Joann." I poured myself a triple. I was so wired I couldn't think of eating. "How can you eat, Tom-Tom?"

"I'm hungry. Besides, the food will calm you down better than the booze."

"Tom-Tom, did you see the look on Sonny's face when you pushed him against the wall?"

Tom-Tom laughed. "You should have seen the look on his face when I walked in with the gun at his driver's head."

The doorbell rang. "Wait, Tom-Tom. Vinnie's gonna want to hear all this."

"I need a drink," Vinnie said as he walked in the door.

"A single, double, or triple?" I asked as I poured.

"Just keep pouring I'll tell you when to stop." Vinnie drained the glass, looked at Tom-Tom and said. "How the hell can you eat, Tom-Tom?"

Tom-Tom looked up with a meatball half in his mouth. "Why don't you two guys go count the money and stop breaking my balls?"

Vinnie and I laughed, went into the living room and emptied the laundry bag onto the coffee table. We separated the cash into 10, 20, 50, and 100-dollar bills and began to count.

"A little over $28,000, Tom-Tom;" I said.

Tom-Tom stopped eating, got up from the table and began to bless us.

I didn't see my ring, so I turned the bag upside down and shook it. My ring fell out, along with some folded bills. There were two ten-dollar bills on top and ten $1,000 bills under the tens. None of us had ever seen a $1,000 bill.

"Make that $38,000, Tom-Tom."

Tom-Tom dropped to his knees and said. "It's time for a prayer."

We counted out the $18,000 to pay Sonny. I put the money in a brown paper bag and handed it to Vinnie. "Don't forget to tell Cosmo not to give it to Sonny all at once. Stick to the plan."

"Okay, Butch, I'll tell him again."

Then I said, "There's twenty grand left. I think we should give Cosmo and Joanne $2,500 apiece and whack up the rest between us. That's five grand each. What do you guys think?"

"I think that's very cool," Tom-Tom said. Vinnie agreed.

"Now tell us what happened, Tom-Tom."

"Well, not long after I got there the shift at the precinct started to change. I thought that wasn't supposed to happen until midnight, but I guess they knock off early. Anyway, I was waiting in front of the club, when one of the cops walks over to me and says, 'Hello, Father, can I help you, are you waiting for someone?'

" 'Yes,' " I said. 'As a matter of fact, I'm waiting for Father O'Reilly to pick me up. I got here a little early, but he will be here soon. Thank you for asking,' I said.

"Okay Father, I just wanted to make sure you were all right.'

"'That's very kind of you.' I said, 'I'm fine, thank you. Goodnight Officer.'"

Tom-Tom sounded like a Harvard graduate. I couldn't believe my ears. "Where did you learn to speak like that?"

"You mean English."

"Well, yeah!

"I was also educated by the Jesuits. Street English is my second language. Anyway I decided not to wait in front of the club. I didn't want any more cops coming over to check on me. I look too young to be a priest and I didn't want to take any more chances. I crossed the street and waited on the stoop of the building directly across from the club.

"A green Bonneville pulled up in front of the club. One guy got out and stood in the doorway of the club, while the driver went to park the car. A few minutes later I saw the driver walking up the street, but I wasn't sure if he was the driver or one of the cops reporting for work. I thought, *Oh shit, how am I going to do this without them seeing my face.* I thought about giving the whole thing a pass, but I didn't want to go through all this again, so I took out my piece and covered it with my ski mask and pulled my hat down.

"I waited until the driver reached the club door. When I saw him reach for his keys, I started walking across the street yelling, 'Excuse me, excuse me!' Both of them turned towards me and waited as I crossed the street. I kept looking down at my hand as if I was looking at an address and was going to ask them for directions. When I got close enough to them, I pulled the mask off the gun and stuck it into the driver's stomach. They both looked down at the gun, which is what I hoped they would do. 'Turn around, open the door and don't look back. Miss a beat and your both dead.' As they stepped inside. I put the mask on."

"Holy shit, Tom-Tom, are you sure they didn't get a good look at you?" I interrupted.

"The only thing they saw was the gun. They were bewildered that I was a priest. I walked them to the staircase in the back of the club. I was about to go down but decided it would be better if I got Sonny to come upstairs because I didn't know where he would be in the room downstairs. So I put the gun in the back of driver's head and told him to call Sonny and ask him to come up here for a minute. When Sonny walked through the door and saw me with the gun in the driver's head, he didn't know whether to shit or go blind." Vinnie and I started laughing.

"I pointed the gun at Sonny's face. He was wearing a beautiful navy blue, mohair suit. I told him to lay face down on the floor with his hands behind his head. He was carrying a snub nose .38 special in the small of his back. I motioned the driver and the player towards the stairs. I put the barrel of my gun against the back of Sonny's head and cocked the hammer back. I put my hand between the back of his neck and his shirt and lifted him to his feet, never taking the cold barrel off his head. I motioned the other two to start walking down the stairs in front of us, then whispered in Sonny's ear, 'Go down very slow. If I trip, the first thing to go is your head. Got it?' He nodded his head.

"The four of us stepped into the room. The players were all huddled around the crap table placing bets and yelling at the dice. I marched Sonny to the back door and pushed him to the floor and put my foot on his back. When the players looked up and saw Sonny and me, I had Sonny's gun pointed at them and my gun pointed at Sonny's head. Then everything went quiet. That's when I opened the door to let you in."

CHAPTER 10

A DUMMY WILL BREAK YOU QUICKER THAN A THIEF

It was Saturday morning, a week after the score, when my mother got a call from my aunt Millie, Big John's wife. My mother, who lived a floor below me, knocked on my door and handed me Big John's phone number. "Big John wants you to call him. Why would he want to talk to you, Butch?"

"I don't know. Give me the number and I'll find out." I knew what the call was about, and my mother knew that I knew what the call was about. The chances of Big John wanting or needing to talk to me, was less than zero.

Before I called Big John, I called Vinnie and Tom-Tom to see what they knew, if anything. I couldn't reach either of them. I called John's house and my aunt Millie answered the phone.

"Hello! Aunt Millie? It's Butch. How are you?"

"I am just fine, Butch. John wants you to come to the house."

"When?"

"Right now."

John lived in Lido Beach, Long Island, about thirty-five miles from me.

"I don't have any way of getting there right now, Aunt Millie. I don't have a car."

"Hang on a minute, Butch. I'll tell him."

My stomach started to do flips as I waited on the line.

"Butch, John said to take a cab."

"Okay! Aunt Millie. Tell him I'm leaving right now."

"Good, I'll tell him."

I tried giving Vinnie and Tom-Tom another call, but no luck.

I got a cab and headed out to Long Island.

John and his boss, Tom (a.k.a. Three-finger Brown) Lucchese had built homes next to one another. I couldn't imagine John would involve Lucchese in anything like our score. The problem I had was that I didn't know exactly what John knew or how he knew it. I was at a big disadvantage. On the way to John's house, my mind began to flip through everything I had heard about John and then my first-hand experience of him.

John had just come out of hiding. He had attended the infamous Appalachian meeting of all the important Mafia members nationwide where they got busted. John was one of the men who got away.

My father had told me that Vito Genovese called the Appalachia meeting and had two things on his agenda: first, to unseat my cousin Charlie and install himself as head of the Commission; second, to lift the band on the drug business that Charlie had imposed - in that order. It made sense because Big John and Vito were already in the heroin business, but the meeting turned out to be a huge blunder for Vito. They got busted with all the bosses around the country.

Since the authorities had nothing on Big John, he was advised by his attorney to disappear while they proceeded without him. It was good advice.

All reports indicated that Big John had left the country. The authorities suspected he went to South America or another foreign place. For all intents and purposes, he had left, but he was actually in the Bronx for two years.

He beat the case and had just emerged, but it would not be long before he was indicted again on drug conspiracy.

Big John was probably less than five foot, seven inches tall, but he was close to 250 pounds. He always had a tan when I saw him for some reason. He looked very much like George Raft, with his black hair parted just left of center. His skin was smooth and dark, his eyes dark brown, slightly bulged, with dark circles under them. He had a smoker's raspy voice, which I loved listening to. He wore the finest handmade suits, and the jewelry he wore on any given day could buy the average American home.

John loved money and power, and he had both. He controlled the trucking business in the New York garment district and owned one of the trucking companies. Through his relationship with Johnny (Dio) Dioguardi, who controlled the Teamsters Union in New York at the time, John was able to dictate which clothes manufactures would be organized by the union and which manufactures wouldn't.

They were on both sides of the deal. As a result, the manufactures would pay Big John to keep the unions out of their shops. The manufactures that were organized would pay Johnny Dio to avoid strikes and to keep wages low. My whole family was connected to the garment business in various ways. Some owned factories; others were union organizers and delegates.

I watched John stir up some pretty heated discussions at the dinner table, all the time knowing how it really worked. He loved it. Anyway, this cozy arrangement brought in $100,000 a week, not counting the cash flow from union dues.

I heard that John was also a silent partner in various nightclubs in New York and that he and Frank Costello were the real owners of the famous Copa Cabana nightclub. It made sense, because when my sister went to her high school prom, John arranged a front row table for her and three of her friends. When they arrived at the club, they waited in line for about a half hour before they got to the maître-de, who refused to seat them. My sister had given him her name but failed to mention who she was.

It was ten thirty and already thirty minutes past show time. The audience was getting restless and the manager was in a panic. My sister's escort overheard the manager telling the Maître d, "If we don't find John's niece, heads are going to roll." My sister's escort said to my sister. "Boy I wish you was this guy John's niece."

"But I am John's niece."

When she told the manager who she was, he acted as if he was just given a reprieve from a death sentence. "Why didn't you tell me who you were? Thank God you're here."

By time they were seated, it was almost forty-five minutes past show time. When Jimmy Durante walked out on the stage, he walked over to my sister's table and asked, "Is it all right if we start the show now?"

For the rest of the evening, the audience kept looking over at my sister's table, wondering who they were. Every once in a while during his performance, Durante walked over to my sister's table and asked. "Are you enjoying yourself? You know I can't afford any bad reviews." It was a very exciting evening for her. When her escort asked for the check, he was told. "You are a guest of the club." Even the waiters wouldn't accept tips. She was truly a princess that night.

John had a fierce reputation. He was Genovese's right-hand man and was feared and respected by everyone, including Genovese. When he wasn't in jail, he was home entertaining and spending time with his two children. He was a generous, funny man and loved playing practical jokes.

One summer, he and his friend "Tom Mix" decided to go to the races at Saratoga Springs, New York, to watch a couple of horses they had just bought run that track. For the occasion he and Tom bought a brand-new Cadillac to make the trip.

After about five days of partying, neither one of them felt like driving back to the city, so, John decided to call Jerry the Greek and Casti, (short for Castilano) and have them take the train up to Saratoga Springs to drive them back. John knew the two men hated each other and loved the idea that they would be sitting together for six hours.

Jerry was a short, stubby, bald-headed man, who had a lisp and stuttered when he was nervous. Casti was a serious guy who couldn't stand being around Jerry. They were told to come up on important business. When they got to the hotel, John told them that they weren't needed after all.

They left the next morning with John and Tom sitting in the back seat, while Jerry and Casti took turns driving. Jerry was steaming and wanted to get home as soon as possible. Speeding toward New York at 90 mph, he was pulled over by a motorcycle cop. When the cop asked for Jerry's license, John noticed that the cop also had a lisp like Jerry's. That's all John needed to know.

"Whathh thh trouble offither?" Jerry asked the cop.

The cop who sounded like Elmer Fudd said, "You know god... god dam well whathh thh trouble is."

Then John said to Jerry, "Jerry, give the officer your license and stop making fun of him."

"Are you makthhing fun of me, you litthhil bathtard?"

"No Offither."

"C'mon, Jerry, don't be disrespectful." The more John taunted Jerry, the worse Jerry's speech became and the more furious the cop became. At one point the cop got so pissed off, he grabbed Jerry by his neck and tried to pull him out of the car through the window. John finally got out of the car and told the cop that Jerry really did have a lisp and apologized then gave the cop five hundred bucks. John loved telling that story.

I rang Big John's doorbell. My aunt, who was not quite five feet tall, opened the door, looked at me and shook her head back and forth, as if to say, "What the hell did you do?"

"Where is he?"

"He's downstairs in the lounge."

"Is he mad?" She just rolled her eyes. John had built a cocktail lounge in the lower half of his house, complete with rosewood bar, built-in gray velvet seats, art decco wall sconces, and sound system. One wall had eight sliding glass doors that opened the entire wall to the pool and cabana area.

John was standing behind the bar in a beautifully tailored white-on-white shirt, tan gabardine slacks, and oxblood loafers. He had just lit a Camel with his gold Dunhill. Sitting at the bar with him, in a navy-blue, silk suit was a darkly handsome man who looked like he could be John's twin brother, except he was two or three inches taller and hundred pounds lighter. I found out later it was Johnny "Dio," who had just gotten out of prison.

I stood in the doorway of the lounge, afraid to walk in. Drawing on his Camel, he looked at me with the coldest eyes I had ever seen in my life. I broke into a cold sweat. He just kept looking at me without saying a word, then motioned me over to the bar stool that was in front of him. When I walked into the lounge Dio got up from the bar and sat at one of the booths. I looked at him wondering, *Who is this guy and what does he have to do with this?* He avoided any eye contact with me, which sent the temperature in the room down another ten degrees.

There was an open bottle of scotch on the bar. I sat directly in front of John but avoided looking at him.

"Are you a tough -guy?"

"No, Uncle John."

"Don't Uncle John me, you little prick."

His face started turning red; then, like thunder bellowing from deep inside his huge body, his words hit me: "Who the fuck do you think you are?"

His dark eyes bulged out of his head like two little balloons. Blue veins appeared on his forehead. The sheer force of his rage almost sent me off the barstool.

I felt paralyzed.

"Answer me, you little bastard." I couldn't speak, I was terrified. "Where do you get the balls to pull a stunt like this; where, tell me where?"

I could hear my aunt running down the stairs yelling, "John! John!" She stood in the doorway. "John, take it easy." Then in Sicilian she said. "He's just a boy."

John looked at my aunt and yelled, "What I want to know is where this kid gets the nerve to pull a stunt like this?"

Then, this little, blue-eyed women, who hardly weighed one hundred pounds and always sported a smile and an incredible sense of humor, looked at her husband and said. "You gotta be kidding. If you really want to know John, turn around and take a good look." John turned around, not knowing what she was getting at and found himself staring into a huge deco-etched blue tinted mirror. "That's where," my aunt said, making her point and her getaway at the same time.

Dio, who had known John since they were kids, could not stop himself from laughing. John was a notorious stickup man early in his "career." Once, while running from the cops after a robbery, he ran past my mother, threw his gun into my sister's carriage with my sister in it then ran into my grandfather's barbershop, out the back door and into the yard to make his getaway.

John was caught off guard by my aunt's comment and Dio's laughter. He even had what appeared to be a slight smile on his face, but it didn't stay there very long.

Then, as if on cue, my two partners came walking in with their fathers in tow or maybe it was the other way around. Needless to say, no one looked very happy. Vinnie gave me that "I told you so" look, while Tom-Tom, recognizing Johnny Dio from newspaper pictures and never having met Big John, acted like he was granted an audience with the Pope. For a moment I thought he was going to genuflect and kiss Big John's five-carat diamond pinky ring.

The men ignored us while they greeted one another. Then I saw for the first time, something I had heard about; that Members of this Secret Society kissed one another on the lips. It was not uncommon for a father and son to kiss on the lips, but never, ever, anyone else. It was something they never did publicly, and I was surprised they did it in front of us.

I felt oddly privileged. I saw in that moment, that these men lived in a very different world than the rest of us. They had their own laws, culture, and rituals; it was not just a Secret Society, but a Sacred one. It was a Secret and Sacred Holy Order to them, so secret that they never named it.

Amongst themselves it was referred to as "our thing" or in Sicilian "La Cosa Nostra." If a Member was introduced to another Member he had never met, the introduction would be, "This is a friend of ours," rather than, "This is a friend of mine." If a Member took a non-member under his wing, the introduction was "He's with me."

Membership required sponsorship and a long apprenticeship. Your sponsor was known as your "Godfather." This commitment was so serious that your Godfather was held accountable for your actions. He could literally be killed, along with you, of course, for something you did.

The Sacred Order came before your wife, your children, even your own life. Up until the early twentieth century, membership required that you be Sicilian and, if you were called upon, to kill for the sake of the Order. My cousin Charlie changed the Sicilian requirement and created the next generation of that Order. Big John, Vito Genovese, Meyer Lansky, Ben "Bugsy" Segal and the nationwide members attending the meeting at Appalachia were that next generation.

"Wait outside," John said, motioning us towards the cabanas. When we got out of hearing range, I asked Vinnie,

"How the fuck did John find out about this, and how does he know it was us?"

"I'll give you three guesses." Tom-Tom chimed in.

"It was Cosmo, right?" I said

"Yeah, it was Cosmo." Vinnie groaned.

"What the fuck happened?"

"Puggie, as Sonny's boss and Big John's lieutenant, told Sonny he would have to make good for everyone's losses that night, so he came down hard on Cosmo and Cosmo paid him our whole eighteen grand. I guess Puggie put two and two together."

"You guess he put two and two together? An idiot could've done that, Vinnie. Cosmo knew damn well that's what would happen. You know, Vinnie, we would've been better off if we had told Sonny to go fuck himself and let your cousin and Sonny take the hit for the whole fuckin' thing. That's the way it should've gone down anyway, and Sonny knows it. Your cousin has a pair of prunes for balls.

Carl was right, I thought to myself. *A dummy will break you quicker than a thief.*

"What difference does it make now?" Tom-Tom said.

"Tom-Tom's right, Butch, the question is what are we going do now?"

"Wrong, Vinnie. The question is what is John going to do now?" I said shaking my head in disbelief.

"Well, one thing for sure, he's not going to kill us. You had that one right, Butch." Tom-Tom said.

"I wonder why your old man isn't here, Butch." Vinnie said.

"Maybe, John's just going to kill Butch." Tom-Tom laughed.

"That's probably who their waiting for right now," I said.

"It's been almost an hour. What the fuck are they doing in there?" Vinnie asked nervously.

We could hear a lot laughing. "Listen, they sound like they're having a party in there. Butch, here comes your old man and he ain't laughing," Tom-Tom said.

"Let's go," My father said sternly. When we got into the room, no one was laughing. It looked like a funeral - ours.

"Between the players and the house, you cowboys owe fifty grand." John said looking at me.

"What! Wait a minute, Uncle John, all we got was $28,000. I wasn't going to admit to the other ten grand in thousand dollar bills. "And we already gave Sonny 18k and ..."

"Who's Sonny?" John interrupted; then I realized John didn't know everything.

"He works the game for Puggie." I said.

John turned to my father and said, "Carl, call Puggie and ask him to meet me here tomorrow morning before ten."

"Okay, John," my father agreed.

"There's a lot more to this, Uncle John..." I was about to tell him the whole story, but he stopped me cold.

"I don't want to hear it. Whatever the story is, it doesn't change a fuckin' thing for you guys. You knew the game belonged to me, so your reasons aren't an excuse."

I was going to explain anyway, but I thought, *I better keep my mouth shut until I knew more myself.*

"You gangsters are going to pay back every fuckin' dime," Big John informed us.

I thought, *Well this isn't too bad and started to think of ways to get the money.*

Then, as if he was reading my mind Big John said, "But you are going to work for it, and I mean work. Monday morning at 7:30 a.m. you go and see the shop steward at the construction site of the Bronx State Mental Hospital," he said as he handed each of us the address.

"His name is Tony "Cigars." He will be expecting you, and God help you if you don't show up. In fact, God Himself won't be able to help you, if you don't show up. Do you understand me?" he asked, looking at me the whole time he was talking to us. It was almost like Vinnie and Tom-Tom weren't even there. He acted like he knew it was my idea.

"Tony will get your union books, and you will start work that day. Every week you will give half of your pay to Tony until you've paid back every fuckin' dime."

Just the thought of being a laborer made me sick. Not only was the work hard, but also the winters were brutal, and winter was almost here. I knew I was being relegated to the life of the ordinary citizen, fifty weeks of work a year with two weeks off - prison.

I was sure John didn't have a clue what laborers made. The numbers were flashing in front of my eyes. "Uncle John, do you have any idea what a laborer makes?"

"No, and I don't give a fuck either."

I explained, "$3.65 an hour. That's $126.50 a week, after taxes maybe 100 bucks. It would take us almost four years to pay that back." I was squirming in my seat, and he loved every minute of it. I looked at Tom-Tom and Vinnie to see if they had anything to say. They didn't want any part of this.

"You guys might have to get a second job." Big John said laughing. So that's what these guys were laughing about for an hour.

There was only one way John had heard about this, and that was from Puggie, but why didn't Puggie mention Sonny or the eighteen grand? Something smelled here, and I was going to get to the bottom of it. The only thing I wanted to do then was get the fuck out of there.

"Can we go now, Uncle John?"

"Yeah sure, better get some rest, you're going to need it." He could hardly contain his laughter. I didn't answer him. I was really pissed off and he knew it.

I turned to Vinnie and said, "Vinnie, I need a ride home, and we need to talk."

"Okay, Butch, but I gotta drop my father off in Yonkers. Why don't you ride up with me?"

"No, drop me home first. I want to change and check-in with my wife, I'll meet you at Joe's.

"Tom-Tom, are you coming with us?" I asked.

"No, I'm going to ride back with my old man."

"Okay, I'll see you at Joe's." I said.

It was three in the afternoon when I got home. Louise was anxious to know what was going on.

"What was that all about, Butch?"

"Big John got me, Tom-Tom and Vinnie construction jobs. We start work Monday."

"That's great news baby," she smiled. "We should celebrate."

"Yeah, we should, but let's wait until I get my first paycheck." I said. feeling like I was going to vomit.

CHAPTER 11

THE LIFE OF THE ORDINARY CITIZEN

Tom-Tom was already at Joe's Bar when I got there. "Where's Vinnie? He should be here by now."

"I don't know, Butch. I was just wondering the same thing. Did you eat? I'm starving."

"Nothing stops your appetite. You amaze me."

"What? We gotta eat."

"Right now, I want a double scotch and Cosmo's two little prunes he has for balls on a plate," I said.

"I rather have spaghetti and meat balls. You can have spaghetti and Cosmo's balls and Vinnie can have spaghetti and Sonny's balls." Tom-Tom laughed and made me laugh. Tom-Tom was always good at making me laugh. It was a quality I really appreciated in him.

He added, "Look at the bright side, Butch. We're alive and we still have our balls."

"Yeah, but Monday those balls will be hanging, and when winter comes, they will shrink to the size of Como's two prunes.," I said laughing.

"Vinnie's here, Butch. I just saw his car go by. Let's grab a table and talk over dinner."

"Okay, Tom-Tom, find something in the back where no one can hear us."

"Right," he agreed leading the way.

Vinnie sat down and ordered a drink. The same question kept bouncing around in my head. "Vinnie, why do you think Puggie never mentioned that prick Sonny to Big John?"

"I know exactly why," Vinnie said. "Do you know a guy named Steve?"

"Yeah, I know that reckless asshole," I answered. "What's he got to do with it?"

"Well, he and Sonny are friends. In fact, he was the one that got Sonny the job with Puggie. Anyway, Sonny ran to Steve when this whole thing went down and made a deal with him. If Steve would get him off the hook with Puggie, he would give Steve our inventory. What I don't get is how this guy has that kind of juice with Puggie. Who the fuck is Steve?"

"First, tell me how you know all this." I said.

"My father told me on the way home."

"How does he know all this?"

"I don't know. He didn't tell me, and I didn't ask."

"I'll tell you how he has that much juice. He's Puggie's brother-in-law."

"What are you talking about, I know Puggie's brother in-law and it ain't him," Vinnie said.

"Okay, then let's call him Puggie's illegitimate brother in-law. Steve's sister has been Puggie's mistress for years and they have two children together. I've been seeing him come out of her building across the street from Jimmy's store for years, but I never put it together until now."

"Are you kidding me? Puggie's wife and three kids live only a block away."

"I know. What's even scarier is that the children look so much alike."

Tom-Tom said, "Okay, now we know what happened. So what? We still have to show up Monday for work."

"Yeah, I know, but this is the second time Steve put himself where he didn't belong. I walked away from a numbers business because of him. He's reckless, dangerous and a legend in his own mind. What he doesn't understand is that 'what goes around comes around.' No one is exempt."

"That's great philosophy, Butch, but how does it get us out of this fuckin' job?"

"It doesn't."

"Then, will you put some of that brain power to work on that problem. The last thing we need is a fuckin' job."

"Just off the top of my head, Tom-Tom, we could get ourselves fired."

"How are we going to do that?"

"I don't know yet, but it shouldn't be that hard."

CHAPTER 12

"Where the hell is Vinnie?" I asked. "I know he's always running late."

"Not this time, Butch. He's not coming. His old man got him a job in a print shop."

"How did he get away with that?"

"I don't know, but he still has to pay his end of the deal.

A half hour went by then a two hundred pound, 50-year-old, cigar-smoking gorilla approached us wearing a gray fedora hat and brown overalls. "You da guys dhat I gotta put ta work?"

"Yeah," I said.

"Falla me."

"Is he speaking English, Butch?" Tom-Tom asked me.

"I'm not sure. He's probably from Brooklyn. Let's just follow him." He led us to an open gate where a flatbed trailer truck loaded with two hundred cement bags was waiting to be unloaded. He pointed to a spot about twenty yards away. "Put it ova dare," he said and walked away.

The bags weighed ninety-four pounds each. The driver stood on top of truck and loaded the bags on our backs as if we were mules. The first bag buckled my knees. By lunchtime we still had half the load left, and the first layer of the skin on my shoulders was gone.

"We gotta get out of this Butch, and I mean now. I'd rather spend six months in a hospital than carry one more fuckin' bag."

"Me too," I said. Before the idea of being in the citizen class was just a fear. Now I could taste it

After lunch the gorilla took us to the just-completed first floor of the T-shaped building. The building was so long it took a few minutes to walk from end to the other. "Stay here," the gorilla mumbled.

A crane loaded with sixteen-foot-long, 3 by 4-inch pieces of lumber lowered the load to the floor where Tom-Tom and I were standing. The gorilla then ordered us to carry the heavy "ribs," as they were called, two at a time, to the other end of the building.

Tom-Tom observed, "Butch, that prick could have dumped this load on the other side of the building. He's just fucking with us. Look at him, with that shit eatin' grin on his face. I'd like to throw him right off the fuckin' building."

"Why don't we do that?" I laughed. "It would get us fired."

"You gotta be kiddin'. We couldn't get away with that." Tom-Tom objected.

"We could if it was an accident," I assured him.

"But that prick would know it wasn't an accident," said Tom-Tom.

"That's right. So what? Knowing and proving are two different things," I said.

Tom-Tom agreed. "Your right, if he really thought it was an accident, we wouldn't get fired. Brilliant."

"Please Tom-Tom; don't say that word, my last brilliant idea got us here."

Tom-Tom smiled. "I'll try to remember that," he said and asked, "So what's the plan?"

I had already thought it out. "Simple," I said. "When he stands at the edge of the building to signal the crane operator, I'll just turn around with the lumber on my shoulder and knock him off, like I didn't see him. You were on the other end of the building and didn't see anything."

"Why do you get to do it and not me?" complained Tom-Tom.

"Because it was my idea."

"No it wasn't," he argued. "It was my idea. I was the one who said I felt like throwing him off the building."

"Okay, Tom-Tom, but, if he dies, who's gonna fire us?" I reasoned.

He got my point. "You're right. I didn't think of that. I'll just hit him softly, so he falls slowly to the ground."

"Good idea," I smiled giving Tom-Tom his way.

The gorilla landed feet first in soft excavated dirt that was around the foundation and broke both his legs. While waiting for the ambulance, he accused Tom-Tom of doing it on purpose and had the foreman fire Tom-Tom and lay me off. I was ecstatic. It was two in the afternoon when Tom-Tom and I walked off our new job.

"Let's go to Joe's and celebrate, Butch. I'm glad that prick didn't die, but I have to admit, I had mixed feelings about that," Tom-Tom said.

"Yeah, I know what you mean."

We got to Joe's around three in the afternoon. After a few drinks, Tom-Tom said. "You know, Butch, the more I think about it, the more pissed off I get about Sonny and this guy Steve. We pay Sonny eighteen grand, then he takes eighteen grand of our inventory and gives it to Steve, and Steve gets Sonny a pass. Even worse, we have to pick up the tab."

"You forgot the part about we are supposed to bust our asses working to pay everything back." I reminded him.

"Boy, if that's not adding insult to injury, I don't know what is. We gotta do something about this. Got any more brilliant ideas?"

"Lots, but none of them makes us any money. Right now that's the first order of business for me. Don't forget, I have a wife and a kid on the way."

"Yeah, I do forget," Tom-Tom nodded. "I still can't believe you're married."

"Neither can I. Speaking about married, I better get home and break the news to Louise."

It was six by time I got home. Louise was cooking and looking happy. I hated to drop this bomb on her.

"Hi, Baby. What are you making?"

"Spaghetti and clams."

"Really? That's great!" I said even though my stomach turned at the thought of it.

"I got some bad news, honey," I told her. "I was fired from the job today. I was involved in an accident and...."

"I know," she interrupted me.

"How do you know?"

"Your Aunt Millie called and said that Big John straightened everything out and you can go back to work tomorrow." I couldn't believe what I was hearing. That son of a bitch really means business.

The phone rang. It was Tom-Tom. He said, "Do you believe this shit? Now I wish that bastard had died."

The next day we reported for work where we were to join a crew building the Bronx State Mental Hospital. They split Tom-Tom and me up. Tom-Tom went to work with the carpenters, and I was assigned to the "bull gang." The bull gang consisted of an all-black crew of about twelve "strippers." It was their job to knock out the T-shaped 4 by 4 inch "jacks" that supported the entire weight of the concrete slabs.

It was very hard and dangerous work. Those doing it were paid 25 cents an hour over union scale because no one wanted to do it.

The bull gang stripped the wooden forms from the concrete after it dried, pulled all the nails out, and stacked the 4 by 8 sheets of plywood between each column. The "ribs" which supported the decking, 3 by 4 inch, sixteen feet long heavy pieces of lumber, were stacked in the next column.

I walked up to the first floor where all the lumber was being stacked and waited there for "Tu Beau," pronounced two-bow, the head of the stripping gang. Tu-Beau arrived and introduced himself. Then he called out to a group of men that were standing by the staircase.

"Chort Dic, come on over here. I want you to meet your new partner."

Chort Dic, his nickname, was really Short Dick. He was five-foot-tall and five-foot-wide. He looked to be around 40 years old. I could barely understand his thick southern accent. I have learned from and been influenced by many different people in my life, but Short Dick, unbeknownst to him, or maybe not, taught me some things that I used my entire life.

Every day, we walked from one pile of lumber to the next lifting the heavy plywood and passing it to the next floor. A few times the wind blew the plywood right out of our hands, almost taking us with it. We had to lift the sixteen-foot-long pieces of lumber from the ends leaving 80 percent of the wood hanging off the building, which tripled the weight. My body would shake because of the strength it took to pass these long pieces to the next floor.

Every morning I would stand at the end of the building and look at the stacks of lumber and go into a complete depression thinking that this was going to be the rest of my life. I was locked in the citizen class and saw no way out.

One day, after a week of this unbearable work, Short Dick said to me, "Don't look at it, boy. Just walk on into it." Each and every morning as the gray winter came upon us, Short Dick said the same thing, "Don't look it, boy. Just walk on into it." It was his way of saying, "The best thing to do, when you are overwhelmed by what's ahead of you, is just do what's in front of you."

He worked hard and effortlessly, demonstrating to me what he was preaching. He didn't just talk the talk, he walked the walk. I admired and respected him for that. He couldn't read or write but was very wise. He taught me to take life as it comes and that sometimes, "When you got too much problems and you don't know what to do, it's better to wait until you do know what to do."

I used my real name, Sal, in the "outside world" but Short Dick could never quite rap his tongue around it. He pronounced it Soul. It was a November morning and the temperatures were dropping into the low twenties, when Short Dick announced "Um goin' home, Soul"

I was taken back by the news. I didn't realize how attached to him I had become. He made my life bearable and taught me patience and endurance.

"Why, Short Dick?" I asked him. "There's at least two years work here."

"It's time to retire, Soul, and go home to my family."

"Retire?" I objected. "You're too young to retire. Besides, what are you going to do for the rest of your life?"

"Soul, I'm seventy-two years old, not much more life left to worry about that." He could see I was surprised and upset. I couldn't believe he was that old, but as those thoughts were running through my mind, his eyes changed and suddenly I could see his age. He was letting go of his life right in front of me. His eyes became soft and loving.

I began to cry like a little boy who was losing his father. He put out his left hand, and, like a little boy, I held his warm hand and we walked hand in hand to the staircase. I felt sad and afraid. We said nothing to each other until we reached the staircase.

I knew I would never see him again and so did he. He turned and looked into my eyes and said gently, "Don't be afraid, Soul. You gonna be alright."

He squeezed my hand tightly, then turned and descended the staircase. I could feel the warmth of his hand traveling through my whole body and suddenly the fear and sadness disappeared. I felt different and changed in some way I didn't understand.

Years later, whenever I found myself overwhelmed by my life, I would hear Short Dick's soft, caring voice of courage, "Don't look at it, boy. Walk on into it," and when I became afraid I heard him saying, "Don't be afraid Soul. You're gonna be alright." Short Dick restored a sense of faith in me, not in religion or God, but in the mysterious knowledge and spirit of Short Dick. From that day on, everything in my life began to change.

CHAPTER 13

MAFIA JUSTICE: THE SIT DOWN

It was the day before Thanksgiving, when I ran into Puggie coming out of his mistress's building. Puggie was about five feet eight inches tall, with a round chubby face and a naturally pug nose. He was one of my Uncle John's most trusted lieutenants. He had a gentle, soft voice and meticulous manners.

He and my father were childhood friends. He wielded a lot of power in the Teamsters and trade unions and like most powerful men I knew, he never flaunted it. He always made me feel comfortable and important. I never found out what he told Big John at the meeting he had after Big John's meeting with us.

"Hi Puggie. How are you?" I greeted him.

"Hello Butch. How are you doing?"

"I'm doing well. Say, Puggie, do you have a minute?" I ventured.

"Sure Butch. Walk with me to the car." As we walked together, he asked, "What's up?"

"First, I want to apologize for knocking off the game. I owe you an explanation." I wanted to find out what he had told Big John and if Sonny had told him the real story. It didn't make sense to me why Sonny got a pass even if Steve went to bat for him, but I had to be careful.

"That's not necessary, Butch. You're doing the right thing by making good the money," Puggie chuckled and continued, "But I am curious, why would you knock off my game, knowing it belonged to your uncle?" His question told me that he didn't know the real story. He motioned me to get in the car with him. I could see he was cold.

"We wanted to get to Sonny for fucking us around."

"What are you talking about?" Now, I knew that Sonny didn't tell him the whole story.

"What did Sonny tell you?" I asked him.

He responded, "Never mind what Sonny told me. I want to know why you wanted to get to Sonny." I could see he was getting irritated, but he didn't seem irritated with me.

I ran the whole story by him starting with Kelly's bust without mentioning Kelly's name, and I told him that Sonny knew the rules but wouldn't follow them and that Sonny had smacked Cosmo in front of his son. Puggie cringed when he heard that.

I went on, "And Sonny wouldn't give us back the eighteen grand in inventory so we could sell it and pay him back."

I explained that Cosmo first told us that Sonny put the money up to be a 50 percent partner, but when the deal went bad Sonny told him it was a loan, and he had to pay it back with interest. He had it both ways.

I added that Sonny even tried to intimidate us at Rao's. I ended by explaining, "Tom-Tom wanted to kill him rather than pay him what he didn't deserve. Given the way it worked out, I should have let him do it."

I could see Puggie's blood boiling. "Why, didn't you tell John all this?"

"I tried, but he didn't want to hear it. He was so pissed off, he didn't want to hear anything."

"That's because you disrespected and embarrassed him. The story that his nephew didn't go to him to straighten this out and instead robbed his business made him look bad. If you guys weren't family, you'd be dead right now. You know that, don't you?"

"I was counting on it."

Puggie shook his head, looked at me, chuckled and said, "John was right. You got some pair of balls." His next question was the $64,000 question.

"What happened to the inventory?"

"Well, I can only tell you what I heard. I don't know if it's true, but I heard that Sonny made a deal with Steve to sell the inventory and split the money with him if Steve would get him off the hook with you."

Puggie started shaking his head up and down as he was absorbing all this and kept saying., "I see, I see, I see. So let me get this straight. You gave Sonny eighteen grand that you got from the game and he kept the inventory?"

"Yeah, that's fuckin' wrong, Puggie, no matter how you look at it. If he'd done the right thing in the first place, none of this would've ever happened. Besides, it's not like he had to go into his pocket or yours. He made at least as much money as we did, and we made over twenty-five grand, so where's the fuckin' loss?"

"Butch, give me your phone number. I'll give you a call in a couple of days." I could see that the shit was going to hit the fan for Sonny and Steve.

"Sure Puggie. I just didn't want you and my uncle to think that all this came out of nowhere."

"I understand, Butch. I'm glad you told me this. I will talk to John about it after I talk to Sonny and Steve. I don't think it will change his mind about you guys working to make things right, but at least he won't think you're a bunch of wise ass cowboys."

"Thanks, Puggie."

"Sure Butch, I'll be in touch."

I went to Jimmy's across the street and called Tom-Tom and Vinnie to set up a meeting for Friday. I wanted to give them a nice Thanksgiving, but I didn't want to talk over Jimmy's phone. Steve had become Jimmy's partner in the candy store as well as in the numbers business.

When I came out of the phone booth, Steve was standing behind the soda fountain in a white apron, making an egg cream, a drink with chocolate syrup, milk and seltzer. He started right out being the asshole that he was. "Hey, Jimmy," he sneered, "look whose here, the big shot himself."

I could tell Jimmy wasn't comfortable with Steve fucking with me. It felt good to know that I had just buried the asshole in very deep shit.

One thing I knew for sure: if it turned out that Steve got paid to run interference for Sonny, Puggie was going to skin him alive.

I responded to Steve in kind." I see you're moving up in the world, Steve. Now you're a soda jerk." To Jimmy I advised, "Jimmy, don't move him up too fast. He may get a big head." I hated this guy. I don't know what it was about him, but I always had a sense of doom whenever I was around him. He was a criminal.

I ran into Charlie Conroy and Steve's wife Ann as I left the candy store. She was a beautiful woman, about five foot four inches tall, with bright blue eyes, dark brown hair, smooth white skin and a very pleasant personality.

She and Charlie had gone to school together. In fact, I think it was Charlie who had introduced Steve to Ann. I always thought they looked more like a couple than Steve and she did. I never could see what that women saw in Steve.

Later I set up a meeting with Vinnie and Tom-Tom for Friday noon at Rao's. Friday morning, I got a call from Puggie: "Butch, I want to have a meeting with you Tom-Tom, and Vinnie today." I could hear the anger in his voice. He was on a warpath.

"OK, Puggie, as a matter of fact, we're having lunch at Rao's at noon today. Can you make it?"

"Yeah I can make it," he agreed.

When I got to Rao's, Vinnie and Tom-Tom were already there. They didn't know yet that Puggie was coming.

"What are you guys drinking?" I asked.

"Grappa. You want some?"

"No thanks. You're supposed to drink that after you eat."

"So sue me." Tom-Tom joked.

"Tell us what's going on, Butch," Vinnie asked anxiously.

Just as I was about to give them the run down, in walked Puggie, Steve, and Sonny.

"What the fuck is this, Butch? Did you know those guys were coming here?" Tom-Tom asked stunned.

"No, I knew Puggie was coming, but not those two pricks. This should be interesting."

"I don't think interesting is the right word for this, Butch." Tom-Tom whispered.

Puggie motioned Steve and Sonny to pull up a couple of chairs at our table. They looked solemn and worried. "Sorry to interrupt your lunch, guys, but this couldn't wait." Puggie said respectfully.

"It's okay, but if we knew you were bringing these two guys, we'd a baked a cake." Puggie gave Tom-Tom a look that could've killed.

"Shut up, Tom-Tom." Vinnie growled

Puggie explained, "Butch, I want you to lay out the whole story and don't leave anything out, including what happened to Cosmo." That seemed to disturb Puggie the most.

So I went through the whole matter, except about the money Sonny gave to Steve. When I was done, Puggie looked at Sonny and asked, "Is there anything that Butch said here that is not true? And if I catch you lying, I'll rip your fucking throat out. Do you understand me, Sonny?"

Sonny was shitting in his pants. "No, Puggie. He's telling you the truth," he admitted.

I couldn't believe what I was seeing. Sonny had his head down and didn't look at Puggie. Under the circumstances, it would have been an act of disrespect and defiance.

Then Puggie turned to Steve. "Did Sonny give you money to cover his fuckin' ass with me?" Puggie was livid

"Yes he did, Angelo," Steve referred to Puggie by his real name.

"How much did he give you?" asked Puggie.

"Ten grand."

"Did you know that money came from the inventory that belonged to them?" Puggie demanded. "I'm warning you. Steve. Don't lie to me."

"No, I didn't know," Steve lied.

Sonny's reaction was very subtle but visible. Puggie knew Steve was lying. He told Steve, "You have until noon tomorrow to give them back that ten grand. You hear what I'm saying Steve and don't be a fuckin' minute late. Now get the fuck out of my sight."

Man, I had never seen anything like this in my life. It was Sicilian justice at its best. As Steve got up he gave me a deadly look, Puggie caught it and said,

"I want to make something very clear to you, Steve. These young men are of "Royal Blood," and they are not touchable. You will have to answer to me, and I will have to answer to Big John, Butch's uncle, if anything happens to them."

Steve's face turned white when he heard Big John's name. He looked back at me stunned. I thought for sure Jimmy had told Steve who I was, but it was clear that he hadn't. I respected Jimmy for that.

Now Steve and Jimmy's numbers business was in jeopardy because it was Big John's bank and permission that Puggie had put in place. Without that, they would have to close shop. This was getting better by the minute.

Sonny was getting up to leave with Steve. "Where the fuck do you think you're going?" Puggie yelled at Sonny. "Sit the fuck down." Sonny's hands were shaking as he lit a cigarette. When Puggie yelled at Sonny, Vincent Rao, who was also a "member" of John's Family, went to the door and locked it and put the "closed" sign up even though it was lunchtime.

Suddenly, without another word Puggie slapped Sonny in the face. He purposely slapped Sonny to humiliate him in front of us the same way Sonny had humiliated Cosmo in front of Cosmo's son. I'm sure Puggie would have rather hit him with a baseball bat because he was that outraged, but he was right to slap him. Anyway, it hurt Sonny far more than a baseball bat would have.

Puggie demanded, "Before noon tomorrow I want you to give Steve ten grand so that he delivers twenty grand to Butch by noon. Then bring the eighteen grand that Cosmo gave you and leave it here with Rao by 6:00 tonight."

The last thing Puggie said to Sonny was the real punishment. "I want you out of Harlem. Go back to the Bronx where you belong, and if I ever hear that you've been back in Harlem, I will have your feet sawed off at the ankles. Do you understand me?"

"Yes, I'm sorry....." Sonny stammered.

"Save it. Now get out of my sight, you low life," Puggie said.

Sonny left with his tail between his legs, and as far as I was concerned, he got off lucky. I had a feeling that Puggie wasn't going to let it go that easily. I think he was just trying to drop Sonny's guard down, but I could be wrong. In any case I would never know. Puggie was the judge, and he was going to rule in his own way.

Puggie turned to me. He said, "Butch, I want you to bring the twenty grand that Steve gives you and leave it here with Vincent. That's a total of $38,000. As far as I am concerned, we are square with each other, but John wanted you to pay back fifty grand. I'm going to tell him what happened and see what he says about the other twelve grand."

"Thanks Puggie," I said, "but given all the problems we've caused we're going to pay the rest of it." I knew it was the right thing to do.

Puggie looked at me, smiled and nodded his approval.

"I'm going to tell John you said that, Butch. I am sure that will mean more to him than the twelve grand."

"And please tell him we're sorry."

"I will, Butch." Puggie got up, hugged me and said "You've got balls, Butch, and you've also handled this with class. John will see that." Puggie then hugged Vinnie and Tom-Tom and left.

"Do you think John will let us off the hook for the twelve grand, Butch?" Tom-Tom asked

"I don't know, but we should pay it anyway. Believe me, it will go a long way, Tom-Tom." I knew that it would change how we were seen.

"Yeah, I think your right. I'm starving, can we eat now?"

"Boy, Tom-Tom, nothing kills that appetite of yours. C'mon let's order." When I got home from lunch there was a message from Andy, Steve's brother, to call him.

"What's up Andy?" I asked when I returned his call.

"Steve wanted to know if it would be all right if I met with you tomorrow at Joe's at noon instead of him."

"Yeah sure, that's fine with me," I agreed. "I'll see you then." I was glad it worked out that way. Nothing good could have come from a meeting with Steve. I also thought it was interesting that Steve was asking my permission for Andy to meet with me.

I met with Andy the next day at Joe's. We got a table and ordered a drink. Then Andy handed me a brown paper bag.

"Here, Butch. I've counted it, but you might want to check it yourself."

"I'll check it later and let you know if there is a problem."

"Will someone tell me what's going on?" he asked.

"That's up to your brother, Andy. It's not my place to do that. I hope you understand."

"I do, Butch, but my brother seems very worried about losing the numbers business. Why would he be worried about that?"

"I know why he is worried about it. Tell him that I am not interested in seeing that happen. First of all, I don't want Jimmy to lose the income, and second they still owe me eight grand."

"Okay Butch, I'll tell him. I'm sure he will be glad to hear that."

Just as Andy and I were leaving Joe's, an ambulance pulled up in front the restaurant. The medics entered the building next to Joe's, and a gathering in front of the building to see what was going on. Within a few minutes the medics carried out Steve's friend Charlie Conroy on a stretcher, George Conroy, Charlie's younger brother, following behind them.

Andy and I approached George. He was in a state of shock. "What happened?" Andy asked.

George kept looking back and forth at Andy and me. Tears began running down his face, and he could barely speak. Then looking at Andy blurted out, "Your brother just shot Charlie"

"What the fuck are you talking about?" Andy shouted at him. "Steve would never do anything like that to Charlie."

"He did, Andy. I was there. Steve rang the downstairs doorbell. Charlie buzzed him in and went out into the hallway to see who it was. I heard Steve yelling at Charlie, 'Come down here! I want to talk to you.'

"Then I heard shots. When I got out into the hall Charlie was on the floor bleeding. All he said was 'I'm sorry' and then went unconscious.

"Where's my brother?" Andy asked. George didn't answer. He just looked at Andy and then climbed into the ambulance.

I turned to Andy and said. "I don't believe this. It doesn't make any sense. Were Charlie and Steve in a rift about something?"

"Not that I know of, but even if they were Steve would never hurt Charlie, let alone try to kill him."

"Why don't you call Steve's house and see if he's there or what Ann knows?"

"Let's just go there, Butch," Andy responded. Steve lived just around the corner. Andy knocked on the apartment door. We could hear the kids crying. One cried, "What's wrong mommy?"

Ann opened the door. She was hysterical. Her face was completely drained of life; her eyes looked wild, almost insane. I'd never seen anyone look like that before.

"Ann, have you seen Steve?" Andy asked.

She blurted out, "Is it true, Andy? Is it true? Did Steve kill Charlie?" There was no way Ann could have known what just happened unless Steve had told her.

"Charlie's on the way to the hospital, Ann. He's not dead."

"Thank God," she sighed.

"Ann, do you know where my brother is?" Andy asked her.

"He's on his way to the 23rd precinct to turn himself in," she said

"Are you sure? How do you know that?' he asked

"He told me. He said that he just killed Charlie and was going to turn himself in."

"How long ago did he leave?"

"A few minutes ago."

"Do you know why he did it?" Andy asked. When Ann turned away and didn't answer him I knew why. I flashed on running into Charlie and her a few days earlier and how I thought they would've made a better couple than Steve and she did. She was having an affair with Charlie, as unimaginable as it was. It was the only thing that would explain why Steve would turn himself in and why Charlie said he was sorry before he went unconscious.

"C'mon Andy. Let's see if we can catch him, before he gets to the station house," I said.

Andy and I scaled down the three flights of stairs and into the cold winter streets. The whole thing was becoming surreal. I'll never forget the wild look on Ann's face and the fear in her children's eyes. I always knew that Steve's recklessness would catch up with him someday, but never would I have ever predicted anything like this.

As Andy and I ran along Third Avenue, fear replaced any sense of well-being I had. I didn't understand why I was feeling this way. I wasn't the one in trouble. My adrenalin started replacing the fear, just like Tom-Tom said it would. Then, that familiar slow motion that always seemed to accompany these dangerous situations kicked in.

It was Saturday afternoon, and the sidewalks were crowded, as they always were on Saturday. We stepped into the street and started running alongside the traffic on Third Avenue while searching the crowd for Steve.

"Butch, why would Steve do something like this and then turn himself in?"

I wasn't about to get into that with Andy. "I don't know" I answered.

When we arrived at the station house, I let Andy go in by himself, and I waited outside. It was about ten minutes before Andy came out.

"They've got him, but that's all they would tell me," he said.

"Let's go to the hospital Andy and see how Charlie is doing," I suggested.

"Jesus, Butch, I can't believe this is happening. My brother loved Charlie. They were in first grade together. I just don't understand." Tear's started running down Andy's face as reality sank in. When I put my arms around Andy and hugged him, I couldn't stop my own tears.

It was about a six-block walk to Flower Fifth Avenue Hospital, the same hospital I was taken to when I was beaten and stabbed. The day was sunny, but cold and windy, and I was beginning to feel nauseous like I was going to vomit. Going to this hospital was triggering all the symptoms I had the last time I was there as a patient.

When we got there, George was in the emergency waiting room being questioned by Clancy and another detective named Brian O'Malley from homicide. As Andy and I approached them, O'Malley stopped us. Clancy looked up, and when he saw who we were, told O'Malley, "It's okay, Brian, I want to talk to them." Clancy introduced us to O'Malley and told him who we were.

"How is he, George?" I asked.

"We don't know yet, Butch. He's in the operating room right now." Clancy motioned me over to the other side of the waiting room. "What do you know about this, Butch?" Clancy asked me.

"Nothing, Clancy. Andy and I were having a drink at Joe's, when we heard the ambulance pull up. A few minutes later, they wheeled Charlie out on a gurney and put him in the ambulance. Before George jumped into the back of the ambulance with Charlie, he told us that Steve shot Charlie. Neither one of us believed him".

I went on to explain, "Andy and I went to Steve's house to find him, and that's when Ann told us that Steve killed Charlie and turned himself in. She didn't know that Charlie was still alive until we told her. Then we came straight here. Is it true, Clancy? Did Steve admit to shooting Charlie?"

"Yeah, he did. He didn't know Charlie was still alive. He told me that he just killed Charlie."

"Did he say why?"

"Yeah, he found out that Ann and Charlie had been having an affair for years, and he just went nuts. It's strange. He knows and admits he did it but can't recall any of the details. We want to hear what Charlie has to say."

"Suppose Charlie doesn't make it? What then?" I asked.

"Let's pray that doesn't happen, Butch."

It was about an hour before the doctor appeared. He walked over to George.

"How is he Doc? Is he going to be all right?" George demanded.

"He's lost a lot of blood. We were able to remove the bullets and stop the internal bleeding. He's stable and conscious. He's been moved to a recovery room. The fact that he's not in a comma is very encouraging. It's wait and see now. The only thing that concerns me is that he is extremely depressed."

Andy and I gave a sigh of relief. Clancy looked over at me and gave me a smiling wink and nodded his head in relief. Clancy had known every one of us and our families for years. He watched a lot of us grow up. He was a friend and very concerned about us.

"Can I see him?" asked George.

"It would be better if you waited until tomorrow, Mr. Conroy," the doctor responded.

Clancy moved forward saying, "Doctor Mendelson, I'm Detective Clancy from the 23rd Precinct and this is Detective O'Malley. It is important that we get a statement from your patient as soon as possible and that we do that before any visitors are allowed. Is he in any condition to talk now?"

"I understand, Detective Clancy. If you can limit your visit to ten minutes, you can see him. He needs rest, not stress,' the doctor said.

"I understand, doctor. You have my word. Thank you."

The three of us waited downstairs for Clancy and O'Malley. They were back in less than ten minutes. Clancy wanted to talk to us, but didn't want O'Malley in on the conversation. He was an "outsider." He looked at the other officer. "Brian, will you bring the car around and then inform headquarters that we are done and will be back in the office in twenty minutes?"

"Yes sir." Clancy started shaking his head back and forth in disbelief. He looked at George and said, "Your brother swears it wasn't Steve who shot him. He said it was two Puerto Rican guys and clammed up. I told him that Steve turned himself in and made a full confession, but he didn't want to hear it. He said it wasn't true, closed his eyes and wouldn't say another word."

Clancy added, "Before he stopped talking, he asked if you were still here. I told him that the three of you were down here, but the doctor didn't want any visitors until tomorrow. He said he needs to talk to you guys right now. He's in room 204. Go ahead up. I'll handle the doctor. Keep me posted, George, okay?"

"I will, Clancy, and thanks," said George.

I hated the sweet, but conflicting smell of flowers and antiseptics that permeates hospitals. It reminded me of the conflicting smell of orange peels and kerosene fumes from my mother's attempt to sweeten the smell of our kerosene stove.

Charlie's room was full of natural light. He was lying flat on his back with two IV's in his arms and a couple of wires taped to his chest and hooked into a heart monitor. His eyes were puffy and closed. He didn't notice we were in the room until George whispered, "Charlie, it's George."

Charlie opened his blood shot eyes slowly and then shut them immediately. I could see the light in the room was hurting his eyes. I walked over to the windows and pulled the shades down. George stood alongside of the bed and took Charlie's hand. Charlie opened his eyes and looked up at his brother.

"How are you doing? The doctor said you're going to be okay." Charlie started crying uncontrollably. His pain filled the room and overwhelmed us. I felt devastated by the sound of his voice, and I didn't want to stay in the room, but I couldn't bring myself to leave.

"I'm not okay. I will never be okay. I'm so sorry. I'm so ashamed." Then looking at Andy he said, "Forgive me. Forgive me."

"It's going to be all right, Charlie." Andy said softly, trying to ease Charlie's anguish.

"Andy, please tell your brother not to talk to the cops. This is entirely my fault, and I don't want him in trouble. I've caused him enough trouble. Tell him I love him. Will you tell him?"

"I will Charlie. I'll do whatever I can. Right now you need to rest and take care of yourself."

The three of us left the hospital and walked back to the neighborhood together without saying a word. After George left us, Andy asked, "Butch, do you know any criminal attorneys?"

"Not off hand, but I'm sure my father will know some. Give me a day to check around and I'll call you."

"Thanks, Butch, and thanks for comin' with me."

"Sure Andy. If you need anything let me know, okay?

"Okay, I will and thanks again."

I went into Jimmy's store to call Tom-Tom and Vinnie to tell them what had happened. The first policy number from the horse races was just out, and about a dozen of the runners that worked for Jimmy and Steve were meeting there to see if any of their customers hit. All kinds of rumors were flying around, but no one knew what was going on.

Before I could get to the phone booth in back of the store, Jimmy cornered me. "Butch, I need to talk to you." We went into Jimmy's living quarters in back of the store. I pulled up a chair, and he sat on his bed. He looked very worried and understandably confused. "Steve told me what happened between him and Puggie. Was Charlie involved in some way?"

"Not that I know of."

"Do you know why Steve shot Charlie?" he asked.

"Yeah, Charlie was having an affair with Ann."

"I don't believe it. Is he out of his fuckin' mind?"

"Maybe, but from what I can tell, he and Ann were in love."

"Steve told me what happened in that perfume deal, and he was worried about losing our numbers business. Do you know what's going to happen with that?

"Well, given what just happened, I wouldn't worry about it. Were you involved in any way?" I asked him.

"No, Butch. I found out about it after Steve had the sit down with you and Puggie. Steve knew better than to tell me about it, Butch. I would not have approved."

"That's what I thought because he seemed very surprised when he found out Big John was my uncle. I was glad you kept my confidence. On the other hand, had he known, he might have stayed out of it."

"Before today, I would've agreed with you, but you were right about his recklessness. I'm sorry, Butch, I should have listened to you."

"You don't have to apologize, Jimmy. If the matter comes up about the business, I will do what I can to keep it in place."

"Thanks, Butch," he said and offered, "You are welcome to have your half back. I never wanted you out of the deal. You know that."

"I know that Jimmy, and I appreciate the offer. Right now I'd rather have the eight grand Steve owes me, but let me think about it."

"OK, Butch. I just want you to know. I'll cover the eight grand if you decide to stay out, okay?"

"OK Jimmy." I wanted to stay in the deal, but I didn't want anything to spill over on me. I went to Rao's and dropped off the twenty grand. Then I called Vinnie and Tom-Tom and filled them in. I was still spun around by the day's events. I was learning how unpredictable life was, and I didn't like it.

I got home around five o'clock. I told Louise what happened. We had dinner, and I fell asleep on the couch.

The phone rang at 1 a.m. It was Andy. "Butch, Charlie's dead."

I was stunned and couldn't speak for a moment. Then I rattled off a bunch of questions? "Are you sure? When? How do you know?"

"I just got a call from George." Andy's voice was quivering I could hardly understand him.

"I can't believe it. He didn't look that bad, Andy."

"He wasn't that bad, Butch. He killed himself."

"What? Whadda' ya mean he killed himself? How could he possibly do that?"

"He pulled out all the IV's during the night. The nurse found him on the floor in the hallway outside his room. That stupid gutless cocksucker. First, he fucks my brother's wife and now, because he can't live with himself, he puts Steve in jail for life."

I was speechless. I didn't know what to say. I asked, "Is there anything I can do, Andy?"

"Yeah, please get a lawyer down there before Steve talks anymore."

"I got it. I'll get right on it." I called my old man and got a name for Andy and called him right back.

CHAPTER 14

THE FUNERAL

The room where Charlie's body was laid out was packed. It was the saddest thing I had ever seen in my life. So many lives were shattered by this tragedy. I walked down the center aisle toward the coffin. I had been to funerals before as a young boy when older relatives and friends of my parents died, but I would never go in the room where the bodies were laid out. I didn't want to see death. It scared me.

When I reached the coffin, I looked down at Charlie. He didn't look dead. His skin was young and still appeared to have color. I reached out and touched Charlie's hands that were folded around black and silver rosary beads, and they were ice cold. I quickly withdrew my hand, as if I had touched a hot flame. I stood there still hoping I would see him take a breath.

The smell of flowers and embalming fluid was making me sick, like the smell of flowers and hospital antiseptics and my mother's orange peels and kerosene fumes. From that time on, I have always associated the smell flowers with death. I couldn't feel anything until I turned around and saw Charlie and Steve's mother sitting together holding Steve's three children and crying.

I walked over to them, tears falling from my eyes, my throat in a knot, my hands and legs unsteady. I leaned over to kiss them both and express my condolences. They wrapped their arms around me and brought me to my knees in front of them. Ann summoned the children from them.

The unbearable pain from their broken hearts erupted into a guttural howling, penetrating the very core of my heart, their arms squeezing tighter around me as my heart absorbed their terrible grief.

They held me until their breathing began to calm down. I kissed them and stood up. Looking into their swollen, bewildered eyes, I searched for something to say that would make it all right. But nothing was going to make this all right. Finally, I said," If you need anything at all, call me, okay? Promise me that you will call me."

Steve's mother said, "We will, Butch, and thank you for being there for Charlie and Steve. Andy told us that you were at the hospital and that you handled things with Clancy and got Steve a lawyer. Steve wanted me to tell you he was sorry for any trouble he caused you."

"Thank you," I responded, "Tell him things are all right between us."

I turned away and walked over to Ann, who was sitting with her children. "I am so sorry about all this Ann. I wish I could do something to make it all go away."

"Thank you, Butch. Andy told me you were there with him at the jail and hospital. That was very kind of you."

"If you need anything, don't hesitate to call me."

"I will and thanks again for your help," she said.

I looked up and saw people I knew and had grown up with. It was like flashing on my whole life all at once. I could feel their eyes on me, but I couldn't look at them. That day changed my life forever. I didn't know what the change was, only that I didn't feel like my old self anymore.

I saw Jimmy standing in the back of the room by the door. I walked up to him and asked, "You got a minute Jimmy?"

"Yeah sure, Butch. What's up?"

"I'm out," I said.

He stood there looking at me for a second then said, "I understand."

I walked out of the funeral home feeling like my heart was going to explode. I was holding back the tears.

I headed for the East River where I could let it all go. I just walked along the river for a very long time. I couldn't understand my feelings. I wasn't that close to Charlie because he was one of the older guys. When I thought about him, I didn't feel anything, but when I thought about his mother and Steve's three children, I broke down and cried uncontrollably for a very long time.

Hours passed before I stopped walking. I was more determined than ever to get out of Harlem. I needed money. Jimmy wouldn't be able to keep the numbers business going without me, and given what happened with the perfume deal, neither Puggy nor Big John was going to give me the okay to operate. I started to feel anxious and depressed, maybe desperate is a better word because I felt trapped.

I started thinking, *"Is this what my life is going to be like: carrying cement bags. I'd rather be dead.*

I had one child and another on the way. I had just gotten fired from a spot-welding job in Queens. It was Monday morning when Huntz, one of the owners approached me. The managers had found out I wasn't old enough to work in a factory. I liked the job. I had increased the company's production by 18 percent and was elected shop steward by seventy co-workers. It didn't pay anything - $1.80 an hour - and probably never would, but I was finding out that I was smart. I could figure things out. I liked solving problems, and, more importantly, people listened to me.

"Salvatore, I'm afraid I must let you go," my boss told me. "Please, you must believe me that it is not something I want to do. You have been a fine employee, and I want to acknowledge the things you've done for the company. But you are not of legal age to work here, and we could get in a lot of trouble if the labor board finds out. But I would like you to consider returning when you are of age."

"I understand, Huntz," I assured him, "and thank you for the opportunity. I must say, Huntz, I didn't think getting fired would be so pleasurable." I laughed. He smiled, but I could tell he didn't quite get it.

CHAPTER 15

DESCENT INTO THE OBSCURITY OF THE ORDINARY CITIZEN'S LIFE

My first son was born in April of 1960, and my second son was born in 1962. During that time, I had two jobs. One was in a factory, spot welding commercial, stainless steel refrigerators, where I was solicited by a Cuban co-worker to join him in the failed invasion of Cuba - where he was killed - for $300 a week.

The other was on construction working in below freezing temperatures or unbearably hot humid summers and losing my weekly pay in the Friday crap games that took place on the job site. The combination of those two experiences drove me to one more illegal and dangerous venture.

One day, Sammy, one of the carpenters on my job, asked me if I had any connections in the heroin business. He knew Big John controlled that business in Harlem. He also knew I had a lot of connections on 116th Streets, where the heroin business was based. But I don't believe he knew my "Family" connections.

Big John had already been convicted on drug conspiracy charges. Vito Genovese was already doing fifteen years for drugs. Sometime in 1961, Genovese ordered a hit on Joe Valachi and caused Valachi to kill someone he thought Genovese ordered to kill him. That mistake got Valachi a life sentence and later put Valachi on national TV for two months spilling his guts all over the airwaves. Most of what Valachi said wasn't enough to convict anyone of anything, but it did shine the spotlight on the existence of organized crime "Families" and who the players were.

It was forbidden for "Members" of a "Family" or anyone connected to a "Family" to be in the drug business under the penalty of death. That's the rule that Genovese and Big John were trying to do away with at the meeting at Appalachia.

It didn't matter to them that they were in the heroin business themselves. It would not have stopped them from killing lower level family members like me if they were caught. It was in this environment that I decided to check out the possibilities of making a heroin deal, a truly desperate and stupid decision.

Sammy lived two blocks from me and on occasions would give me a ride home. It was Friday. I'd just lost half my pay in the crap game after work. I had also borrowed money from the Shylock that worked the construction site. Every construction job in the city had its Shylock.

On the way home Sammy asked, "Hey Butch, do you have any connections for "smack?"

I shot back, "Sammy, that's a very dangerous business, and I don't know anything about it," which wasn't entirely true. I knew that a kilo of pure heroin could be bought for $2,500 in Marseille, France. It would be shipped to Canada and then brought over the border into Buffalo, New York. It hit Harlem in lots of about two hundred kilos at $8,000 a kilo.

The drug could then be cut 8 to 12 times, meaning you could make 8 to 12 kilos out of one kilo and still get 15k per kilo, and that was wholesale. The profits were staggering. But there was far more to know technically, namely, how to cut and test the drug, which I knew nothing about, and Sammy knew less.

Big John was on appeal from his conspiracy conviction. If I were to get busted during his appeal, the press would have a field day. "The Genovese/ Luciano Family" names would be splashed all over the country. The last thing Big John wanted was his name in the papers especially connected to Genovese, who was already doing fifteen years. It would also be a virtual death sentence for me.

I asked Sammy, "Who is your connection?"

"He's a Puerto Rican guy named Spanish Tony. This guy is in the position to take over the distribution in the Puerto Rican neighborhoods."

"If his business is that big, he must already have connections," I objected. "Why is he coming to you?"

"I asked him that, and he told me, 'Because you're Italian.' Right now he buys from a black Harlem connection, but for him to expand, he needs contacts with the higher sources, the Italians."

"What is he looking for?"

"A quarter of a Kilo of a 3-to-1 cut. He's willing to pay five grand, and if it works out, he will buy that every week."

"Okay. Sammy." I agreed. "Let me check around and see what I can do,"

Of course, I knew the higher up guys in the business. They all hung out at Rao's. The dilemma was that they knew my father, Big John and who I was. I'd get the beating of my life just for asking. That's if I was stupid enough to ask.

I went to see Johnny Pecarro, a.k.a Johnny Peck, an old friend since early childhood. His mother Mary and my mother grew up together, and until recently I thought we were cousins. Johnny was four or five years older than I was. He was Andy Garcia handsome with jet-black hair and eyes and an olive complexion. He was five foot, eight inches tall and buffed out like most guys coming out of prison where he had spent a lot of time. Peck had just gotten out and was clean.

Dealing with Peck was a double-edged sword. The upside was that he was a junkie and knew the quality of heroin better than the guys who sold it, and he also knew how to cut it. The downside was that he was a junkie, and when it came to heroin no junkie could or should be trusted. I knew that, but I was determined to get the fuck out of Harlem and the subjugated life of the ordinary citizen. I needed money to do it.

Coincidently, Johnny Peck's mother asked my mother if I could get him a job where I was working. *Perfect timing,* I thought. Peck lived with his mother a block from me and across the street from the famous Julliard School of Music on 105th Street. On a sunny Saturday morning in late June, Peck sat on his stoop, and I ran the whole deal down to him. He looked great, but I had a real concern that he might go back to using again, and I didn't want to be responsible for that.

"Butch, you know this is a dangerous business. More guys get beat for their money than make real deals."

"I know that, Johnny. That's why I came to you. I have two kids, and I don't want to raise them in Harlem.

"Okay, Butch, give me a day or two, and I'll get back to you."

"Thanks Johnny." I left Johnny feeling uneasy. I was in a game I didn't know much about, and I wasn't in control. My gut was telling me don't do it. Two days later, after I got home from work, Johnny rang my doorbell,

"Who's that, Butch?" Louise asked

"It's Johnny Peck. I told you about him. I'm trying to get him on my job site. I'm going to talk to him, and I'll be right back."

"Why don't you ask him to come up?"

"I'll go down and ask him." I never talked business in front of Louise, and I especially didn't want talk this business in front of her.

When I got down to Johnny, I asked him, "What's happening?"

"I can get a quarter kilo of a three cut for $3,500. If you can get five grand, we got a deal."

"That's great, Johnny. I'll split 50/50 with you."

"Okay, Butch. How long will take it you to put the money together?"

"I don't know yet, but I'll see my man tomorrow at work and call you."

I spoke to Sammy at lunch and made arrangements to pick up the money at 7 p.m. at Joe's. I called Johnny and set it up for 8 p.m. in front of Saint Cecilia's church a block away.

Sammy handed me the money and asked, "How long will it take to get this done? I need to let my people know. I don't want them getting nervous. Are you sure about the people you are dealing with?"

"I have known this guy since I was a boy. His mother and mine grew up together," I assured Sammy, but I was getting the jitters.

"I'm meeting him at eight, and I should be done in about an hour."

"Why so long?"

"He's got to test it, Sammy. He's the only one who knows what he's doing."

"Right, that makes sense. I'll tell Tony and meet you back at Joe's at 9:30 p.m., and, Butch, make sure nothing goes wrong. The last thing we need is trouble with this spic."

"OK, Sammy." My stomach turned when he used that word, and my instincts told me to call the deal off, but it was too late for that now. Besides, I wanted the money. I took out my cut and handed him $4,250.

When I went to meet Johnny Peck, I asked him, "Johnny, are you sure about the people you're dealing with? If anything goes wrong, I'm going to have serious problems."

"Don't worry, Butch. Nothing is going to go wrong. If the quality is not right, I won't do the deal, and we'll just give back the money."

I felt a lot better when Johnny said that. "Good. Listen, Johnny, I'll be inside the church when you get back. I'll be praying the whole time you're gone." We both laughed. I went back to Joe's, had a few drinks and waited.

I got back to the church at nine and sat in the back. The church was having a Novena service with about fifty people in attendance. It was an odd experience, the smell of incense bringing back my altar boy days. The priest that caught me going into the tabernacle, the same one who married Louise and me, was performing the service.

I thought about what I was doing in the church and didn't feel right about it. Then I thought about how I had to bribe that asshole to allow Louise to wear a white gown. He was no better than me, I thought. In fact, he was worse than me. He was a thief pretending to be a holy man, a true criminal.

Johnny never showed. I met with Sammy and told him what happened. "Give me a day to find out what's going on, and tell your guys whatever happens I'll make good on it."

I knew deep down this was a bad move on my part. I didn't have any place to get four or five grand. I had the $750 I took out of the five grand, but that wasn't going to solve my problem. I met with Tom-Tom and told him what had happened. He said, "I don't have five grand to cover you Butch, but maybe we can work something out." Then asked me, "Who are these people?"

"Well, the middle-man is Sammy, the carpenter. He worked on the same job we did. Remember? He's from 108th street."

"Yeah, I know who he is. He's a good guy. Let's meet with him and see what we can do."

"I've already met with him," I explained. "He's not the problem. He's just stuck in the middle of it. Do you know who Spanish Tony is?

"I've heard of him, but I don't know him. Why did you go to Johnny Peck when you're wired into many other sources? You know them all."

"Yeah and they know me. If I went to any of them, they'd pretend they didn't know what I was talking about, then break my fuckin' legs for asking. You know it's a death sentence for any mafia members or family connected to them to be fuckin' with junk. Having big shot relatives is not what you think, Tom-Tom. It's 'Do what I say, not what I do.' I am sure you've heard that before."

"Yeah, but fuck them. They ain't living by those rules. It's the worse kept secret in New York. Too bad you didn't come to me first."

"You're in no better position than me to approach those guys."

"Yes, I am, but that's not the problem right now. When are you supposed to meet with Spanish Tony?

"I don't know. I'm supposed to call Sammy and bring him up speed, but what am I going to tell him?"

"Just tell him you will meet him Thursday night at eight in front of your building and let me see what I can do. No matter what, I'll be there packing and you should do the same. I've heard about Spanish Tony, and from what I hear, he's a serious guy."

I called Sammy and set the meeting up. He told me that Spanish Tony expected his money or the "goods." He said, "Butch, this guy is bad news. If he's beat for his money, please don't put me on the spot."

"I am doing everything I can, Sammy. I will make good for the money, one way or another, but it may take more time."

"This guy is not into waiting."

It was 8:15 when I saw Sammy and Spanish Tony standing across the street on Second Ave. I was standing in the doorway of my building next to Mary's Pizzeria. I had a small revolver in my hand and a brown paper bag over it. Tom-Tom hadn't shown up yet, and it looked like I was on my own.

Sammy crossed the street alone to talk with me while Tony waited on the other side with his hand in his jacket like he was packing, and I'm sure he was.

"What's happening Butch? You know your mother is looking out the window watching all this."

"No, I didn't know. Just what I need. Listen, Sammy, I'm waiting for someone, but he's late. I'm sure he will be here. Just tell Tony to wait about twenty minutes."

"I told you, Butch, he's not into waiting." Sammy said to me in a threatening tone, which I didn't like coming from him. I could feel my adrenalin starting to rev-up. I was very nervous and didn't know how to handle this. I kept looking up and down the street for Tom-Tom.

"Sammy, if I was going to beat Tony for his money, I wouldn't be here, so stop the bullshit. We are talking about five grand here, not fifty grand. If this is going to come down to a shootout, you better decide whose side you're on right now."

I told him this as I pulled the brown bag off my piece and put it in my belt. I left my jacket open, so Sammy understood what was coming. Sammy was facing me with his back to the street. I could look past him and see Tony watching us.

"Wait a minute, Butch. I'm in the middle of this....."

"Right," I interrupted him, so stay in the middle and don't talk to me like that. You go back across the street and tell him I'm an honorable guy and if there is a problem, I will make it right, but if he chooses to play gangster with me, all bets are off, and I will never cover his losses.

"This is crazy, Butch."

"Yes, it is. Tell that to Tony."

Sammy walked back across the street. I could see him and Tony arguing, and then Tony pushed Sammy aside and started walking across Second Ave. towards me, his hand in his jacket.

I started shaking. My first thought was to go into my building and just get away. I sure as hell didn't want a shootout in the middle of Second Ave. with my mother watching, but it was too late. I really didn't have a choice. I thought to myself, *Sooner or later you'll have to deal with this. You might as well do it now.*" I remembered what Tom-Tom told me about fear when we were knocking off the crap game. "It will all turn into pure adrenalin when the action starts."

I cocked the hammer of the gun and slipped my hand back into the brown paper bag then dropped my arm to my side.

As I stepped off the curb into the street, a 1961 powder blue Oldsmobile convertible pulled up between Spanish Tony and me. It was Tom-Tom and Johnny Echoes. Johnny was married to one of the Selerno brothers' daughters and was in the heroin business. The Selerno brothers were members of Big John's family. Johnny was ten years older than I was and lived in Tom-Tom's building right around the corner from me. I knew him from the neighborhood, but only to say hello. I'm sure Tom-Tom told him who I was. They both got out of the car and looked at Tony who was halfway across the street.

Johnny said, "Stay here, Butch and put that gun away." Then he and Tom-Tom turned and walked toward Tony. Johnny started waving his hand at Tony and calling his name out. "It's Okay. Tony. Everything is cool."

Within a few minutes, Tony got into Johnny's car and they pulled away. I was relieved but couldn't figure out what was going on. Tom-Tom came over and filled me in. "Johnny Echoes just gave Tony the goods he ordered from you but of an even much better quality than what he paid for. Tony's going to be one happy spic."

I told Tom-Tom, "Thanks. It came pretty close to a blood bath. What do I have to give Echoes for doing this?"

"Nothing. Tony is his customer now. Echoes was looking for a "spic" connection and knows who Tony is, so it works out perfect. They both get what they want, and you're off the hook. Echoes will make that money back in a couple of days. Come on let's have a pizza." Tom-Tom put his arm around me and laughed as we walked into Mary's pizzeria.

"You know, Tom-Tom, I'm beginning to believe that dangerous situations actually give you an appetite." We both laughed and ordered a pie.

About twenty minutes later, Echoes walked in and sat with us. It was the first time we ever had a conversation. I had seen him many times and he always acknowledged me, usually with a nod or a smile. Tom-Tom introduced us, and the first words out of my mouth were, "I owe you Johnny. Thanks."

"It's okay, Butch. It worked out for everyone but let me give you a little advice. Stay away from this business. It's dangerous and especially dangerous for you, and you know what I mean."

That meant he knew who I was, which meant Tom-Tom had told him about me. I decided then and there that now was the time to get out of Harlem with or without money.

"Thanks, Johnny, I'm going to take your advice."

I had the $750 from the deal but didn't feel right about just keeping it, so I handed it to Johnny and said, "This is what I was supposed to make on the deal, Johnny. It belongs to you."

He looked at me with a warm, amused smile and said, "I'll tell you what Butch, how about we split it three ways, you, me and Tom-Tom."

"That's very cool, Johnny. Are you sure? I can't say I don't need the money."

"Don't mention it, Butch. I'll do very well with Tony." Johnny got up to leave the restaurant. When he got to the door he turned around and walked back to the table, took a slice of pizza, and said, "Butch, take your family and get out of this fuckin' place. It's not a place for a guy like you."

"You know something, Johnny? I've felt that way about this place all my life."

I kept hearing Johnny's voice saying, "This is not a place for a guy like you." What did he mean by "a guy like me?" I wondered. I thought it was an odd thing to say to me, since he really didn't know me. Then he shook my hand and said, "Take care of yourself, Butch," and left.

I turned to Tom-Tom and said, "Tom-Tom, Johnny seems to know a lot about me, what did you tell him?"

"I didn't have to tell him anything, Butch. This is our neighborhood. Everybody knows everything about everybody. You don't really think no one knows who your family is do you? Johnny is married to Mike Salerno's daughter and Mike works for your Uncle, Big John. Where do you think he got the junk from?"

I did know Mike Salerno worked for Big John because my father told me that when he took me to the parking lots to straighten out the guys who shot me. Mike was the guy who stopped me from hitting that bastard in his parking lot on 110th Street. I just hadn't connected the two things.

"Do you think Johnny knows about the whole perfume and crap game story?"

Tom-Tom laughed at me and said, "You know, Butch, you are the smartest guy I've ever known, but you're also the most naive."

Twenty-five years later, while I was in federal prison camp, I met a Puerto Rican name Hector from my old neighborhood. I was excited to meet someone who grew up where I did. He was finishing a twenty-year sentence for heroin. I asked him "Do you know Spanish Tony?

He looked at me very surprised and asked "How do you know Spanish Tony?"

I told him the story.

"So you are the guy who brought Tony and Echoes together."

I laughed and said, "Yeah, I guess you could say that."

Then he told me, "I got busted with them. They are both finishing twenty like me and should be getting out in a couple of months. We are going to have a hell of a party when we are all out. It would blow their mind if you showed up. Wait til they hear this story."

"I'd like to see them again" I said, "but my present schedule will not allow it. Say hello for me, will you?

CHAPTER 16

To say the town of Shirley, Long Island, was small would take a huge leap of imagination. More people lived on my block in Harlem than in the whole "town." It was located seventy-five miles from New York City. I moved to Shirley with my family and lived just a block from the Fire Island Bridge and less than twenty miles from West Hampton Beach, which provided me with a unique perspective.

With the help of my father's sister, who gave me a $1,000 for the down payment, I was able to buy a seven room gray Cape Cod house. I paid $9,500 for it and moved there with my family, including my mother and my failing grandfather, who died shortly after the move. My mortgage payment was $90 month.

Louise was pregnant again and gave birth to my third son a few months later. I was all of twenty years old and had three children, no job, no degrees, or skills yet felt oddly liberated.

The next couple of years were a huge transition for me. The country was also going through a huge transition. The sixties were thumping: Vietnam was heating up, and Dylan and the Beatles were on the scene, and, for the first time, I was in a place where no one knew anything about me. I had no image to represent, protect, or defend. I could be whoever I wanted to be. I didn't know who or what that might be, but I knew I had a chance not to be Butch anymore. I was Sal from now on. I never liked that name, but it was better than Butch.

Letting go of the name Butch was the same as letting go of the person called Butch. So dramatic was the change that it literally changed the way I experienced my life. I realized the way others related to Butch prevented me from ever evolving. Butch was expected to respond in predictable ways, which made others feel safe but forced me into a psychological and emotional box.

I took a job hanging sheet rock for eleven dollars a day, a humbling experience to say the least. It was hard work that paid nothing, but within a year I had learned enough to go into business for myself. By the second year, I had four employees. Just the fact that I'd learned something that quick and had the balls to go on my own gave substance to the confidence I always felt and exuded.

One of my employees was the road manager for the Young Rascals rock band. They lived six miles away from me in the next town called Bellport. That connection renewed my interest in music, and, although I was older than the baby boomers, I got into the music, the pot smoking, and the changing psychology, culture and politics of the time.

By the summer of 1962, I was getting bored and restless. I began spending weekends in West Hampton Beach. I became the pot connection for my favorite band, but for the life of me I can't remember their name. Pot at that time sold for $15 a "lid" (an ounce), but I could buy it in Harlem for $90 a kilo 35 ounces.

Every couple of weeks the five members of the band and I would chip in $15 apiece, which covered the price of a kilo. Then, I would divide the kilo evenly among us, so for the price of one ounce we all got almost six ounces. In those days, if you got a good amount of pot for your money just a little more than an ounce, people would say, "It's a good count."

One Friday night, I walked into the club in West Hampton Beach. My guys were on stage in the middle of a song. There were at least a hundred people on the dance floor. Suddenly, the band stopped playing, and I heard Frankie, the lead singer, say, "the Count is here. Let him through." He was referring to me. It looked like the parting of the Red Sea. I walked up to the stage and threw the five brown paper bags up to them one at a time as the crowd, knowing what was in the bags, cheered. From that time on, the band referred to me as "The Count."

I never made any money on the pot, but supplying it had its privileges: no waiting in lines, no cover charge in any place the band played, and inclusion in their social scene. I never got pot for anyone else except a few personal friends I hung out with in Shirley, namely, Vinnie Moraldo, and Frankie Pasqua.

I loved smoking pot, and on Sunday afternoons four or five of us would meet at Vinnie's house and play conga drums to jazz and Latin records. It was very tribal and primitive, almost sacred. It reminded me of the nights in Harlem I used to spend singing with my friends, but this music was in a different head space altogether. It was much more sophisticated and complex.

I was changing rapidly, far more rapidly than I realized. I was a truth seeker by nature and curious about everything, and the pot increased my self-awareness. It was the beginning of introspection and exploring this new person called Sal.

The weekends in West Hampton put me in touch with a different social and economic stratum - college educated men and women my own age. Most were successful professionals or on their way to being successful New Yorkers: lawyers, stockbrokers, actors, young film makers and writers, not the kind of people I would've met in Rao's or Jimmy's candy store in East Harlem.

Some of them would chip in and rent houses for the summer, sometimes as many as twelve people to a house.

They came to party and let off steam, and they knew how to do that.

I fell in with a small group of outrageously funny and zany guys from Brooklyn. Six of them had a house together. Danny O'Brian and Ritchie De Marco were on the summer lease and were the wildest of the bunch. They made the ninety-mile trip from the city on a motorcycle.

Ritchie rode as a passenger and insisted on riding the last fifteen miles naked from the waist down. Danny, a more-than-willing Irish lunatic, would drive his bike into the house, make the required legal stop at the stop sign they placed at the foot of the stairs, drive up the stairs, and park the bike in his bedroom. We became fast friends. I was accepted for whom I was and had an open invitation to all their parties.

I was having a very different kind of fun, a carefree fun without danger. Danny was completely irreverent and had no boundaries when it came to getting a laugh. I arrived at the beach one Saturday afternoon to find Danny giving "The Sermon on the Mount" in a very realistic Hebrew dialect, which no one understood, including Danny. He was dressed in a white robe - white sheets from the house - and was crowned with thorns - tree branches.

After the sermon, he proceeded to change water into wine or rather *bash*. *Bash* consisted of two cases of vodka, four cases each of orange and cranberry juice, and four, 25-pound bags of ice cubes stirred carefully with a canoe oar in a couple of large garbage cans.

As the audience grew, both in size and intoxication, the "Lord" decided to heal the blind and the crippled. Eager to get into the act, Ritchie, pretending he was blind, crawled over every beautiful woman in his path and made his way to the Lord who baptized him by pouring *bash* over his head and singing like a Cantor. He was actually very good. Then miraculously Ritchie could see again.

Danny, crossing the line from irreverence to outrageous, saw a woman in the audience who was actually crippled.

After singing his prayer to heal the crippled a number of times, he demanded that she walk, and then looking at the audience said, "Well, no one's perfect." It was so outrageous the crowd couldn't help but laugh. Surprisingly, the girl herself was laughing hysterically.

Later, I saw Danny talking to her, and that night I saw them having dinner together. He told me later he was so impressed with the way she handled herself that he had to know more about her.

In the fall of '62 my cousin Nicky flew in from Las Vegas where he'd been working as a crap dealer for the last five years. He hadn't been home for more than a few weeks in the last ten years. He had joined the Army when he was seventeen and was stationed in Hawaii. After he finished his service, he remained in Hawaii and worked as a bartender, then moved to Las Vegas. He needed a change of venue and decided to see if the East Coast had something for him.

Nicky and I had been very close when we were younger. In 1952 when Nicky lived in Queens, my father got his father, Dominick, a job stocking cigarettes into the newly invented vending machines. It was the business my cousin Charlie (Lucky) had offered to give my father 50 cent of, if he would run it, but my father had turned him down.

In those days, cigarettes were twenty-three cents a pack. When you put a quarter in the machine you got your cigarettes with two cents slid inside the cellophane wrapper. On weekends, Nicky and I would sit in his father's basement for hours inserting the two pennies into cellophane the packs were wrapped in.

A high-ranking member of the Gambino Family owned the "company." It turned out that Nicky's father, my uncle Dominick, had been stealing from the company for years. Uncle Dominick did it by buying his own cigarettes and filling half the machines with them and keeping the profits.

He got caught when he got sick and couldn't go to work for ten days and the profits doubled.

Nicky's father was a major asshole and wreaked havoc with everyone's life, but my father had to step in and save his life. He had little choice since Uncle Dominic was family. When Nicky came back to New York, I brought him into the business with me as a partner. Nicky was six foot tall and weighed about one hundred-eighty pounds. He had blue eyes, black curly hair, and a dry sense of humor. He was one of my favorite people. It had been a long time since we had seen one another, and we spent many hours catching up.

A year went by before Nicky told me he was going back to Vegas. He explained to me, "Butch, I can't take the hard work here, the weather and most of all my old man."

"I understand, Nicky, and I don't blame you," I told him. "I only wish I was going with you."

"Why don't you come with me?" he asked. "I can get you a job, and when you're set up you can send for Louise and the kids."

"I wish it was that easy, but I also have my mother and a mortgage. I feel like I'm in jail. When I look to the future, I don't see one. I just get depressed."

"Yeah, I don't know how you do it," he sympathized.

"It's getting harder and harder."

"How much time do you need to get a replacement for me?" he asked.

"Don't worry about it, Nicky. Winter is coming and the work is slowing down. We just need to finish up the house we're working on. A week should be enough time." I added, "I'm sure going to miss having you around."

"Yeah, it's been good for me, too. I'll call you after I'm set up with a place. I have no problem getting work. Think about moving out to Vegas. Talk to Louise and see what she thinks."

"I'll think about it," I agreed.

Nicky left a week later. The idea of moving to a warmer climate really appealed to me, but I couldn't see how it was possible. The dark winter passed slowly, and my depression got worse. I kept thinking about Vegas and how great it could be, but the only thing that would really change for me would be the weather. My problems were far more complex. I wanted to be free. I was twenty-two years old. I had a family that I loved, a business that I hated and a mortgage. I felt like my life was cast in stone.

The summer came just in time. Ritchie and Danny had already reserved the house before they left last summer. It was mid-June when I got a call from Ritchie. "Hey Sal, how the hell are you?"

"I'm fine, Ritchie. What's up?"

"I just wanted to let you know we're having a party this weekend."

"Ritchie, you guys have a party every weekend, so what's new?"

"Do you remember the Sermon on the Mount?"

"I'll remember that for the rest of my life, Ritchie."

"So will Danny. He's getting engaged to "Mary Magdalene" this weekend."

"You don't mean that crippled girl on the beach he tried to make walk?"

"Yep. I warned him about healing the sick and helping the poor, but he just wouldn't listen."

"That's great. What a love story that would make."

"Yeah," he agreed. "She's really a great gal, and, wouldn't you know it, she's filthy rich. Listen, I'm coming out Friday, and I wanted to know if you could help me get things together for Saturday night. Danny is going to pop the question and give her a ring. It's a surprise."

"What if she says no?"

"Then we'll throw her out and have the party anyway," he laughed.

I got to the house just as Ritchie was pulling up. He was driving a blue Corvette convertible. Beside him was a beautiful woman. She had olive skin, Ritchie introduced her, "Sal, this is Margaret. She's here to help."

"Hello Margaret. It's very nice to meet you."

Her eyes locked on to mine as she smiled and said, "Is it Saul?'

"No, it's Sal for Salvatore."

"Salvatore, I do like that better. Do you mind if I call you Salvatore?"

"You can call me anything you want." I said, flirting with her.

I was instantly smitten, and I was surprised at what tumbled out of my mouth. She smiled at my obvious flirt and held my eyes with hers.

We all got into my car and went shopping for food, booze, and a few decorations. That night the three of us went out for a drink. It was obvious that she was just as attracted to me as I was to her. I didn't know what to do.

I took Ritchie aside, "Does she know I'm married and have three kids?"

"I told her you were."

"What did she say?"

"She said, 'I'm not looking for a husband.'"

Now I was really in trouble. I was nervous, excited and ambivalent. The three of us went to the club that night and danced our asses off. Margaret and I got pretty high and wound up walking on the beach. There was nothing shy about this woman even before she was high.

We were walking hand in hand along the shore like a couple in love. The summer nights on Long Island were warm and intoxicating. The cool moist air was filled with the scent of honeysuckle.

I was trying to think of something to say when she turned, threw her arms around me, and kissed me. Her tongue was hot, moist, and passionate. She pulled me down into the sand and got on top of me never taking her tongue out of my mouth.

I was on fire. Still on top of me, she reached down and unbuckled her shorts. She sucked my tongue into her mouth and held me there while she pushed her shorts down around her knees. I grabbed the cheeks of her ass and pulled them apart, she let out cry then moaned and came.

She started panting and sucking on my ear, then my neck and then my cock. She was completely out of control, and I loved it. I came in her mouth, and I could tell she was cuming at the same time. I turned her over on her back. She raised her legs and put them behind her head like a contortionist and lay there completely spread apart. It was hours before our passion began to rest into a warm glow. I felt weightless as we walked back to the club, which was closing.

Still, I couldn't think of anything to say to her. I took her back to the house and walked her to the door. She turned and kissed me. Then she looked into my eyes and said, "Thank you, Salvatore, for an evening I will never forget."

I stood there speechless then realized there was nothing to say but goodnight. We both knew it couldn't go anywhere, but that night made me more restless than I already was. I hadn't been with another women other than Louise.

My passionate one-night stand with Margaret was a sexual awakening for me. I started looking at my life and questioning everything about it: my marriage, fatherhood, where I lived, what I did for a living, and what the future held for "a guy like me." I knew the times were changing, and I wanted to be part of the change.

One Friday morning I woke up and could not connect with anything in my life. It was like waking up in someone else's house and life.

I decided to go to Las Vegas. I felt out of control, and I just wanted to leave the life I was living. I called Nicky and told him I was coming. I thought I would get set up in Las Vegas and send for Louise and the kids later. I told Louise what I was going to do. Needless to say, she was very upset, and so was I.

She said, "I don't understand. What did I do?"

"You didn't do anything, Baby. It really has nothing to do with you. I just need a break from my life the way it is now. I have no idea who I am, and I'll never find out in this situation." We were both crying.

It was difficult and painful, but we were too young and inexperienced. I knew I would never be happy if I didn't leave and explore life. I felt terrible for thinking only about myself. It was not in my nature to be that way, but I felt an urgency and desperation I couldn't explain at the time.

I called my uncle Carl and went to see him. I told him what I was going through and what I was going to do. He said, "I can understand what you are going through. You were too young to take on the responsibility of a family, but what's done is done, and you can't undo it."

"I know, Uncle Carl," I agreed, "but I just can't do it anymore. I feel like I'm losing my mind. I just need a break for a while."

"Okay, Butch, I can't stop you. Maybe a break will make you see things better, but you can't abandon your family. You must either send for them or come home, do you understand?"

"I have no intentions of abandoning them. I just need a break." The truth is I had nothing planned other than leaving. I couldn't think past that. Two weeks later I left.

CHAPTER 17

VEGAS TO SCIENTOLOGY

I got to Las Vegas in 1964 and went to work at the Carousel Casino, a twenty-five-cent crap game. The clientele spent a whole day there with a $2 bankroll. It was training for me. It was also where I met a great cast of characters, starting with Tony Maronni from Steubenville, Ohio. Sixty-four years old at the time, he had worked gambling places all over the country for forty years. Gambling, while illegal in those days, operated openly in cities all over the country.

Tony had three great talents: He could roll a joint with one hand and stand it straight up on its end. He could throw a pair of dice in such a way that only field bets would come up, very profitable if you bet field bets. Even more impressive, he could play poker and win $80 to $100 a day, and that was 1960's money.

When I asked him, "How do you know you will have the luck to get the cards to win? He said, 'Winning has nothing to do with luck or cards. It's about betting, reading your opponent's face and mannerisms, and counting cards."

The pit boss at the Carousel where I worked was an Italian who changed his name to Silver Rich. He, too, was from Steubenville. He was about five feet nine inches, a hundred-seventy pounds, and wore expensive sharkskin suits. He had jet-black hair, which he parted just right of center, and he looked like George Raft.

When we weren't busy Silver would display his card talents. He could deal five poker hands, one to each of us, and he would always win. He said to us, "I'm dealing seconds," meaning not off the top of the deck.

No matter how closely we all watched, we couldn't see him do it. Finally, he turned the top card over face up and continued to deal five hands with the face up card at the top of the deck, and we still couldn't see him do it.

I asked him, "Silver, why can't we see you do it?"

He said, "You've heard 'the hand is quicker than the eye'? Well, there's a time laps between the time something happens and when you actually see it. You have to operate faster than that. Magicians learn how to do it."

Even more amazing when I asked who had taught him the trick and how long it took to master it he said, "No one taught me. I stood in front of the mirror on top of my dresser and dealt the cards until I couldn't see myself doing it anymore. I mastered it by the time I was 11 years old. I even learned how to muzzle the sound you might hear when the second card slides out from under the top card."

Joey Maxim, the 1950 heavy weight champion, was imported from Florida where he had retired. He became the host of the new Bonanza Hotel. He later lost his job and came to live with me.

A friend of mine got a job at the Tower of Pizza on The Strip. It was the restaurant where Sinatra and friends went to eat after a night of partying. The owner was Jasper Martin.

Jasper ran the illegal nationwide wire service for years. He knew all the big-time bookies and players. Caesars Palace had just opened, and Fat Tony Salerno owned ten points in Caesars at the time. Jasper was made the host of Caesars Casino at $150,000 a year, plus commissions on the players' losses.

This was the world I walked into after leaving New York. There were a lot of New Yorkers and guys from Chicago there watching the money for their investors. The hotels and casinos back then were almost completely financed by the

Teamsters Union pension funds, which according to Bobby Kennedy was synonymous with organized crime.

The Teamsters Union consisted of truck-drivers, construction workers and other blue-collar workers, none of whom went to Harvard. Most of them never got passed the seventh grade. When the Senate and Bobby Kennedy were holding their investigation into the Teamsters' pension funds, they made it appear as though the funds were stolen or somehow gotten illegally because they had financed the casinos. The investigators never mention the fact those funds were paid back with hefty interests and profits.

It is my opinion that after the hotels and casinos were so successful the banks got pissed off and jealous because they didn't get in on it. That's why they sent in the Ivy League mob after the teamsters to put them out of the banking business. There was nothing wrong or illegal about what the Teamsters did. What bothered Kennedy was that the money came from the Teamsters. To Bobby Kennedy organized unions and organized crime were the same thing even though there was not one shred of evidence to support this conclusion.

Of course, the bankers wouldn't finance those hotels and casinos. It was "too risky" for them. I think there might have even been a trace of morality in them. I suspect, though, apart from a complete lack of vision, it had more to do with the nature of the business, for which they had no experience, not to mention that they didn't like who was running it.

It reminds me of when off-track betting became legal in New York. The State hired their own employees and lost millions. They wound up hiring all the illegal bookies to take it over.

The pension fund managers weren't the only ones with vision. The Catholic Church also had vision. It, too, invested in the casinos. I don't know how deeply they were involved, and I doubt if anyone could find out because of the way they went about it.

I went to pick up my cousin Nicky at the Sands one day. I was waiting for him at the bar and got to talking to the guy next to me. The usual chitchat. He asked, "What do you do?"

I said," I'm a crap dealer." Then he asked me a lot for questions about the game, why different numbers had different odds and questions like that. He obviously knew a lot about numbers.

He was Italian but dressed horribly, which is why I probably remember him.

When I asked him what he did, he said, "I represent investors from the East Coast and I'm out here negotiating a deal with the people building the Landmark Hotel Casino."

I said, "Oh yeah? It's under construction now. I would think they'd have all their money in place."

"That's true but they're running a little short" he chuckled.

"If you don't mind me asking, who are these high rollers? They must have a ton of money."

He laughed, then leaned over and whispered, "The Archdiocese of New York."

I watched the Scientology documentary "Going Clear" last night. I was not surprised how crazy it was, but I was surprised how much wealth they had. My story with Scientology, if you can call it that, took place fifty years ago, when there was very little of that kind of money around.

It was in Las Vegas, of all places, where I found out about Dianetics, the precursor to Scientology. My cousin Nicky introduced me to the Kaplans, a husband and wife team that ran a Dianetics franchise in Las Vegas. In those days franchises didn't have Scientology services. Indeed, Scientology was not yet fully developed and there were few practitioners in the country, most of them in New York and Saint Hill, England.

Dianetics was my first exposure to anything like therapy, if it could be called that. Dianetics was a best-selling book in the fifties and still is a big seller, having sold over 20 million copies in the last fifty years.

The ideas were very helpful to me because I was able to speak openly about things I had never told anyone before. That, in itself, was liberating. It was a simple process of repeating traumatic life experiences over and over until there was no longer any charge or emotion connected to them anymore. It's akin to saying something over and over until your bored with it.

In a Dianetics session, I was asked by a practitioner to memorize the definition of an Engram. An Engram is any traumatizing life experience one has in life, including birth. I held two cans, one in each hand. The cans were connected by wires to a box with a meter on it. A small current of electricity ran through the cans, the meter, and me. The meter measured any change on the needle the practitioner was monitoring. Lie detectors worked on the same principle.

The practitioner or auditor, as the role was called, then asked me to "recall an Engram." I would answer and the auditor would say "thank you." If the needle showed a high charge, the question would be asked again and again, until the needle "floated," meaning there was no longer any charge (emotion) on the incident.

Once that happened, the next question would be "recall a similar Engram." I would recall another trauma, usually further back in my life or "time track." The sessions would last about an hour or so. Then more sessions would be scheduled.

The auditor was looking for chains of Engrams, which could release, theoretically, large chunks of trauma at one time. In those days, when no more charge could be found you were "clear." Scientology was still being developed back then, and it would be a few years before all courses would be available.

After Dianetics auditing you went on to the early stages of Scientology auditing, which consisted of seven levels to the new Clear. Then on to six more levels called O.T (Operating Thetan), "Thetan" is Scientology's name for the soul or spirit.

I got to Las Vegas with $20 in my pocket. I walked into the Four Queens Casino downtown and put it down on the crap table. Thirty minutes later I walked out with $750, enough to put down on a car and get an apartment down the street from the Desert Inn, two bedrooms $150 a month.

A year later I was working the swing shift at the Fremont Hotel just across the street from the Four Queens. I went to pick up my paycheck before I started my shift. Instead of a paycheck I found two documents. One was a notice that my check was taken by the New York State Franchise Tax Board. The other was a draft notice, telling me to appear at White Hall Street in NYC within thirty days for induction. Needless to say, it was not a good start to my day.

My entire cash situation equaled $3.50. I needed to buy a plane ticket and figure out how I would live when I got to New York.

In Vegas dealers worked one hour on and twenty minutes off for a break. During my break I ran across the street with my bankroll of $3.50 to the Four Queens and shot craps. You were not allowed to gamble where you worked. By the end of my shift that day, I had won $750, enough to buy the ticket and have pocket money when I got to New York.

By that time I was very interested in Scientology. It was a church and I thought about becoming a minister to get a deferment. Apparently that had been tried, but the military didn't recognize Scientology as a church and didn't give a shit either.

At the induction center in New York, I remember being put into several ear-testing booths, which no one else had to do. I was asked if I had any hearing problems, to which I answered no. I found out much later in life that I had nerve damage from a gunshot that was fired inches from my head, so I could hear but I couldn't make out what you were saying nor could I hear high pitch sounds.

As it turned out, I was reclassified and didn't have to go, I was married and had three kids, but it didn't stop them from drafting me in the first place. I'm not sure why the deferment was given.

CHAPTER 18

SCIENTOLOGY

I went to work for the Scientology organization in the Martinique Hotel in Midtown Manhattan. They had two shifts. Day shift was 10:00 a.m. to 5:00 p.m.; night shift was 5:00 p.m. to 10:00 p.m. and weekends. I worked both shifts, including weekends, in different capacities. No one made much money working for Scientology

During the day I was head of promotion, creating ways of bringing people into the early evening lectures. The attendance when I took over was five to eight people a night. I printed up Gold Cordial invitations that looked like formal wedding invitations and had them passed out all day on 6th Avenue in Midtown Manhattan. I spent the rest of time as an ethics officer and a little time as an intelligence officer, a very eye-opening experience.

Eric Barnes, an unemployed off-Broadway actor, was a lecturer for Scientology. His signups for courses were low even after the attendance shot up. Eric got himself a part in a show and resigned his post. Bob Thomas, the Executive Director of the New York organization at the time, asked me to take over the lecture until he could find a replacement, and I agreed.

During the evenings I gave the introduction lectures. As a result of the "Cordial Invitations," attendance shot up to an average of thirty people a night with sign-ups going from two or three to fifteen to twenty. Income quadrupled in a week. After the lecture, I studied and became a practitioner or auditor as they called them.

The financial results of my work brought the income of the New York organization from 5k a week to 18k a week and shot me into the limelight of the powers that be. It was here that I realized I had a talent for public speaking and sales.

The staff was paid in units. Different jobs paid a different number of units. The value of each unit was the same and was established by deducting all costs from the gross income then dividing what was left, the net, by the gross number of units being paid to the entire staff.

Most staff made little more than twenty to thirty dollars a week. After I took over, their pay quadrupled, which made me popular with the staff.

As a result of my success, L Ron Hubbard promoted Bob Thomas, the Executive Director of the New York organization, to the post of "Assistant Guardian," the head of Scientology in the United States, and he would be located in Los Angeles. Bob was replaced by Dave Ecker whom I later found out sold promotional advertising gifts, like pens, for a living.

Bob was a strange looking bird. He was about six foot four with black scraggly hair, small, pitch black eyes with invisible pupils. He had long narrow fingers and a white bloodless complexion. He looked like a character you might find in vampire movie.

Before Bob left for his new position in Los Angeles, I spent a short time working in Scientology's intelligence post and was quite surprised about their activities, which included break-ins into the state mental health facilities that used shock treatments, something Hubbard was vehemently against.

I also found one of Scientology's written interrogation policies. Policies typically were numbered. This one was called policy SP 45. SP means a Suppressive Person. That was Scientology lingo for dangerous enemy and fair game, anything goes.

The instructions for dealing with the Suppressive Person went something like this: remove his or her top so they are bare chested. Then strap the enemy to a chair by wrapping a leather belt around the chest, leaving both arms free. Then place the e-meter cans under the armpits making sure to have good skin contact. Then take a .45-caliber pistol and put to the enemy's head and begin interrogation.

Frankly, I didn't take the policy seriously at the time. I didn't know what to think about it, so I stopped thinking about it. I learned about the break-ins to state mental health facilities by reading the files I had access to. It was only later I realized how dangerous and serious Scientology was.

I spent the rest of my time studying Scientology's technology and taking the training courses to be an auditor, which I completed. I would say the most beneficial course I had in Scientology was the communication course. It included what they called the TR-0 exercise, which consisted of two people sitting across from one another, hands on lap for two hours, just looking into each other's eyes, saying nothing. You'd be surprised how difficult it is.

After a few days of practicing the TR- 0 exercise, you'd move to the next level. The next level was to bait each other, trying to break each other's concentration. You could tell jokes, insult each other, and sing if you liked. In effect you learned how to be still and listen without reacting.

In the beginning of the baiting you would try not to listen, so you won't break up, but that misses the point. It was a very powerful experience for most people and the reason why they got drawn into Scientology, even though their experience may have even been downhill after that. It's important to understand how and why people got involved. You cannot throw the baby out with the bathwater. To assume there was no real value to Scientology's teachings and people were just stupid and duped would be a mistake.

The documentary "Going Clear" never really got into any of that. It concentrated only on all the craziness about it and all the damage it did to its members and their families.

My training as an auditor was much more technical, intense, and subtle. Here's why it was intense: in auditing sessions, the client is opening up about a lot of sensitive things, probably for the first time in his or her life. You are in a small quiet room together. Should the auditor react to what he is hearing, the client will experience it as a judgment and close down. Mind you the auditor never really speaks, other than asking very specific questions and acknowledging the answer with a simple "Thank you."

The auditor must become a mirror with nothing else going on. He must be completely in present time for the process to be beneficial to the client. This is a very useful ability for anyone, and people got a lot out of it. It affected and improved every aspect of their lives, including their jobs, relationships, and overall self-confidence.

You can understand why Tom Cruise and John Travolta as actors got so drawn to it. Their craft depends on their ability to be present and listen without distraction and respond appropriately. That's the essence of acting.

As to why they are still involved and defending it, the answer is simple: Blackmail and loss of face. The auditing sessions are fundamentally confessionals, similar to Catholic Church practices, only far more invasive, especially when the organization has their own agenda.

You need only look at what Bob Thomas did when Franklin asked for his money back. His first response was to blackmail me, and that was fifty years ago.

It was Bob Thomas who started the celebrity organization Scientology has been running in Hollywood. He hated the weather in New York and used this opportunity to move to L.A. To Bob, Scientology was a business, and he wanted to go where the pickings were good and the weather was better.

Bob had two Scientology franchises that he opened in New York, one in a high-end apartment building on 72nd Street between First Avenue and the East River Drive, the other on 74th between Lexington and Madison, another high-end apartment.

Bob needed money for his move to L.A., so he offered to sell both franchises to me for $20,000. I wasn't particularly interested and didn't have the money anyway. But a commercial printer named Bernard Schwartz, a Scientology member and groupie, offered to buy them and make me a full partner if I would agree to run them. I agreed and took them over.

I left the Scientology staff to run the franchisees. As a result of my leaving, the income of the New York organization. dropped almost to what it was before I took over. Shortly after, Hubbard sent in his Sea Organization to investigate. The Sea Org was Hubbard's version of the Black Shirt Gestapo, only they didn't wear black shirts. Instead, these clowns wore white jump suits and white construction helmets.

They were the elite of Scientology, the OT's and were personally trained by Hubbard. Everyone in the organization was in awe of them. They were on a witch-hunt looking for the "Suppressive Person," a dangerous enemy and fair game, a term you would hear a lot of in Scientology. The members of the Sea Org were the most obnoxious assholes you'd ever want to meet. They were full of themselves, completely brain washed and, as such, very dangerous.

They found out very quickly that the money had dropped because I had left, but that wasn't good enough. They knew Hubbard wanted someone to hang. So the Gestapo reported to Hubbard that I was siphoning off the Org's clients and feeding them into my franchises. Of course, they didn't have a shred of evidence because it wasn't true.

Not only was it not true, but also the franchises were dying. Bob Thomas had completely misrepresented the income and the client base. It was outright fraud. During the same time the Sea Org were investigating, Franklin Jones and I left for LA for two weeks to complete all the "upper levels."

Around 1965 or 1966, I met and became close friends with John McMaster. He was on a world tour and spent a lot of time in New York. I let him stay at one of my apartments while he was in New York.

John was a South African man. He had a slight build, a charming English accent, large beautiful blue eyes, and pure white wavy hair. We used to refer to him as the white dove. He was the epitome of elegance. He loved to drink and be social.

One night John and I were alone having a few drinks at my place. He seemed upset. I asked him, "What's wrong, John? I've never seen you like this before. You look worried."

"There's a lot wrong, Sal," he confided in me, "and I don't know what to do about it, or who I can really trust. You are the only one I feel safe enough to tell, but you must not tell anyone. I'm very fearful."

John was child-like in many ways, meaning innocent. He drank a couple more drinks and began to open up. First he said, "I don't believe Ron is in charge of Scientology any longer."

"What makes you say that?"

"Well, there is always a lot of politics going on around Ron. Everyone wants to be the closest to him. It is all about power. The closer you are to him the more power you have. Before, Ron never let anyone get between us. We were friends, and I am eternally indebted to him for saving my life." It was clear to me John attributed his cancer remission to Ron and Dianetics, which may in fact be true. The mind can turn off illnesses if it believes it can. Otherwise, placeboes wouldn't work.

John went on to explain, "Now, I no longer have direct contact with Ron, and I've been ordered back to 'The Ship.'"

"The Ship" in Scientology was a term for about six actual boats serving as Ron L. Hubbard's seat of power. Hubbard had to live on one of the boats because he was wanted by the law in so many countries. More significantly, "The Ship" was the FBI of Scientology. It was run by the Sea Org, the enforcers, the secret police. The members of the Sea Org were fanatics, capable of anything.

I asked John, "What do you think is going on?

"Sal, you must not tell anyone, but Ron is addicted to drugs and has been for a long time."

"What kind of drugs?"

"I'm not sure, but given his behavior and some of his comments, I would say cocaine or something like it."

"What comments?"

"Well, he would often mention how Freud and his colleagues spent years injecting cocaine and that the character Sherlock Holmes was also addicted to cocaine. The last time I saw him I urged him to be careful. I believe the senior staff has taken control of everything and isolated him in some way."

"What are you afraid of John?"

"I'm afraid if I go back to The Ship you will never see me again"

"What do you mean? Do you think they would kill you? I wouldn't worry too much about that John. You bring in too much money," I laughed. He was a major fundraiser for Scientology

"I don't know what they would do, but if Ron is isolated and someone else is in control, anything could happen."

John had been diagnosed with cancer and apparently went into remission during the time he was working with Hubbard on Dianetics. He became the first "clear." He claimed, and truly believed, that his remission was because of Dianetics. Hubbard smartly made him the ambassador for Scientology around the world.

John McMaster, more than anyone else, was responsible for Scientology's success around the world. He was also gay. I didn't know if anyone else knew it at that time. Things like that were kept very secret in those days. John was not a macho guy by any stretch of the imagination, but he wasn't at all effeminate.

John had the demeanor of a gentle doctor. He was a benign soul with an angelic aura about him. The only reason I know he was gay is that he slept with another friend of mine, Larry, while he lived at my place in New York. I didn't know Larry was so inclined since he was living with his long-time girlfriend at the time.

The levels of Scientology ran from one to seven or "Clear." Then there were six more levels above Clear called OT (Operating Thetan), Thetan being synonymous with soul or spirit. "Clear" was someone who no longer had a "reactive mind, meaning someone who was free from the trauma of his entire past.

OT was someone who could be anywhere in the world in real-time just by putting his attention there. He wasn't there bodily, but he would have all his senses still available to him in that place; that was the claim.

Most of my courses were free because I worked for the organization. The upper level courses of Scientology cost $10,000 at the time, I believe. I had to pay for those levels, and they were only available in Los Angeles. I didn't have the money, but my partner Bernie insisted that I go, and he would pay for it.

I said, "Bernie I don't feel comfortable about you paying for it. Why would you want to do that?"

"Well first of all, you are my friend and second, I believe it would be good for our business. If you were at the highest level of Scientology, think of it as a good business move." So, I accepted Bernie's generous offer.

Not long after I went to work for Scientology, I met Franklin Jones. He had just gotten back from India visiting a guru called Muktanda, later to be well-known Guru in the US.

Franklin had also spent five years as a disciple of a gay Jewish guru who called himself Rudrananda or Rudy. Rudy owned an eastern art store in Greenwich Village. When Franklin became aware of the fact that Rudy's Guru was Muktanda, he decided to go around Rudy and visit the Man himself. Franklin had just returned from that visit when he came to check out Scientology. He asked to speak to someone about Scientology, and I was asked to explain it to him.

Franklin and I sat down in the waiting room at the Martinique Hotel and talked for six hours, then spent the next eleven years together. A few years later I moved to California and established him as an American guru, calling himself Bubba Free John, then Free John.

Over the next twenty years he changed his name at least ten times. But that's another story that many people have been asking me to write about for years. It should probably be in another book, but I will try to get it into this one.

Franklin and I went to L.A. together to do all the "OT" levels. He paid the $10,000. The so-called upper levels were a self-audit or solo audit. One morning I walked into Franklin's room. He was lying on the floor in his underwear, with his e-meter. He looked up at me and said, "Sal, this is total bullshit!" We must have laughed on and off for hours.

We had been hoodwinked.

CHAPTER 19

OT 6 AND THE LAND OF OZ

The documentary "Going Clear" about Scientology accurately described the e-meter and its function in the auditing process.

The OT levels were a complete fantasy, which is why they were secret. I wish I could remember all the course materials in that psychotic journey.

While Franklin and I were in Los Angeles, the Sea Org came to New York to investigate why the income had dropped so dramatically. At the same time, Franklin and I had realized that Scientology was complete bullshit and had decided to leave the organization and return to New York, but Franklin wanted his money back.

Once Franklin and I got back to New York, we went to the office of Dave Ecker, who had replaced Bob Thomas as Executive Director, to demand Franklin's money back. After Dave recovered from the shock of our demand, he was at a loss as to what to do about it, so he called Bob Thomas in L.A.

I spoke to Bob briefly on the phone, and he threatened me. He knew I was the cousin and namesake of Lucky Luciano, and, of course, that meant I was somehow a member of the Mafia. I wasn't a member, and I believe he knew it but couldn't really be sure.

He said, "How would it look, Sal, if it was made public that the Mafia was shaking down churches."

Without a pause I replied, "I guess it would look something like a church trying to undermine the U.S. government like breaking into government mental health facilities as well as FBI offices and stealing their files." He knew I had the goods on them.

After a long silence I said, "If this is the way you want to play it, let's do it," and hung up. It was only about ten minutes before he called back and told Dave Ecker he was flying into New York in a couple of days and wanted to meet with us.

During the course of that year Franklin and his wife, Nina, who were now both on the Scientology staff, split up. At that time Nina was having an affair with Dave Ecker and worked for him in the executive offices.

At 4 a.m. a couple of days before Franklin and I were to meet Bob Thomas, I got a call from Franklin. He told me, "I just got a call from Nina. She's at Dave Ecker's office right now. She said, 'Milton Gordon just left here with your pistol, claiming you are a killer.'

Milton Gordon and his wife worked for me, running my New York Franchise. Nina also told Franklin that Milton and his wife were working with the Sea Org to prove that I was stealing the NY Org's clients.

She said that Milton found the gun in my desk drawer. He was using it as evidence that I should be kicked out of Scientology. I didn't know whether to laugh or go off like a bomb.

How ironic: Bob Thomas had just tried to blackmail me and my employee was trying to frame me so I would get thrown out of Scientology, and he could take over my franchises for himself. And I was supposedly the criminal!

After that I knew what I was dealing with. Franklin was not a tough guy and never had much of a stomach for confrontation. He was a Stanford and Columbia graduate and had spent a year in a Lutheran seminary. I, on the other hand, was a street guy and used to confrontation.

I said to Franklin. "These people are really crazy." I did keep a little .25 automatic pistol in the drawer of my desk that I had brought with me from Las Vegas but didn't even remember I had it.

Milton in real life was a garden-variety salesman and, I was told, jealous of me because of my fast rise in the Scientology organization. I knew immediately what he was up to. If I was to be thrown out of Scientology, I could no longer own those franchises. He would then take them over for nothing.

I told Franklin to grab a cab and meet me at the 74th Street offices. It was about 5 a.m. when Franklin and I walked into the apartment. All the lights were on. The entire staff was there, and all the client files were spread out on the desks.

The first person I ran into was Milton's wife Frannie. I thought she would have a heart attack when she saw me. "Hi, Frannie," I greeted her. "What are you guys doing here?"

Stumbling over her words she said, "Working, Boss."

Knowing what she was doing there, I wanted to raise her temperature a little.

"What exactly are you working on?" I pushed.

She turned pale and started to hyperventilate. "We are examining all the clients' files to see if there are any auditing mistakes."

"Very good, Frannie, I'm impressed and glad to see you're on it. Where's Milton?"

"He's in your office working." I walked to the back of the apartment where my office was. I walked in and found Milton sitting at my desk in the big leather executive chair, no doubt trying it out.

On the desk were the two corporate books representing my two franchises. Next to them was my little .25 automatic pistol. The clip was full and lay alongside the pistol.

Franklin walked into the room behind me. I walked calmly toward Milton and sat in the chair alongside the desk. I knew he had just gotten there, and he knew it was no accident that I was there.

I stared at him for about a minute without saying a word, just watching him squirm in the chair. Then I picked up the pistol, looked at it, and asked him, "What are you doing with this out?" I was curious to see how much of his bullshit he believed about me.

He said in a quivering voice, "I was just cleaning it." Then I picked up the clip, loaded into the gun, put a bullet in the chamber, and put it against his head between his eyes.

Franklin immediately left the room. Then I said to Milton, "Tell me something, Milton, what if everything you just said about me is true? What do you think your life is worth right about now?"

Milton fainted and pissed in his pants. When he regained his senses, I picked up the two corporate books and dropped them on his lap. "Is this what it's all about, Milton?" I knew Milton was a well-educated Jewish boy with an ego as large as his stomach, which was large.

He felt entitled to more than he had accomplished, and it bothered him that I was an Italian, clearly lower class, a high school drop out from the streets of Harlem. I wanted to hurt him, but not physically, although that ran through my mind more than once.

I said to him, "You can have these franchises, Milton. They're yours." I knew I wouldn't have them in a couple of days anyway.

I continued, "But I want you to know something. Guys like you do not make it in life without guys like me. You mark my words. You will be broke in a year, because you're a fuckin' loser and a thief."

In saying that, I remembered what my Uncle Carl had told me about arrogance and stupidity. Here was an example right before my eyes.

Then Franklin and I left the apartment

When I got home around 6 that morning, I got a call from a Roger Stone, the Sea Org "commander" in charge of my investigation. He asked me in a very authoritative voice, "Is this Mr. Luciano? "

I didn't know what was coming, but I knew what it was about. I had no intention of being polite to this clown. Correcting him I said, "No, this is Mr. Lucania. Who the hell are you?"

"I'm commander Roger Stone from the Sea Org," he announced as if expecting applause.

"Well, bully for you," I said. "What's on your mind, Commander?" It better be good calling me at this time of the morning."

"You are commanded to report immediately to the New York office to answer serious charges made against you."

"Really? What are these charges, and who made them?"

"Never mind that. You will be told when you arrive here." I couldn't believe the audacity of this idiot. I thought, *If he believes all this shit, he has to be psychotic.*

Knowing how the Scientology inquisition worked, I knew there would be at least three or four members of what would amount to a tribunal, so I asked, "Tell me, Commander, are all the members of this tribunal from the Sea Org?"

"Of course, and they are all OT as required by the Admiral."

Oh this is going to be good, I thought.

"By the Admiral, you mean Hubbard?"

"Yes, of course. You are wasting my time and the time of six others who have very important things to do."

Little did I know one of those important things they had to do was kidnap John McMaster and bring him back to the ship.

"Yeah, like what?" I asked.

"That's none of your business. You have an hour to get down here."

I wanted to ask, *or what?* but had a much better idea. I was going to put these assholes in their place once and for all.

"You said you and the others are all O.T. I realize now how important your time is. So, I suggest we all get out of our bodies and meet at the top of the Empire State Building in, say, ten minutes."

The silence was defining, and I wasn't going to fill the empty space for him. So I waited in silence to see how he would handle it.

Finally I asked, "Roger, Roger are you there?" He was still there but obviously speechless. I then added, "Give the Admiral my regards, you idiot," and hung up.

Sometimes in life, just sometimes, there is poetic justice. A few years later I was checking into the Fontainebleau Hotel in Miami, and there was Milton, the head bellhop at the hotel.

He recognized me. He knew I saw him. I could have approached him and rubbed it in his face, which he most certainly would have deserved. But I thought that would be classless on my part. Instead, knowing the size of Milton's ego, I walked past him like he wasn't there, and he didn't matter. And he didn't.

Franklin and I met Bob Thomas at his old office. He leaned back in the big leather chair with the attitude of a king. In a very condescending manner he said, "Well Sal, have you thought about what I said?" He meant the image of the Mafia shaking down a church.

I didn't believe my father when he told me I would have trouble because of my name and family connection. I didn't know then that I was a member of the outlaw class. But here was another example that my father was right.

My first thought was to walk over to Bob and slap him off his chair. I just had no patience for this arrogant asshole. I don't know where these jerks originated from, but it wasn't Harlem.

"You mean that threat? Did you ever consider how the Mafia might react to such an accusation? Probably not, I suspect." I knew he was full of shit. He was scared, I could smell it. He didn't travel three thousand miles to tell me this. He could have done that over the phone, and he had, no doubt, spoken to Roger.

I said, "You have five minutes to write the check to return Franklin's $10,000. Then I'm leaving here and walking over to the *Daily News* first and the FBI second. You're over your head, Bob." Then I turned to leave.

He jumped off his throne, and said, "Okay Sal, but you and Franklin will sign an agreement never to disclose anything about Scientology or its technology." He was more concerned about what I could reveal than about the money.

"Not a fuckin chance," I said, "but what I will sign is a mutual *hold harmless agreement.*" He agreed and wrote the check.

It turned out that "Commander" Roger did have something important to do in New York. He was there to go after John Mac Master.

A week or so after I left Scientology, I got a call from a couple that ran a franchise in the Boston area. " Hi ,Sal, my name is Mary Higgins. You don't know me, but I run the Scientology franchise in the Boston area."

"Yes, Mary. What can I do for you?"

"John McMaster showed up here a few days ago and was in a panic. He told me the Sea Org was after him. He asked me to call and tell you. Do you have any idea what's going on?"

"Yes I do. Is he OK?"

"Oh, yes. He's staying with me at our house. It's wonderful having him with us."

"OK, good. Tell him not to worry. I'll call him in a couple days. Keep him out of the franchise and give me your home number and address."

"OK, Sal, I will and thanks."

When I got off the phone, I got Bob Thomas' home number and address. He was listed, believe or not. I waited until midnight to call him at home. After Bob had tried to blackmail me, and I found the Sea Org was really out to kidnap John and possibly kill him, I knew what I was dealing with.

When these people can't bury you with lawyers, they seem to have no problem just burying you. I got Bob on the line and asked, "Do you remember the conversation we had the last time I saw you?"

"Yes, I do. Why? Is there something wrong?"

"There is a lot wrong. The Sea Org is trying to kidnap John McMaster."

"That's absurd. Where did you hear that?'

"He told me that himself, Bob, and he believes they will kill him and so do I." Bob knew I was to be taken seriously. I also wanted those clowns from the Sea Org to understand what they were dealing with.

I said, "Listen close, Bob, and don't play stupid with me. I want you to call off those Sea Org idiots. I want them back on their fuckin' rowboat and out of New York. I told you I would go to the press and the FBI about your intelligence activities, and now I can add kidnapping and possibly murder as your present activity. But more importantly to you is, if anything happens to John, I'm going to hold you personally responsible, meaning, whatever happens to him will happen to you."

"Listen, Sal ….

"I don't want to hear it," I said and hung up. It was the last time I ever heard from anyone in Scientology again. These people were outright criminals. I noticed watching the "Going Clear" documentary that none of Scientology's victims knew how to deal with the higher ups. They were of the citizen class and afraid of them.

The only way to deal with Scientology is to put them in fear of losing their lives. At least that was my experience.

CHAPTER 20

S.E.R.A.—SERVICES, EDUCATION, REHABILITATION, ADDICTION DRUG PROGRAM

After I left Scientology, my wife and I decided to get back together. After all, I didn't leave her because of any problems we had. I left because I felt suffocated by my circumstance. Looking at it in retrospect, I would say I had left because I was having a nervous breakdown.

When I left, I was twenty-five years old and already married for eight years. I had three children by the time I was twenty, and I spent four years in the drywall business as contractor and hated it. I was much too young to settle for that ordinary citizen kind of life, and I saw no future in it for me.

I knew I was smarter and more capable than swinging a hammer for the rest of my life. I wanted and needed change, but I had no idea what I wanted to do or even what I could do, but I was determined to find out. I figured it was better to walk into the unknown than to live the way I was living.

It was the mid-sixties. The country was in an upheaval and changing rapidly, and I wanted to be part of it. Leaving got me to Vegas. Vegas got me to Scientology, which got me to Franklin Jones and back with my wife. She got me into the poverty programs of the sixties, and the poverty programs got me into the drug rehabilitation field. There I learned about the deadliness of politics in the real world and a great many things about myself.

I maintained a close relationship with Franklin for many years. He had become my closest friend and the strong positive influence on me. After our stint in Scientology he moved into a loft in Soho Manhattan with his wife Nina and his former lover Pat Morley.

At the time Soho had light industrial spaces being vacated then rented out to artists, writers, and others who needed large, quiet spaces but couldn't afford such spaces anywhere else in New York. Franklin and I worked hard on weekends, painting the floors and walls, making beds out of old doors and foam mattresses.

Franklin returned to his spiritual practice in Eastern traditions of enlightenment and began to teach me what he had learned. We dreamed and talked about starting an experimental, self-contained community where we would live free from ruling class suppression. We researched available land and found 1,500 acres in Canada. We even wrote to Buckminster Fuller to participate in the design of a new community. We were hungry for knowledge. I wanted to be "enlightened" (happy) but didn't have a clue of what that meant or even if there was such a thing.

The only strength I had to go on was Franklin's personality. I had never met anyone like him before. I was drawn to him by his sense of humor, which I found to be unique and incredibly liberating. By the time he and I met, he had spent five years with Albert Rudolph or Swami Rudrananda.

Rudy had made Franklin work very hard in his antique shop in Greenwich Village. Franklin then entered a Lutheran seminary for a year at Rudy's request. Franklin's search for truth was honest and sincere.

It was after seeing a picture of Rudy's guru Muktananda in Rudy's shop that Franklin decided to go to India to meet the man himself. At the time he was employed as a ticket agent for an international airline, and so was able to fly practically free. Upon his return, he decided to look into Scientology, which is where I first met him.

Louise worked for a truck rental company in the Bronx as a bookkeeper. Franklin's wife Nina wrote grants for various non-profit organizations, and I was creating a drug program in the South Bronx. Later, this core group of Franklin, Nina, Pat Morley, Louise, and I incorporated as a religious organization and started a community in California that still exists today.

My wife had moved to the Bronx while I was in Vegas. She was involved with school politics and was seeing a Puerto Rican man who was somehow connected to the poverty programs. Through her connections I got a job in the Neighborhood Youth Corp, a small agency giving out subsidized summer jobs to young people.

One day the director of my agency, Mike Grau, asked me if I would attend a meeting for him at the Hunt's Point Community Corp in the South Bronx. I was surprised since I hadn't been working there very long. I didn't think I was there to do anything other than to fill his chair.

This agency funded sixty satellite agencies throughout the South Bronx. Those satellite agencies were all bilingual and acted as liaisons to all government services: welfare, health care, housing, and more.

The meeting was held in a center that was once a supermarket. I walked in and saw folding tables and chairs in a large circle with about fifty people sitting and waiting for Bobby Munoz, the Executive Director of the Hunt's Point Community Corp. Munoz's agency received money from the Federal War on Poverty funds. He had a couple of million-dollar budgets, which was used to fund the sixty satellite agencies. The center was a large space with old, worn out green tiles interrupted by long swatches of concrete where the shelves had once stood.

The directors introduced themselves and the agencies they represented. I was the only white guy in the meeting. I told them who I was and said I was representing Mike Grau. Bobby Munoz, who was running the meeting, was about 50 years old. His experience was in union organizing. He had a degree from Cornell University, but then again everyone there seemed to have a degree from Cornell. To me, he seemed much more like an Italian American than a Puerto Rican.

Bobby was smart and strong. He was not afraid to take on anything. He wore very ordinary accountant glasses and was appropriately paunchy for his age. He looked very much like Lewis Black the comedian.

Bobby was sincere and passionate about his responsibilities, which is why he was very effective. There were two poverty agencies in the South Bronx, his and Multi-Services Corp. headed by Ramon Valez. Valez had a bigger agency with more money and, therefore, more political power.

Valez had gotten Bobby his job through political connections and, therefore, considered that Bobby worked for him. Technically, of course, it wasn't true. Valez had already made it known he was going to run for Congress against a priest named Father Gigante. I was told Valez wanted to be governor of Puerto Rico, and Congress was going to be his stepping-stone.

Ramon Valez was about five foot five inches tall with a fifty-inch waist. He had black short-cropped hair on a very small head compared to the rest of his body. The thing that stood out the most to me was his very white skin. I don't know why, but his appearance just didn't come together right for me. He had a Napoleonic air about him. He walked with a swagger but still spoke with a strong Spanish accent.

Bobby opened the meeting announcing he wanted to establish a bilingual drug program in the South Bronx. He went around the table asking for everyone's input, focusing on where they thought it should be located or how many clients it could or should serve. It was more show than anything else. He didn't need or want their input.

By the time he got to me the staff members were already arguing about location, management, and money. When Bobby asked me what I thought, I told him, "You haven't got a prayer of getting a program here with this group."

Bobby locked onto my eyes with a very slight smile on his face and asked, "Why do you say that?"

"Because this group is already fighting over the money and the program doesn't even exist." Needless to say that didn't go over well with the other directors. Bobby knew I was right, and I'm sure he knew it long before I said anything.

Bobby asked me to stay after the meeting. We went into his office and he told me, "I want you to come to work for me as my Executive Assistant."

I was taken by surprise. I had no idea what that meant, "but what about my job?"

"Don't worry about that," he assured me. "I'll take care of it. Starting tomorrow you come to work here, and I'll have a desk for you in my office. You'll stay on Mike's payroll until I can get you into my budget. I'll let him know what's going on."

"What's my job here supposed to be?"

"You have only one job, Sully." Bobby called me Sully from the first day I met him. I don't know why, but I liked it better than Sally. "Get me a bilingual drug program here in the South Bronx."

That was it. He just expected me to do it. He never asked about my experience, qualifications, or questioned my ability to get the job done. Maybe my success was a forgone conclusion for him. I've never been short on confidence, but from that moment on, success became a foregone conclusion for me as well.

That one act of confidence in me changed my life and my attitude towards life. I had learned from my experience in Scientology that I could sell and speak publicly in front of fairly large groups. I had also learned a good deal about organization and marketing. The paradox is that I'm painfully shy.

Bobby had plenty of resources and political connections, which I had at my disposal, including Maria Favuzzi, a very literate 28-year-old ex-nun who was Bobby's executive secretary and mistress.

It was obvious that the first order of business was to get a program written. You can't sell something you don't have yet. Maria had the writing skills but neither of us knew anything about the drug rehabilitation business, so learning about it became the next order of business.

I don't think I was at my new job a week when two Puerto Rican clinicians from Phoenix House, the largest drug rehabilitation program in New York, walked into my office with the idea of starting a bilingual drug program in the South Bronx. How's that for luck?

Their names were Frank Gracia and Frank Marrero, whom I came to call Cheech to distinguish him from Frank Gracia. It was common in the Italian culture to have a nickname and anyone named Frank was called Cheech. I have no idea why.

I recognized immediately that all the players necessary to write, run, and fund a drug program were in place: Bobby, Maria, Frank, Cheech, and me. Bobby left the writing of the program to the four of us and spent his time opening doors for us.

We met every day and began to write the program. Frank was the clinical expert. It was his idea to radically change the Phoenix Houses therapeutic model into something never tried before.

He and Cheech had completed Phoenix House's five-year program then worked as clinicians there for another five years. The Phoenix House five-year program had a 5 percent success rate at the time. Frank wanted a one-year program with a 50 percent success rate.

To achieve this rate we couldn't follow the traditional practices in drug rehabilitation. The old therapeutic communities were basically work camps. For free room and board, clients were put to work within the facilities scrubbing floors, doing basic maintenance, or serving in the programs' restaurant and other businesses, basically slave labor.

For us the key to rehabilitation was engaging every part of the clients' lives to equip them to get back into society. That meant basics like preparing them to get a GED, getting a driver's license, cleaning up legal issues, like traffic tickets or other warrants, and finding housing. Thus, we armed the client to survive.

Our therapeutic program required a rigid structure designed to deal with street addicts. There is a difference between making mistakes in society and making mistakes in the program. In the outside world, a mistake would land you in jail. In the program if you did something against the rules, you would be corrected immediately.

Our T.C (therapeutic community) were structured to deal with manipulative behavior. As such, every minute of the day, from the time you got up until you went to bed, you were told what to do. When the client tried to get around the rules he was confronted, first, by the clinician and then by his peers in therapy groups.

The written program was finished in two weeks. It was completely unique. Phoenix House's concept required the clients to show up at the admission center every day for a year before they could be admitted to the program. The idea was to see if they were motivated enough to go through the program. A year was far too long to wait for help as far as Frank was concerned and was one of the reasons Phoenix House had only a 5 percent success rate.

Also at Phoenix House, clients entered a daycare program for two years. They spent seven days a week working without pay for the facility or outside if they had a job. They also attended group therapy sessions then went home at night, assuming they had a home. Many didn't. At the end of the first two years, they entered the live-in facility full time for another two years.

In contrast, our program took only a month or less before admission. Some clients were admitted in a few days. Next, they got to live-in full time for eight months, then daycare for three months, all fairly flexible depending on a client's progress. Frank considered the lengthy five-year programs unnecessary, counterproductive and what amounted to, in his view, involuntary servitude. Those programs tended to become more like religions or cults.

Private, more expensive programs were available for people with money. The clients in those programs were for well-known types or their children. Judy Denson Gerber, the Gerber Baby Food heir, ran one of them.

Our program's name, Services, Education, Rehabilitation, Addiction, (SERA) described our approach to addiction. Frank had a few very novel ideas. He saw addiction as a symptom, not a problem. The problem was being poor, uneducated and having no opportunity to integrate into society. The responsibility for addiction, lay with the community. He felt that the drug problem started in the community and, therefore, must be resolved there, but first there had to be a community. To graduate from S.E.R.A., you had to have all your legal problems cleared up, a G.E.D., a driver's license, a place to live and a job. We had our own teachers on staff as well as a legal department to clear up warrants and other legal problems.

Cheech wore many hats, as we all did. He was our man in the city courts when he wasn't working in the facility. He knew almost all the judges from working with them when he was at Phoenix House, not to mention the ones that put him in prison over the years. Both he and Frank had spent twenty years each in prison on and off.

The judges loved Cheech because of the way he had turned his life around. The women working in the Hall of

Justice were nuts about him. They would do anything for him. Theses connections helped in our success

Cheech was a Spanish Cary Grant, but not as tall. He had a full head of dark brown hair with graying temples. He was in great shape, owing to his two-mile run every day and visits to the gym when it was snowing. Although he was Frank's age, he looked ten years younger. He loved to laugh, especially at his own jokes.

He got the community's help by having our residents out on the street patrolling the neighborhood. The residents knew almost all the street junkies who were praying on the residence in the neighborhood. In the beginning, our clients had to administer a few well-deserved beatings to show the local hoods we meant business.

Also we set up a community relations department where people could come to meet their neighbors and speak openly about drug dealers and robberies they saw going on. The community didn't trust the police in the same way they don't trust them now and for the same reasons.

We basically became a community police department embedded in the community. The cops didn't like it at first, but it worked incredibly well and made life easier for them. Eventually they created a position within the police department for a community relations officer. He attended our community meetings and got to know our clients and the people in the neighborhood. The cops were always welcome to have lunch and dinner in our cafeteria with the residents. It was there they found out that "junkies" were human beings that needed help.

As part of the therapy, we set up a community service unit and assigned a few clients each day to work in the unit. Their job was to help local residents wherever and whenever it was possible. We also established a "hustle unit" made up of clients whose job was to solicit goods and/or services from large companies such as foods from super markets or clothes from department stores, which we distributed to poor families in the community.

Local neighbors could call us with requests for help. Our guys carried groceries, walked the kids to school and even helped their kids with their homework because many parents didn't know enough English to be of help. It was heartwarming to be a part of it.

Working in the neighborhood was a great experience for our clients. It built their self-esteem, which was in short supply for people trying to rebuild their lives. We virtually eliminated burglaries, muggings, and drug dealing on the streets where we operated. We made the neighborhood safe for everybody, including the cops.

We opened our facility to the neighborhood where they could hold meetings, organize events and, most important, we could listen to what they had to say. They were the key to solving the drug problem.

We worked with them on any problem they had where we could be of help. Eventually, we had over five hundred volunteers who got to know and care about our residents as well as each another. Our volunteers helped our residents when they were ready to graduate and find jobs and places to stay. In many instances they took them into their homes until they could find a place. It was nothing short of a miracle, and the results were immediate and visible.

CHAPTER 21

THE FUNDING

We needed $1.3 million a year to perform this miracle, and getting it was Bobby's and my job. No program was ever given that kind of money directly. The State Narcotics Commission funneled its grants to New York City's A.S.A (Addiction Service Agency). They in turn funded programs around the city, but most of the funds went to Phoenix House or Black programs, first because they had the biggest program and second because there was very little difference between ASA and Phoenix House, meaning Phoenix House staffed and politically controlled the ASA.

Getting funds for the Spanish-speaking community through the A.S.A. was never going to happen. We would have to go around the A.S.A directly to the State Narcotics Commission, which was responsible for all funding in the state. That had never been done before. The state was allowed to fund only local government agencies, which, in turn, could fund local non-profit programs. That was the political landscape in 1965.

At the time, the courts and jails were overwhelmed, much as they are today and for the same reason: for politicians to get elected. To get elected, politicians declared the War on Drugs. They never understood that the "War on Drugs" was a metaphor. You can't declare war on a drug. It's an inanimate object.

Then, as now, the government was declaring war on the ordinary citizen class. What's worse, they knew it and didn't give a shit, just like now. Today prisons are private profit-making businesses trading on Wall Street. As Bobby Munoz had said, "They're a bunch of whores." It began to change a little when Bobby Kennedy's son, David Kennedy, was found dead of a heroin overdose

There were serious debates going on about decriminalizing heroin the way England did and treating heroin addiction as a medical problem, which is exactly what it is. England issued medical cards for heroin and dispensed the drug for free to anyone who had a card. When England initiated this policy, its crime rate fell out the bottom.

The heroin problem was a political one; how were the politicians going to decriminalize heroin after all the bullshit they had used to terrorize the public in order to get themselves into office. They knew they could solve the crime side of the problem just as England did. The evidence was already there. But it was too politically dangerous for them. Like the politicians of today their first concern was for themselves. Today's War on Drugs is big business and has nothing to do with solving the drug problem.

Ultimately, the United States followed a similar practice to the practice in England by authorizing a substitute drug called methadone and called it an antidote. But methadone is far worse than heroin. Unlike heroin withdrawal, the withdrawals from methadone come from the marrow of the bones, not just the blood stream. It is very painful.

Heroin, ironically, had been introduced as the cure/antidote for morphine addiction. The big difference between heroin and methadone is that heroin has no tolerance level, meaning you have to take more and more heroin to get the same high, which was not true of methadone. Also there is no "high" connected with Methadone, but it is a narcotic and every bit as dangerous and addictive as heroin or Oxycontin.

Frank and I had many fights with the powers that be about replacing one drug addiction with another. People on methadone eventually lose their sex drive and are not very productive. The only relief with methadone for the addict was that he didn't have to steal to get it and that took the pressure off the jails and the courts.

There was a private clinic in the South Bronx that was contracted to dispense methadone for $30 a drink, paid for by the Welfare Department. There were lines around the block day and night for that clinic, bringing in $30,000 a week, all profit to the private clinic. We can see today how it cured the heroin problem.

The State Narcotics Commission had five Commissioners, made up of different ethnic backgrounds covering the five boroughs. The Executive Director, Frank Smith, was Black. He screened and submitted the grant applications to the commissioners. He was the gatekeeper, but no applicants were allowed to speak to any commissioner directly.

Although most of the state funding went to Phoenix House and Black programs, we had a few advantages to get funding. First, the highest rate of addiction per capita was in the Spanish speaking community, and there were no bilingual programs in the country at all. Second, there were only thirteen Spanish-speaking clinicians in the country, and they all worked for Phoenix House, as did Frank and Cheech.

I knew it would be a big advantage if we could get those clinicians to commit to working for us if and when we got funded. It would also prevent Phoenix House from qualifying for those funds because they would then have no Spanish-speaking clinicians.

I told Frank Garcia we needed to attract the Spanish-speaking clinicians from Phoenix House for our Puerto Rican program. It meant the clinicians would have to quit their jobs without knowing if we would get funded.

He said, "Give me a couple days, and I'll get back to you."

Frank was an interesting man. He was about fifty years old and had a face that closely resembled the face of Jack

Palance the actor. He spent most of his life in and out of prison, mostly in and had been a heroin addict almost all of his adult life. He was about five foot, eight and well built, with pure white hair and tan colored skin. His warm, humorous eyes betrayed his well-earned rugged looks. He had an aura about him that one finds in movie stars or heads of state, yet he was humble in his demeanor.

Frank called me a few days later. "Sal, I would like to have my clinicians meet with you, Bobby, and Maria on Saturday. I want to show them that our plan for the program is real, and I want you guys to get to know them."

"You got it, Frank," I agreed. "How about 10 a.m.?"

When we met on Saturday, I was impressed with all of them. I hadn't realized that three of them were women. It was not until then that it occurred to me that we would be treating women as well as men, even though it was written in the program.

At the end of the meeting, they all signed on with us. This was a very big deal for them, because they were willing to take the risk of having no work if our program didn't get funded. Many had families to support, but they believed in Frank Garcia and the future of the program. They were Puerto Ricans and having their own program was a dream for them. Also they agreed with Frank that the recovery time of five years was way too long.

The meeting ended with lots of hugs, even some tears. Frank was their leader, hero, and trusted friend. I told Bobby Munoz we needed to get the politicians to sign on – literally, meaning become members of the "advisory board" we would form just for that purpose. I wanted their names to appear on our new stationary.

At that point, Bobby's union organizing and negotiating skills came into play. He began to call our representatives in Albany to set up appointments for us but was getting the run around. They were too busy to help the people they represented, just like they are today, and Bobby was furious.

He was on the phone when I came to work that morning talking to some Senator's office. "He's in a meeting? Who the fuck does he think he is?" Bobby slammed the phone down looked at me and said, "We're going to Albany tomorrow."

"Who are we meeting with?"

"Anybody we want." He had a plan but he wasn't telling me what it was. We went to Senator Robert Garcia's office. Bobby knew Senator Garcia from the neighborhood and saw a lot of him when the Senator came around begging for help in turning out the vote.

Bobby was still fuming when we walked into the Senator's outer office. He walked past his secretary, opened the door, and found the Senator on the phone. Bobby took the couch from the office wall and slid it in front of the door so no one could leave or enter.

The first words out of Bobby's mouth were, "Who the fuck do you think you are, you fuckin whore?" I stood there with my mouth open not believing what I was witnessing. I didn't know you could talk to senators that way. "You're too busy to help the people who gave you your fuckin' job?"

"Bob, what's wrong? the senator asked, as if he didn't know Bobby was trying to meet with him, which, of course, made Bobby even more pissed off.

"I'll tell you what's wrong. We gave the job to the wrong guy, but we won't make that mistake again. You can be sure of that."

"Bob, please you need to calm down and tell me what you want or need." I could see Bobby was still fuming and frankly I thought he was going to slap the senator around. I'm sure he wanted to, but I didn't think it would help our cause, so I stepped in and told the senator who I was, what we were doing, and what we wanted from him.

"Senator, we need broad political support, not just from you but also from everyone holding political office covering the Bronx. We would like you to go on our Advisory Board and solicit your colleagues to do the same."

Bobby was looking at the senator very closely and waiting for the wrong answer, which fortunately didn't come. I think it was very clear to the young senator what would happen if he refused to get involved.

"Sure," agreed the senator. "I'll do whatever I can."

When I suggested he call a public hearing at the Hunt's Point Community Corporation, he said, "I'll have to think about that."

Bobby asked, "What's there to think about?"

"I've never done anything like that before, Bob. I wouldn't know how to make it happen." Public hearings in neighborhoods where the problems existed were virtually unheard of in those days. They were usually conducted in some government building somewhere which was hard to get to even assuming you knew about them.

Just then I noticed the Senator's stationery sitting on a breakaway in his office and thought, *I know how to make it happen.* As Bobby and the Senator discussed the matter, I grabbed about ten pieces of the stationery and slipped them into the back of my pants under my suit jacket.

When Bobby and I left the Senator's office, he took me into the Senate chamber. The chamber had thirty-foot long, burgundy velvet drapes, ceiling to floor, covering all the walls . Bobby poured lighter fluid everywhere he could and lit the curtains.

I said to him," Now I know the secret of your negotiating skills." He smiled at me and we left. He had no fear.

On the way home I pulled out the stationery. "What do you have there, Sully?"

"The solution to organizing the public hearing. The senator is going to put out a press release on his special stationery announcing the public hearings he's having in two weeks. We will send it to all the radio and TV stations and every newspaper in NYC."

Bobby loved it and said, "I knew I picked the right guy for this job."

I learned a lot about Bobby that day, and he learned a lot about me. We were both willing to step over the line to shake things up.

For whatever reason that press release spread like a virus everywhere. The politicians and media showed up in droves, including U.S. Senator Jacob Javits, four congressmen, and a slew of assemblymen and state senators, not to mention officials from the Mayor's office.

When the Senator saw the announcement about his public hearing, he began to panic. He called Bobby's office. Bobby passed the call to me. "Yes, Senator what can I do for you?"

He asked, "Have you guys lost your minds? I already have plans for the day you scheduled *my* public hearing."

"Well, I guess you need to change your plans, Senator, or maybe Bobby can chair it for you. You don't know it yet, but we have done you a real favor. We've taken you out of obscurity and put you in the political limelight."

"Oh yeah, what if no one shows up?"

"Well, that's the chance we'll have to take," I said and hung up.

At the hearing, TV cameras showed one Spanish assemblyman sitting with an eleven-year-old addict on his lap. The child had recently been arrested holding a knife trying to mug someone twice his size in a hallway. The assemblyman was hugging the child, kissing him, and crying. No one could have scripted that scene better.

Senator Garcia was a bit unsettled that we would do something like that without his knowledge or permission until everyone started to show up. He couldn't believe his eyes and neither could we frankly. He became a star overnight, known for his leadership against drug addiction.

He spoke to those in attendance and said, "We will never solve this problem by putting everyone in jail." Pointing to the child on the assemblyman's lap he said, "Do you want to put him in jail?

The event also projected Bobby Munoz into the limelight, which didn't go over well with Raymond Valez who felt Bobby should have gotten the press for him because he was the one running for Congress. It was the beginning of the end of their relationship.

Between the Hunt's Point agency that Bobby ran and our S.E.R.A drug program, Bobby would become bigger and stronger than Valez. Bobby eventually controlled more money, which meant more jobs and more troops. With the staff of both programs, the clients, and the five hundred volunteers, we could put many people behind any political campaign. We had the power to control the Senate, Assembly, and congressional seats in our district, but we had no such interest.

Needless to say, Senator Garcia became our man. He did everything we wanted him to do from then on. His office was getting calls from other elected officials asking to be on our advisory board. Bobby was right about politicians. They're nothing but a bunch of whores. Two weeks before, Bobby couldn't even get the Senator on the phone.

The hearing went far beyond what anyone would have expected. Rudy Garcia, a *Daily News* reporter became a huge supporter of S.E.R.A. and eventually became a member of our Board of Directors, as did Victor Risso, Director of Community Relations for the Justice Department for the entire East Coast and Puerto Rico. He became Vice Chairmen of S.E.R.A. and a friend of mine.

CHAPTER 22

THE MONEY

Shortly before our media blitz, I got a generic public relations newsletter from the governor's public relations office telling us the State Narcotics Commission was spending $285 million a year on drug programs in the state and praising the success they were having fighting addiction.

The newsletter inspired me to write a response. I sent off a scathing letter to the Governor's office starting with "How dare you send this bullshit to me when the highest rate of addiction is among Spanish speaking citizens, and you haven't spent ten cents on bilingual programs." Then I ended it with accusing Frank Smith, the Executive Director of the State Narcotics Commission, of being a racist and concluded, "Don't ever send bullshit like this to me ever again."

We had already submitted our program to the State-funding agency. I was calling Frank Smith, executive director of the New York Narcotics Commission, almost every day to get an appointment. Then one day about a week after I sent off that letter, I got a call from Frank Smith calling me by my first name.

"Sal, we need to talk right away. Please do not send any more letters. I'll be in the city tomorrow and will come to your office." He was clearly in a panic about something. I couldn't imagine why he was calling me. Even more bizarre, he was coming to see us.

I told Bobby we were meeting with him in the morning. "What do you think this is about, Bobby?"

"I don't know. What did you say in that letter?"

I started to worry that I might have gone too far. "You don't want to know."

"Don't worry about it, Sully. He wouldn't be coming here if you blew him off. We'll find out when he gets here." Bobby didn't seem concerned at all, or at least he wasn't showing it.

The next day Smith showed up with a complete approval of our funding request and a contract. The budget was prorated to $800,000 because we were so far into the physical year. Somehow my letter had found its way to Governor Rockefeller's desk. Then it was sent to Smith's office with a note written on it by Rockefeller himself, which simply said, "Fund this program now."

Rockefeller had a soft spot for his Spanish-speaking constituency. He spoke Spanish fluently and conducted his campaigns in the Puerto Rican community in Spanish. That was it. Just like that it was done.

Frank Smith congratulated Bobby and me then said while shaking my hand, "Sal, you have to promise me, if you have any problems regarding the funding, you will call me directly. No more letters to the governor's office or anyone else. Do you promise?"

"Okay, Frank"

"Okay what, Sal? Say it."

"Okay, Frank. No more letters to the Governor or anyone else. You have my word."

"Good, here's my direct private office number. It doesn't go through the switchboard. I'm going to have a Miss Taft from my office contact you. She will walk you through the contract and set up how the funds will be dispersed to you."

"When can we access the funds, Frank?" I asked. "We have a lot to do."

"As soon as the contracts are signed, but I recommend you have a lawyer take it from here, Sal, and hire a CPA who knows his way around these funding contracts."

"OK, Frank I will and thanks. We'll make you proud of us, Frank. I promise."

It was a great moment for all of us and for me personally. When Frank left, Bobby came over put his arms around me and hugged me like a father would a son. "I'm so proud of you, Sully. You have no idea what you have accomplished. It's not just a drug program. It's real power for this community."

Maria ran into the office and started jumping up and down. I asked her to call Frank and Cheech to let them know and make dinner reservations somewhere nice. Bobby asked, "Sully, what did you say in that fuckin' letter?"

Maria got it out and showed it to Bobby. "Holy shit, Sully, and the governor read it? No wonder Frank is shitting in his pants." Bobby couldn't stop laughing.

Frank Gracia became the Executive Director of the S.E.R.A program. Cheech became Clinical Director and I became the Administrator. Our salaries were very modest. Frank made $18,000, Cheech $16,000, and I made $16,000.

Bobby remained the Executive Director of the Hunt's Point Community Corp, and we also made him Chairman of the Board of S.E.R.A.

Now our work was in the unknown future.

CHAPTER 23

THE REAL WORK BEGINS

The first thing we did was call in all the clinicians to inform them that we were in business. It was an exciting moment. Frank said to them, "We've talked and dreamed about this for years and now it has happened." He had named our program SERÁ for the expression, *Que será, será*, what will be will be," and now more than ever it fit our efforts.

Then Frank turned and pointed to Bobby, Maria, and me and said, "These are the people that made it happen. They believe in us. Now it's our turn to show them they were right." They cheered us and gave us lots of hugs. I'll never forget that day.

There were a lot of abandoned buildings in the South Bronx. It had been described as a bombed-out war zone. Rent control was very stringent in those days and costs for maintaining and heating the buildings grew far higher than the rents could support.

Frank knew the area well. He and I walked there for hours looking for facilities to house our program. We found two buildings next to each other on a 147th Street and Hoe Avenue and a third building just around the corner. They were empty with no squatters in them. Maria located the landlord and had him meet us at the site.

Big Sal Terranova, the owner of the buildings, was in his early sixties. He had a difficult time getting in and out of the Cadillac his son was driving. Sal was obese and couldn't drive because he didn't fit behind the steering wheel. He was a very nice guy who could take a ribbing, which Frank Gracia enjoyed doing. Frank would describe big Sal's weight and size not in inches and pounds but in yards, as in concrete.

We told Sal what we were doing and that we wanted to buy the buildings and fix them up but the government contract would not allow us to buy, renovate or own anything with government money. We could only lease the space for $3.50 a square foot. I don't remember how much space we leased, but we wound up with three four-story tenement buildings with large basements costing us $235,000 a year.

Big Sal was willing to do the deal for a lot less money, but the contract wouldn't allow it; go figure. He was very interested in helping us for a lot of reasons, not the least of which was that he would make a killing. The lease money would cover the renovations in the first two years then give him a hefty profit. When the lease was over, he would have three newly renovated buildings that had previously been abandoned.

Standing in front of the buildings, he made us an offer we couldn't refuse. "I tell you what: I'll renovate the buildings to your specifications for a five-year lease." Frank looked at me to see what I thought. I nodded my assent. Then Frank stuck out his hand and said, "You got a deal, Big Sal." It was a shame to just give all that money away, but we both knew it saved us a lot of time and headaches.

In a few months the first building was completed, and we opened for business while Big Sal worked on the other two. We got him to hire some of our clients to help with the renovations, which gave them WAM or "Walk Around Money."

All the bed space was booked before we finished the construction, and we had a waiting list. The judges were more than happy to sentence their convicts to us rather than to prison. They were under pressure to find alternatives, and the city was going broke. Many of the judges came to visit our facilities and became real supporters of what we were doing.

Senator Javits sent some of his staff to help us start a HUD housing program to renovate abandoned buildings. Rudy Garcia did a big piece on us for *The Daily News* with pictures of Frank, Cheech and me. The headlines were "Drug Warriors Come to the South Bronx."

He wrote about how we got started and how we got the community involved. We started getting a lot of other press, including radio and television interviews. Then visitors from other communities came to see what we were doing and asking us to help them.

The press brought some old friends from my youth to see me, namely Louie Lump Lump Barone. It had been years since I had seen him. He had always watched out for me like an older brother, and although he was a bit nuts, I liked him. He made an appointment with my secretary to see me not really knowing if I was the same guy he knew only as Butch.

I was really glad to see him. "What are you doing these days Louie?"

"I'm in the insurance game Butch, and I'm here to get your business," he told me. I gave Louie all our business, which was substantial. I was happy to do it for him. He would insist on buying lunch at Rao's occasionally and drop around my office to chat. He was very proud of me, especially since he knew the trouble I was getting into in the past.

I had just bought a new Oldsmobile, and because I had no place to park the car, I asked Louie if he would take care of it for me while I made a trip to Saint Croix for a week then pick me up at the airport when I got back. I'm telling you this little side story because it's indicative of the kind of characters who peppered my life. For better or worse, I just loved them.

Louie said, "Sure I'd be glad to do it. You know, Butch, my brother Paulie and me want to go to Harrisburg to visit our brother in prison. Would you mind if we drove up there with the car while you're gone?"

"No Lou, as long as you pick me up at the airport when I get back."

When I landed at Kennedy, Louie was there but my car wasn't. The story goes like this. Louie flipped the car over doing eighty-five miles an hour. It rolled over seven times landing upside down on the windshield. Paulie, who weighed close to two hundred eighty pounds, snapped the front seat, landing Louie and him in the back seat.

A motorcycle cop watched the whole thing from the side of the road while he was waiting to catch speeders. Gas was pouring from the gas tank as the cop was trying to get them out of the car before it blew up. A passerby stopped to help the cop, and they were able to get them out.

Apart from Louie's fractured collarbone, they escaped with little damage. The first words out of Paulie's mouth as he watched the gas pour out of the car was "Jesus Christ, we just put ten dollars' worth of gas in the fuckin' thing."

My car was two weeks old and had less than a thousand miles on it. Louie flipped out; "We just demolished Sal's car and you're worried about the fuckin' the gas?"

To add to the luck of these two guys, the passerby who had helped the cop get them out of the car was on his way to a small airport where he kept his plane. He first drove them to a hospital and then flew them to Harrisburg.

Louie told me to give him the insurance money, which was $3,500, (I paid $6,500) and he'd get me another car, which he did. He came by my office a few days later with a one-year old, yellow Cadillac Eldorado, with a white leather top and white leather upholstery. It was a classic pimp car.

Our success rate at SERA was off the charts at about 70 percent compared to Phoenix House's five or ten percent. One of the reasons for our success, among other things, was our admission screening. We were only interested in clients we felt were desperate enough to change their life rather than just clean up and go back to the streets. A lot of addicts did that to lower their consumption rate. If they withdrew for a while, it wouldn't take as much heroin to get high.

Our admission staff was very good at recognizing and weeding out the potential failures. They themselves had been there many times because they were all former addicts.

A year into the program the evidence that our system worked was coming in and looked better than good. Dropouts usually happen in the first few months, but by the time we hit that benchmark we had none.

Here's how Frank explained our success to me when I asked him about it: "First of all, Sal, no one wants to spend five years working for nothing. Would you? It's just too long. No other rehabilitation program has the criteria we have for graduating; they just don't have the money. Our clients graduate with high school equivalency diplomas, full time jobs, driver's licenses, and a place to live."

He went on, "Without those benefits, your chance of making it are slim to none, not to mention the friends and support they got from the people who live here. You know some of our graduates grew up here in this neighborhood."

He added, "One of the things that concerns me is the clients' dependency on the program after they leave. I don't want to be another AA program, trading one dependency for another."

I found Frank's awareness of that possibility very interesting. I became interested in the therapeutic community as a concept. I began to participate in the groups and got to know many of the residents very well. I was surprised to find out how sensitive, warm, and smart many of them were. It occurred to me that maybe it was exactly these qualities that made them so susceptible to drugs.

Prior to the idea that ex-addicts were better suited to help other addicts, only professional licensed therapists could get funds to treat addiction. They had little, if any, success, but they had the "credentials." They weren't necessary for our program, but they had the degrees. Thus, as part of our contract, we were compelled to hire a Ph. D. psychologist to justify and legitimize our funding.

I interviewed at least six professionals and asked each one of them if they would enter the program as a resident for one week. I wanted them to better understand what our residents were experiencing. There were no takers. So we paid a psychologist just for his credential. He came once a month for an hour, spoke to Cheech, picked up a check and left. He was completely useless.

I firmly believe future historians will look at the last fifty years of the War on Drugs as one of the most devastating and damaging fiascoes ever perpetrated on our society. The politicians, justice system, police, and prison system had become an industry.

It has been about money and power for politicians and still is. The irony is that legal drugs kill far more of us than all the illicit drugs combined. One has to wonder why the newly appointed head of the Federal Drug Administration was the CEO of Monsanto.

A reporter once asked me, "How do you think so much heroin gets into this country undetected?"

I said, "I don't believe all the heroin is coming from outside the country but is manufactured here from legally imported morphine by our drug companies, then sold out the backdoor to illegal drug distributors."

Nothing like that had ever been suggested before. The reporter got very excited and asked me if I would say that in a TV interview. I said I would, but I never heard from him again. It seemed to me that the drug companies, which spend billions on advertising, had the power to silence this idea.

I remember reading an article by an investigative reporter asking the drug companies to explain why they were manufacturing 200 million amphetamine diet pills, in other words, *speed*, when there were prescriptions for less than nine million. He wanted to know where the rest had gone. He found out the pills were exported to dummy Corporations in Mexico just over the border in thirty- gallon drums, then smuggled back over our borders and sold on the black market.

CHAPTER 24

VALEZ, CONGRESS, AND THE ELECTION

The Congressional elections were at hand. Ramon Valez announced that he was running for Congress. The district where he was running was once Italian but was now half Spanish speaking. He was running against an Italian priest named Father Gigante. Between Ramon Valez's Multi-Service organization and Bobby Munoz's Hunt's Point Community Corp they could put a lot of free manpower behind Valez. Our program had twice the manpower of both of them combined.

Valez called Bobby to a meeting at his office to discuss the election. Bobby asked Frank, Cheech, and me to go along with him. Even though Bobby was the chairman of our board, technically our boss, he recognized that he alone was not the power. He would never commit us to something without our agreement. By this time we were all very close friends.

Valez was surprised Bobby had brought all of us with him without first asking him. It immediately signaled to Valez that the game had changed, and he didn't like it. It was the first time any of us had met him face to face. Bobby introduced us, and Valez started talking to us in Spanish.

Frank interrupted him immediately. "Speak English, Ramon." In that one sentence Frank put him in his place. He addressed him by his first name, which was telling him to get off his high horse. He also told him, rather than asked him, to speak English, giving Valez a lesson in manners.

Valez was only about 37 years old. He was short and fat, which made him look a lot older than he was. He was arrogant and full of himself, but he wasn't stupid. He knew he no longer had the power and control over Bobby he once had, and he would never have control of us. It was a completely unexpected turn of events for Valez.

Frank, seeing the change in Valez's demeanor, changed accordingly. "How can we help you, Ramon?" he asked warmly. Just the fact it was Frank addressing Valez and not Bobby told him where the power lay.

Frank didn't like Valez to begin with, and the word on the street was that Valez hated the fact an Italian had such power and visibility on his turf. I had no doubt he would get rid of me if he had the chance. I also knew Bobby made it very clear to him who brought in the $1.3 million. Valez respected money and anyone who had the talent to bring it in, so he was careful not to offend me.

"Senor Gracia," said Valez

"Call me Frank"

"I'm in need of manpower, as much as you can spare. I need people to put up posters, register the community to vote and, most important, to get them to the polls on Election Day."

"Ramon, I'm in the drug rehabilitation business not politics, but I understand what it means to have friends in office. I will give you all the help I can because Bobby asked me to do it, as long as it doesn't interfere with my work or my funding."

Frank continued, "So you understand, Ramon, Sal is the administrator, and he's in charge of everything that is not clinical. He's very talented and knows his way around politics, and I'm sure, if he agrees, he will be a great help to you." That put Valez in a position to look to me if he was going to get our support.

Then Frank looked at me, and I said. "I will do everything I can to help you win, Ramon. If you will send me a list of what you need and when, I will do my best to make sure you have it."

"Thank you, I appreciate your support." He shook our hands, and the meeting was over. The meeting was not like anything he expected. He got what he needed, but lost what he wanted, which was control over all of us through control over Bobby, but he wasn't giving orders to Bobby anymore, and he knew it. He was not having a good day.

When we all got back to the office, Frank said, "He's a snake, Sal. Be careful"

"Thanks. Frank. Remind me not to attend meetings with you anymore," I laughed then said to Bobby "It looks like we have had a change of power, Bobby. How does it feel to be free of Valez? Are you going to be okay?"

Bobby looked a little disoriented. "I'm not sure how it feels yet, Sully. I knew we would split someday, but I never expected it would be today."

"Neither did he, Bobby." I was about to leave when Frank asked me to attend a clinical meeting he was having with Cheech that night. I didn't usually get involved in clinical meetings, so I knew something was up.

"What's up, Frank?"

"I'm not sure. Cheech said there were a number of clients who were not responding to the program the way they should be."

Cheech was a hands-on clinical director. He didn't go home half the time, and he gave special attention to anyone who needed it. His special gift was that he really cared about the people. Having spent more than twenty years as an addict, he really felt their pain. I admired and respected that about him.

We met in Frank's office that night. The structure of the therapeutic community's program was very tight. It was geared to deal with manipulative behavior.

Usually when a client tried to manipulate his way out of responsibility, he was always caught because the clinicians knew the game better than he did and because the residents he lived with knew and cared about him. They would make him or her conscious of their behavior in groups, not in any "I gotcha" kind of way, but with empathy. These men and women developed very strong emotional bonds.

I think it's reasonable to say that our clients were in a state of manipulation. They had survived that way for so long that they were no longer conscious of it. It was part of their personality. It was who they were. It was the goal and function of group therapy or rap sessions that took place every night to make a client conscious of his behavior, especially the manipulation and then make him responsible for it.

At the meeting Frank asked Cheech, "Okay, what's going on, Cheech?"

He explained, "We have a dozen residents in here that never get dealt with. They follow orders and complete tasks very well. It's like there's nothing wrong with them - except they still want to shoot junk."

Cheech brought out their files and said, "I went through all their files looking for a common thread. They all come from different backgrounds, and I noticed most of them didn't even grow up in cities. They're not street junkies. The only thing that links them is the fact they're all Vietnam vets, and they all got hooked in Nam. And get this, their $15 a week pure heroin habit in Nam is $300 a day here in the streets."

"What do you think, Sal?" Frank asked.

"I think Cheech is right. These guys are not street addicts manipulating their way through life. They're military men who are comfortable being told what to do and carrying out tasks or missions."

"I agree that's a key element" said Cheech. "Yes, it makes sense, but it doesn't solve the problem. How are we going to get to them?"

Then Frank asked me. "What do you think we should do about it?"

"I don't know, Frank. I'm not a clinician."

"So what? Think about it. You too, Cheech?"

After I thought for a moment, I said, "Well, if they are not responding to our modality, we obviously need a new one, but I wouldn't know what that would look like."

Cheech said, "Whatever it looks like, it won't be here," meaning we would need a separate facility.

I could see Frank's light go on, and he said, "Our program is designed to deal with manipulative behavior, but what is manipulative behavior and how does it work? What are you always dealing with, Cheech?"

"Our usual clients are always initiating a new game to stay in control. I'm always trying to stay ahead of them, but the vets never seem to initiate anything."

"Right. That way they don't have to be responsible for anything," said Frank. I was always impressed with his ability to zero in on and pinpoint problems.

Then I watched Cheech spring into action. He said, "I see what you're saying, Frank, and your right. They don't initiate anything. The unconscious logic seems to be 'If I don't initiate anything, I'm not accountable for anything.' That's their game. So all we have to do is create a situation that forces them to initiate."

Frank followed up, "The only way I can see getting these guys to initiate is to give them responsibility, but without a leader to tell them what needs to be done. Then leave them to themselves."

I asked, "How the hell are we going to do that?"

Then Cheech's light went on. "I got it! Why don't we put them to work on the new building we're renovating? We can drop them off at the job site, tell them what needs to be done, and leave them to themselves to figure it out."

Frank started laughing, "That should do it, Cheech. Let's try that and see what happens. Their first big problem will be finding a leader. Someone will have to step up and assume that responsibility or they won't get anything accomplished. Also we will need to separate them from the other rap sessions. They will need their own group."

It worked beautifully. All kinds of issues and arguments came to the floor, which allowed Cheech access to them, so he could hold them accountable. When the new facility was completed, we moved all the vets into it, separating them entirely from the rest of the population.

Cheech started to develop a different clinical approach to the vets. He had to get them to start asserting themselves in groups, so they could be held accountable. This was the antithesis of the model we had created. Once Cheech nailed it, vets started to assert themselves and to become conscious of their game.

CHAPTER 25

THE REAL DEVASTATION OF THE WAR

Dealing with the Vets took us into another realm entirely. In their rap sessions they revealed that the CIA was responsible for supplying them with heroin. These men were doing two, three, sometimes four tours to keep their heroin habit going. Remember, this was not a volunteer army. At that time there was outright rebellion against the war in the streets, and the morale in Nam was deteriorating rapidly.

I was outraged to learn from the vets that were given B.C.D.'s (Bad Conduct Discharges) for taking drugs; they received no benefits even though they were decorated heroes.

I don't think this practice of keeping vets hooked as changed to this day, nor has the use of drugs in the Middle East wars. You can be sure of that. Remember, opium is Afghanistan's biggest cash crop.

Here are the results of the government's lunatic practice: Fifty thousand of our kids were killed in Nam, but 51,000 died in the subsequent ten years after they came home. Post-Traumatic Stress Syndrome wasn't recognized as a medical problem back then; yet that's what caused them to die of drug overdoses, alcohol poisoning, poverty and outright suicide.

Here we are again. It is astonishing to me that we are doing the exact same thing in the Middle East that we did in Vietnam. I can only describe Washington at this point only as psychotic. Right now our veterans are committing suicide at the rate of twenty-two every day. I believe that the death rate will grow by a factor of five when we start to include post-traumatic stress liabilities: drugs, alcohol and poverty over the next ten years.

I watched the Presidential candidate, George W. Bush call for more troops on the ground in order to win, but to win what? No one will answer that question. Bush's conclusion was that without our troops on the ground, it would take another ten to twenty years of our involvement, and god knows how much money to stabilize the Middle East when the Middle East should take care of its own problems.

Over the last eleven years three million of our kids served in the Mid East. We had 300,000 troops on the ground at any one time at the height of the war. Half of them were mercenaries hired by Bush and Cheney and paid for with our taxes. Why weren't the oil companies sent the bill?

To add insult to injury, they paid the mercenaries far more money than they paid our kids. Meanwhile, military families were on food stamps, and they had to buy their own bulletproof vests.

The oil interests spilled the blood of our kids, paid for it with our hard-earned money, made fortunes doing it, and at the same time they refuse to pay taxes. They keep their money outside our country, while our country's infrastructure, which they depend on to make billions, is falling apart. This is an example of the ruling class and the criminal class being the same thing.

The next day I had a meeting with Cheech who was personally leading the Vets' new rap sessions. Cheech had decided to video the sessions as part of the therapy. Taping had never been done before, and he was excited to see the results. I asked him to use some of the sessions to focus on the CIA operation in distributing heroin to our guys and to give me a copy of the tapes. I intended to transcribe them.

CHAPTER 26

DRUGS, POLITICS, AND THE WAR

Our S.E.R.A drug program was getting a huge influx of Vietnam vets, and we were achieving excellent results This advent of a one-year, drug-free Veterans programs was big news. So we were back in the limelight. Letters and inquiries were coming in from everywhere. Nixon was running for a second term and had announced that he was going to end war.

The families of addicted vets were devastated and in an uproar over the fact their kids were coming home junkies and without any medical benefits. They didn't know at that time that our government was the drug dealer and that getting soldiers addicted was deliberate to keep them re-enlisting or extending their tours of duty. Many of our men were highly decorated. They were real heroes, yet they were thrown out into the street without honor or support to fend for themselves.

I watched two of the videos of our vets telling their stories and had to stop. I saw our boys cry holding one another. Even though the dealers they named were military officers, they blamed themselves. They didn't think it was a deliberate strategy to keep them there because it was their decision to do drugs and reenlist. They just didn't make the connection back then.

I cried watching those videos. It was heart breaking. And I was more than furious; I wanted to kill someone. Nixon was getting hell from the families of our boys as they came home since no one would take care of them. They didn't even know the military deliberately addicted their kids. In fact, no one knew about it for years.

I still don't think most Americans know even now. I called Frank and Bobby that night and asked them to come to my office in the morning and watch the videos with me. I had already decided to transcribe and edit them. When we finished watching, Cheech turned on the lights and we all looked at each other in disbelief and disgust.

I opened the conversation saying, "We can't let these low life mother fuckin' politicians get away with this shit."

Bobby asked, "What do you want to do about it, Sully?

"I don't know, Bobby, but I'll tell you what I'd like to do about it. I'd like to go to Washington, lock them all up, and throw the key away."

Frank said, "I haven't had a chance to tell you guys yet, but I got a call yesterday from a guy named Jeff Donfeld from Washington

"Who is he and what the fuck does he want?" I asked angrily still reeling from what we had just watched.

"He said he read about what we were doing for our Veterans. He would like to meet with us and tour the program. I didn't think to ask him who he was exactly, but he wanted to visit. He also asked if it was possible to meet with the heads of the program."

"What'd you tell him?" I asked.

"I told him to leave his number and I'd get back to him."

"Okay, Frank, tell him a week from today. I want time to get the videos transcribed and study them. We should also find out who he is before he gets here. It sounds to me like he has an agenda."

"Why don't I call him now while we're all together and set the date?"

"Good idea" Cheech said, "because I have a heavy week with the Vets coming up."

Frank picked up the phone, dialed the number then put it on speaker phone. A woman answered, "The White House. Where may I direct your call?" We all looked at one another surprised.

"Jeff Donfeld, please."

"Whom may I say is calling?"

"Frank Gracia Executive Director of S.E.R.A." This Donfeld guy was on the phone in an instant.

"Hello Frank. I'm so glad you got right back to me. When will it be possible for me to come and visit?"

"Well, how about a week from today at 10 a.m.?

"That will work just fine"

"Excuse me, Jeff, but who are you and what do you do in the White House?"

"Yes of course; I work for the President as an adviser on all things pertaining to drugs."

"Okay, Jeff. We will be glad to help you any way we can. See you next week."

Jeff was the equivalent of the drug czars of today, which later became cabinet positions.

"Well," I said, "it looks like we hit the big time. I wonder what he wants?"

Ever since I took on the rehab project, things just started dropping into my lap. It was all luck. I mean who knew my letter would wind up in Rockefeller's hands, or that he would respond the way he did. Things seem to go that way in Scientology as well.

I was beginning to look like some sort of wonder boy to people around me. More and more people began to ask my advice about things of which I had no experience. I'd just tell them what I thought and more often than not things worked out for the better. I really didn't understand it at the time. It never occurred to me that I might be smarter than the average bear.

About that time, I got a call from my father asking me to meet him in little Italy for lunch. We met at Angelo's on Mulberry Street. We had been meeting for lunch every couple of months. He was reading all the press we were getting and was very proud of me. I told him the story of how we put the program together and got it funded.

At lunch he said, "I need a favor. Chin Gigante asked me to ask you if you would meet with him."

I immediately recognized Gigante's name and knew he was one of the New York Mafia bosses. "What does he want?" I asked.

"Well, he has a brother running for Congress in your area, and he would like to get some help from your organization."

I wondered if it could be possible that the Mafia boss of New York had a brother that was a priest who was running for Congress. I asked my father, hoping I was wrong, "Is Chin's brother a priest?"

"Yes, his name is Father Gigante. Do you know him?"

"No I don't, and I don't think I want to know him." I said thinking about my meeting with Valez. I knew what was coming and didn't really want to go to a meeting with Chin, but I couldn't say no.

Chin Gigante was the Mafia boss who walked around little Italy for years in a bathrobe and slippers talking to himself to avoid prosecution. He was also the guy who shot Frank Costello on orders from Vito Genovese who was trying to take over my cousin Charlie Luciano's organization in 1957. It was my father who went to see Charlie in Italy for Frank Costello in 1957.

"Why, what's wrong?" my father asked me.

"Nothing yet. When does he want to meet?"

" I was hoping we could go for coffee at his club after we eat."

I thought, *It's better I get this over with now.* I agreed, and we walked over to the club a couple of blocks away.

The club was the classic Italian social club right out of the movies, with men playing cards, drinking espresso, and smoking cigars. Chin was sitting with "fat" Tony Salerno, the boss who owned ten points in Caesar's Palace in Vegas. My father introduced us, and I got the traditional hug and kiss from them.

Chin said to me, "We've been reading about you and your organization in the papers. Your father is very proud of you, and so are we. Do you know my brother Father Gigante?"

"No, I don't, but I know who he is and that he's running for Congress."

"Good, because this is what I wanna to talk to you about. It would be a big favor to me if you would throw the weight of your organization behind my brother. I spoke to him when I found out about your organization. He told me if your organization got behind him he would be sure to win. He believes he's going to win anyway, but with your backing it would be in the bag."

I've been asked many times by friends "How do you get into all these things?" Part of writing this book was to figure out just that. Well here's just one example of how shit happens to me. When a guy like Chin says, "It will be a big favor to me" there are a lot of implications to that request, especially for my father. When you do favors for powerful people, some benefit is likely to come from it.

"You know, Chin," I said. "I would like nothing more than to help your brother. I'd be honored. After all he's a priest and one of us, but I can't and here's why. I do have a lot of power in the organization, but I'm the only Italian in a completely Spanish program. If I came out and backed your brother, my power would evaporate in a heartbeat. Do you see what I mean?"

To his credit Chin understood what I was saying and said, "You're right, Salvatore, I see what you mean. Tell me something. Do you know this spic Valez, the Congressional candidate?" To Chin, Ramon Valez was just a spic.

"I met him once," I said. "What was I going to say, 'I'm providing Valez with all the manpower he needs to run against your brother?'"

"Do you have access to him? I mean can you meet with him in private if you want?"

"Yes, I'm sure I could arrange it."

"Good. Here's what I want you to do. Congress is only a two-year term, I want you to offer him $50,000 to drop out of the race, and we will back him the next time around."

I didn't believe Chin and neither would Valez. When Chin started talking about logistics, like where to meet him, I got very bad feelings, so I told him, "Valez will never go for that, Chin. First of all, he wouldn't believe you, and, second, Valez wants to be governor of Puerto Rico. Congress is just a steppingstone for him."

When we left I told my father, "I believe Chin was thinking about killing Valez."

He said, "No, Sal, if he did something like that it would backfire. If the connection between Chin and his brother becomes public, his brother will lose the election." I agreed it would be a dumb move, but I know it crossed his mind. The last thing I wanted was for Valez or anyone else to make a connection between Chin Gigante and me. I never told anyone about that meeting, I didn't see the point.

Later I got call from Valez wanting to meet with me about the election. I told Frank I was going to meet with him and he said, "Not without me and Cheech."

"Why, what's wrong?"

"Nothing, I just want to make sure it stays that way. I told you I just don't trust him." Apparently, Frank had heard rumors that some of Valez's loyalists were out to get me. Anyway, we went to the meeting.

Frank and I were talking while walking through the hallway towards Valez's office, with Cheech walking behind us talking to one of Valez's staff.

Suddenly, I heard Cheech yell out my name. When I turned around I saw Cheech behind this guy, and he's got him in a choke hold. I didn't see the knife in the guy's hand, but Frank did and took it from him.

Frank said, "C'mon, Sal. Let's get the fuck out of here."

"What about the meeting?" I asked.

"Fuck the meeting and fuck Valez."

I said, "Do you really think that Valez had anything to do with trying to kill me? He wanted and needed my help. It doesn't make sense."

"No, I don't think he was involved with it or even knew about it, but it's given us an out not to help him. It happened on his turf at a meeting he called. How is he going to explain it?"

Valez called Bobby immediately, apologizing for what happened. He wanted me to press charges against the guy, but I told Bobby I wouldn't. "I don't think that press would be good for us or for Valez either. Tell him what I said."

Bobby told Valez what I said, and he was very thankful.

It turned out that the guy wasn't an employee of Valez but was looking to work for him. He thought this attack would put him in Valez's good graces. Then I thought, *Why would this guy think Valez would be glad about it?* Valez must have been shooting of his mouth about me to someone.

I later heard Valez had the guy badly beaten. I never heard from Valez again. As it turned out Father Gigante won the election.

CHAPTER 27

WASHINGTON ARRIVES

Jeff Donfeld arrived on time with his secretary. Cheech took him on a tour of all departments and then invited him to have lunch in our cafeteria with a few veterans and us. He spent about a half hour listening to the veterans and learning what it was like being in the program.

Afterwards, we went to Frank's office to discuss what Donfeld wanted. Frank opened the discussion. "Jeff, what is it you think we can do for you?"

He explained, "The President is starting to bring our troops home. He's aware of their drug problem and would like to do something about it, but frankly we don't know what to do. It's why I was so excited to read about your program. He would like to open up drug centers all over the country, so our guys will have access no matter where they live."

"And do what?" I asked.

"Well, that's what I'm here to find out. I'm impressed with what you've done here. Would you guys consider coming to work for us to expand what you've done here throughout the country?"

I said, "I don't think you understand what's involved here, Jeff. It would take years and hundreds of millions of dollars to duplicate this around the country. Even if you made that kind of money available, there aren't enough qualified clinicians in the country to make it work."

"Couldn't we make methadone available through these centers?"

Frank explained, "The use of methadone was supposed to be the first stage of the rehab process, to be followed by drug-free programs. The drug-free aspect never happened. They just replaced one drug addiction for another. We are completely against methadone."

"Well, wouldn't it be better to have something available for them when they get home? It's better than nothing at all," he argued.

"Yes, I guess that's true," I said, "but you will be doing nothing for our boys. It looks more like political cover for your boss than help for our boys."

Jeff went on to talk about the financial benefits for us personally: twice the salaries, cars, expense accounts, and more. I told him we just didn't have the time, but we would make our expertise available to him whenever we could.

I made no mention to him of the CIA'S involvement in the drug business. I wasn't ready to deal with all that yet. I'd not yet transcribed all the videos, and I wanted to be on firm ground before I let that cat out of the bag.

A week later we got a call from Jeff inviting us to a meeting with the Vice President Spiro Agnew They were bringing out the big guns. By that time I had transcribed enough of the videotapes to make a case. I knew it would be difficult, if not impossible, to convince Agnew of the CIA'S involvement, but what I was really after was the B.C.D.'S (Bad Conduct Discharges) without benefits.

I made twenty copies of the transcribed tapes and, not taking any chances, had them put in twenty different locations.

I was surprised at how loose security was in the White House. When Jeff walked me into Agnew's office, neither my briefcase nor I was searched.

Jeff introduced me. "Mr. Vice President, this is Salvatore Lucania, the administrator of the veterans' program." Jeff had brought Agnew up to speed about our meeting."

"Mr. Lucania, you are of Italian heritage?"

I said, "No, I'm Sicilian."

"I see. First generation?"

"No, second."

"I'm Greek." Agnew was trying to make an ethnic connection with me. Afterward, he became very direct. "Why won't you help us and our troops?

I explained, "We are already helping our troops. It is not that we won't help further, sir. It's that we can't. It's just not possible. As I told Jeff it would take years to put together what is necessary to make any significant impact on the problem. I came here today to inform you that it's our own CIA officers who are responsible for supplying our troops with the heroin."

My statement stunned Agnew. "That's a very serious accusation, Mr. Lucania. Where did you get such information?"

"I pulled it out of these transcribed tapes," I said handing them to him. "These are transcriptions taken from the group therapy sessions of our veterans. I believe they speak for themselves."

Agnew looked skeptical and said, "I find this very hard to believe. Why would the CIA do something like that?"

"Maybe to keep them fighting. That's my guess. Their $15 a week pure heroin habit over there is $300 a day on the streets in New York. I guess it may be hard to prove, but I'm not here to make a case against our CIA," I said.

I explained further, "I am here to end the policy of refusing medical care to our boys if they come up dirty from their drug use. They are given Bad Conduct Discharges which eliminates their medical benefits, and that's easy to prove."

Agnew was truly shocked. He looked at Jeff and said, "Did you know this?

"No, sir, I didn't."

The Vice President told Jeff, "I want you to check this out and get back to me immediately."

I pushed, "Mr. Agnew, I'm not interested in starting an investigation of the CIA, but the B.C.D.'S must stop, and I believe the President has the power to do it."

Jeff turned to me and asked, "Why didn't you tell me about this?"

"Because I hadn't transcribed the tapes yet, and I wanted to be sure nothing stopped the Vice President from hearing it straight from our boys."

A week passed before I heard from Jeff again. Then he told me he was being stonewalled by the military about the B.C.D.'s. He explained that if the President stepped in to straighten this out, he would have to acknowledge that he knew something about it.

He concluded, "It's not going to happen in an election year, Sal, but I promise you I will get to the bottom of it."

I told our staff what had happened. Bobby asked me, "What do you think Sully?"

"I would like to expose the whole dirty business, Bobby, but I'm not sure it will help our vets right now. I think Jeff is right. Nothing is going happen during the election. The ball is in their court now. Let's see what they do with it."

A few days after this discussion we received a letter and a check for fifty thousand dollars from a political supporter of Nixon. The letter simply said he'd heard about the work we were doing from Jeff Donfeld and wanted to help.

Bobby said, "It feels like a payoff to keep a lid on this"

I said, " Maybe it is, but who cares; we can use the money and it's not the reason we tabled it anyway."

We all agreed not to take on the fight just then. It could only distract us from our real work. Who knows where it would go once we let the cat out of the bag.

Years later the military drug connection was exposed, but I never heard anything about the B.C.D.'S again. I don't even know if that policy is still in place today.

CHAPTER 28

OZ AND ME

A year into the drug program my old friend Franklin Jones made a trip from California to New York to see his parents. He visited my program and was intrigued with the community concept and the way we organized ourselves and used study groups, which Franklin and I later used to organize our spiritual community in California

Of course he took credit for all of our community's organization. It was a common practice of his to use ideas from others and take credit for them. It took years for me to catch on.

Since I had left the Catholic religion when I was fifteen years old after I punched out two of their "black robed spiritual vampires" I dismissed all religious beliefs for the rest of my life.

I knew something had to account for the appearance of this world. That was just logical, so I remained fascinated by this mystery. I always felt the answer would somehow come from science, particularly astronomy.

I remember when the Hubble telescope turned its lens toward deep space and heaven was nowhere to be found. I wondered how the religious leaders of the world were going to get out of that one.

The Pope, to his credit, said heaven was 'a state of consciousness,' which I thought was pretty smart and as close to the truth anyone was going to get. The rest of the Christian leadership in this country said nothing; they ignored it and still do.

My spiritual curiosity was re-stimulated when I met Franklin Jones in Scientology ten years later.

A friend I've known for forty years insisted I write the story now, "or it may never get written." I was sure he was right. So, I will be weaving in and out between S.E.R.A. and the Franklin Jones story because both stories overlapped for a period of time.

There is much to tell about the sixties and seventies New Age days. I'm almost looking forward to revisiting those days because they were the most happy and exciting times for me. But first I want to tell you how and why my spiritual search ended.

Since I'm going to deal with the business of religion and god in my life, you should know where I'm at with all of it. So I beg your indulgence, while I address the idea of god and religions. You may believe I have gone off the reservation, and I might have. Still, I see no reason why my view or yours should be subordinated to the will of the three major religions that continue to control the world and prevent access to free thought.

My search came to an end one day when the thought occurred to me, "is it possible that suffering in the spiritual sense, is the sensation of being alive?" I thought, it would be the ultimate cosmic joke, and I laughed out loud. Here, I believe, is the essence of our spiritual dilemma: we are mortal and paradoxically immortal at the same time.

Bear with me on this for a few pages. According to the laws of physics, the universe and everything in it, seen and unseen, including us is made up of atoms or energy. Energy or atoms cannot be created or destroyed, only changed, so says physics. If an atom cannot be created or destroyed, then the atom could not have had a beginning and cannot have an end.

It is, in fact, how all the great spiritual teachers of the world have described the eternal nature of god. Atoms are the invisible, yet-to-be physically formed, eternal nature of existence.

The big bang event could be understood as the moment when atoms took form and the concept of time began.

We all have a profound sense of having an eternal nature, which is true. It's one of the reasons we feel we've lived before, and we will live after we die. At the same time, we know we are going to die.

For instance, when you put a log on a fire, it changes to heat, flames, smoke, and ashes. We've changed the form of the log, but we have not eliminated the atoms of the log from existence. The atoms simply return to their original unformed state. This in my view is exactly what happens when we die.

Therefore, "our suffering," while real as an experience, is not a problem to be solved at all, but to be understood and accepted as "the sensation of being alive" or the nature of reality itself.

No one needs to be saved because no one can be saved; and after death there is no one to be saved. Hence, the religions of the world only serve to obscure the nature of reality. They see the eternal dimension of our human existence as a separate soul, but it is not separate. Atoms are the unformed nature of all physical appearance in the universe.

When I came to this realization, I no longer felt a need for any answers; for me the matter was and is settled. The sensation of being alive or "suffering," if you will, still goes on and will until I'm no longer alive.

I've learned to deal with the paradox of my existence and the endless voice going on in my head, which that paradox creates. I've learned to ignore it like a TV on that I'm not listening to anymore. Someone who successfully masters meditation basically learns to do the same thing.

As far as the "Big Bang" is concerned, which supposedly is the beginning of time and therefore space, it's a theory, even if true. What makes anyone think it's not still going on in each and every minute and will go on forever? If Life and the Universe is an eternal process, then, by definition, there is no such thing as time and space. Therefore, time and space should be eliminated from the "Theory of Everything." Then maybe a new Physics will appear and explain why physics breaks down when we go from micro to macro. It's just a thought.

CHAPTER 29

THE CURTAIN COMES DOWN ON NEW YORK

I spent almost all of my spare time with Franklin at his loft in Soho. He fascinated me. I'd never met anyone like him before; he re-stimulated my interest in spiritual life and taught me about meditation, diet, and fasting. He saw religion as I did: crowd control and a source of political power and wealth for the undeserved.

He spent his time writing, studying, and teaching me about religions, spiritual movements and practices of the world. Mainly we were best friends and grew to love one another.

Franklin had a sense of humor that baffled me. I knew he was coming from a point of view I didn't comprehend, but his humor liberated me from many of my concerns. When I'd go to him with a problem, he'd look at me and fall over laughing; I mean really laughing and holding on to his head as though his brains were going to fall out. It was humor, not comedy.

In those moments - and there were many throughout the years - my mind and my concerns would just disappear; it was like magic. I have been asked for the last thirty-five years to write about Franklin Jones, but I have steadily refused.

Most of the people interested, beside ex-members of the community we formed, were from the academic world of the "Enlightenment Industry." Since it was he and I who started the spiritual organization, and I was the only one who knew him for years before he became "Enlightened," it was thought I was the only one who could expose him as a charlatan, but it is not that simple.

Franklin was not a charlatan to begin with. That happened over years of isolation from anyone who disagreed with him. He became a drug addict, delusional and later mad.

Franklin was my friend; it was a personal relationship. What he was like for those years before his "Enlightenment" was nobody's business but mine. The people who wanted to know were ill intended, just a bunch of gossiping opportunists like the news media of today.

For those of you who are not familiar with Franklin Jones, I suggest you Google Franklin Jones/Sal Lucania. You'll read about the cult his organization became after I left in 1977. Franklin died in November of 2008.

Franklin eventually moved from New York to L.A. and wrote his first book describing his enlightenment experience. I was still in NY running S.E.R.A. and met Nellie, a Columbia student who did her master's thesis on our program.

She was a Puerto Rican woman married to a much older Jewish Columbia professor. I fell in love with Nellie. She was divorcing her husband and getting her own apartment. She started work on her Ph. D. One day she came to me with an offer from Columbia. She said she could get me a master's degree in Public Health Administration if I would take six months of courses.

I asked her, "Why would they want to do something like that? I don't even have a high school diploma"

"Because most people who want a degree like that could only hope to accomplish what you have accomplished in your program." I saw no point in getting such a degree, since I wasn't interested in doing the work, and I was planning to move to California eventually. I can say now it was one of the stupidest decisions I've ever made in my life.

Nellie felt I could easily run for office someday. After my experience with politicians, it was the last thing I'd want to do. When she got an apartment, she thought I would move in with her, even though we never even had a discussion about it.

When I told her I wouldn't leave my family she came apart. She left for Spain, and I didn't see her for six months. When she did return, I was about to leave for California.

I was changing rapidly. I traded in my suits for a navy pea coat and bell bottom denims. I wanted to visit Franklin in California for the summer and made arrangements to do so. I was kept on the payroll of S.E.R.A. while I was gone for two months. When I returned things were different. Cheech was running the program, and Frank was not around.

Frances, Frank's secretary and girlfriend was holding things together for him. I had known Frances for years and, in fact, introduced her to Frank. Frances gave me the story that Frank was being treated for cancer, but something didn't feel right.

I wanted to see him, but Frances kept telling me he didn't want to see anyone just then. I got a hold of Cheech and Bobby and asked them what they knew. They didn't know any more than I did. I wasn't buying the cancer story.

Finally Cheech and I cornered Frances. I said, "I want to know what's going on, and I don't want to hear the cancer story. She finally broke down crying and told us Frank was shooting heroin again. Cheech completely freaked out. I would like to have the usual Hollywood happy ending to this extraordinary adventure, but real life is not full of happy endings. Life seems to have its own agenda.

I was very sad about Frank. I loved him and admired him. I took consolation in all he had accomplished. He had become the leader of an extraordinary drug program, and he had saved a lot of lives. There is a theory some people just cannot handle success. Until then I never believed it. I never found out what happened to Frank after that.

As for Louie lump-lump Barone, I found out about him just a few years ago while reading the *New Yorker Magazine* doing an article on Rao's restaurant in my old neighborhood.

One night, Louie was having a drink in Rao's bar. The restaurant was full of celebrity types. A woman was singing Italian songs. A young mafia type from Jersey sitting next to Louie at the bar yelled, "Do we have to listen to this old bitch?" to which Louie responded, "Hey, you don't act like that in here."

The kid said to Louie, "Oh yeah! Who the fuck are you?"

Louie pulled out his gun and, without a word, shot him dead right off the bar stool. If that kid had known anything about Louie, he would have never opened his mouth.

As for Nellie, I could never find her again. I knew only her married name and was unable to trace her.

I decided to leave and join Franklin in L.A. Cheech stayed and ran the program for a while and eventually came out to California and joined me. He became a lifelong member of the community Franklin and I had established. He married a beautiful woman and had his first and only child with her. He died about five years ago at the age of 80.

As for Bobby Munoz, Senator Bobby Garcia and a couple of congressmen, they were indicted on racketeering charges and received very long sentences. Chin Gigante was finally indicted for being the boss of the New York a mafia family and given a hundred-year sentence. Fat Tony Selerno was also given a hundred years.

Before I left for L.A., I urged my childhood friend Anthony Metoyer to come with me. We had known each other since we were two years old, and I had hired him to be my administrative assistant at S.E.R.A.

At the time I was leaving, he was seeing a recently divorced woman who was living in his building in the Bronx. He didn't want to leave her, so I told him to bring her with him. He finally agreed to come out by Christmas, but for one reason or another he kept getting delayed. I suspect he couldn't get her to agree to come. Finally he called the day after Christmas and said he was coming out alone on New Year's Day.

On New Year's Eve, he and his girlfriend were coming out of the building where they lived, and her ex-husband was waiting for them. He shot them both in the face and killed them. I still get upset when I think about it. After that I permanently lost my taste for New York.

I don't doubt my life would have been very different had I stayed in New York, married Nellie·' and gotten into politics, but I don't think it would have turned out better.

CHAPTER 30

THE MAKING OF A CULT

It was the spring of 1970 when I arrived in Hollywood. Franklin, Nina, and Pat Morley had rented a house in the Hollywood Hills. My wife Louise was finishing up the details of moving and selling my yellow Eldorado pimp car. I was busy finding us a place to live.

I found and rented a large three-bedroom house in North Hollywood just the other side of Laurel Canyon. The rent was $250 a month.

We moved in and we got the kids into school. The boys loved California. Louise got a job as a bookkeeper. I had letters of recommendation from Jeff Donfeld in Washington, Nixon's cabinet guy on drugs and from Dennis Ally from Senator Jacob Javits' office.

I also had character letters from the *Daily News*, the *El Dario* Spanish newspapers and many New York politicians. The letters were directed toward the Army and Navy military commanders in California as well as non-profit organizations.

It was my friends' hope and mine that my drug rehab and fundraising experience could help me find employment. It didn't work out because the military had its own medical services, staffed by federal employees, not to mention they had no drug programs. They did not recognize drug addiction as a medical problem. They saw it as a criminal problem and still do.

Franklin had not yet published his book called *The Knee of Listening* describing in allegorical prose the moment of his enlightenment in a small Vedanta Temple in Hollywood. He was interested in starting his "teaching" career.

I had no idea at the time about what he was up to. He really wanted to be a god/man or Guru, but only Eastern teachers were given that status. In 1970 L.A., the enlightened gurus from India were just starting to make their way over to America. Hollywood and San Francisco became the Mecca for the god business. Those teachers came here already "enlightened" and were steeped in that tradition hundreds of years old.

It was difficult for Americans who wanted to get into the god business to be gurus. There was no culture for it in America. Franklin hid his real ambition cleverly. He criticized the religious institutions of the world as being corrupt and an impediment to true spiritual life.

To establish a public face, Franklin decided we should open a spiritual bookstore and meditation hall. We found a place on Melrose Avenue just down the road from the Bodhi Tree, a very popular Eastern religions bookstore.

Franklin's advantage in the guru business was his five-year long involvement with Swami Rudrananda or Rudi who ran an Eastern antique art store in Greenwich Village and taught a version of Kundalini Yoga in the back of his shop.

Franklin had a scholarly knowledge of Eastern religions and practices. He had the ability to make Eastern philosophy intelligible to the American mind. Also he was bright and a gifted speaker.

Guys like John Rosenberg, a.k.a Werner Erhard, of est or L. Ron Hubbard, of Scientology and many others like them were cult leaders. The difference between cults and traditional religious organizations is that the cult leaders are alive and running things; whereas, a religious leader is not the god/man himself. Religious institutions are established and typically run by close surviving disciples and then passed over generations.

Jesus and his disciples were originally a mystical cult. After the death of Jesus, his followers established the church as an institution to carry on his teachings.

The process of becoming a cult and a god/man is very interesting to me. Essentially it is a brainwash in which the teacher takes over your life completely and requires absolute obedience of you. Then he cuts you off from the outside world, all with the promise that he will make you enlightened.

What's interesting about cults to me is they all go through the exact same process. Indeed, all the religions of the world started the exact same way. Having started Franklin's career, I witnessed and unwittingly helped create and participated in Franklin's cult.

I saw firsthand the process and internal workings of what happened with Jesus, his followers, and Judas Iscariot in particular. Hitler's movement, too, was a cult and he was able to brainwash an entire country the same way. Donald Trump has succeeded in doing the same thing to one third of this country.

Religions, to a lesser degree, are still cults, keeping control over their followers by indoctrinating them from early childhood for political and financial power. You need only to look at the Catholic Church and the wealthy TV evangelists to see that game.

Franklin was very clever in hiding his real aspirations. He spoke against the idea of associating spiritual life with a teacher. He always criticized the Eastern traditions for doing it; for me it was a perfect ploy because I wanted nothing to do with Jesus or anyone who claimed to be a god/man. Yet the first thing Franklin did was hang two 3 by 4-foot pictures of himself in the bookstore window.

I arrived in L.A. with about $15,000, which I used to open the bookstore. Franklin's book was still not published.

During the process of renovating the bookstore, a number of people became interested in what we were up to.

Because I acknowledged him as a teacher, I gave him legitimacy. Gurus can't toot their own horn; someone other than themselves must acknowledge them before they gain any legitimacy.

Before long a small group of people began to form around the store. They helped fix up the place and were invited to my house for meetings and meditation until the renovations were complete.

One of the new guys named Jerry Seinfeld, a real hippie, began to live in a shack we had out back of the store. One day he brought in a friend of his, Neil Panico. Neil owned a successful art print business and was married, had four children but was in the middle of a divorce.

Neil kept a shotgun in the trunk of his car and, according to Jerry Seinfeld, planned to use it to kill himself, so Jerry talked him into meeting with Franklin. He and Franklin clicked almost immediately. Neil was from New York and had twenty years of experience in the book-remainder (over stock) business. He used to go around the country selling books by the train carload. He and I became Franklin's closest friends.

A publisher in Georgia accepted Franklin's manuscript. The editor was so impressed with Franklin that he quit his job flew out to California and camped himself outside Franklin's house in a meditative trance. It was a strange occurrence, which gave Franklin some mystical credibility.

Followers send a copy of the manuscript to Alan Watts asking him to write the forward. Watts was a very well-known author who wrote some twenty-five books on Eastern religion and philosophy. He did write the forward, but it wasn't what Franklin wanted, so a couple of people went to see Watts with Franklin's version of his forward. They partied with Alan Watts and he changed his forward to Franklin's version.

The book was published, and Neil was getting it distributed. Eventually Neil and his partner split their business each keeping half. Then Neil devoted the rest of his life to Franklin.

Franklin gave talks in the meditation hall we built behind the bookstore. I was giving the introductory lectures as I used to do for Scientology and was self- conscious about the way I spoke. I still had a lot of New York in my speech. My accent and manner of speaking didn't matter much in New York because everyone spoke that way, but in California it was out of place.

Franklin and Nina were highly educated with master's degrees in English literature. I asked both of them to correct my speech every time they could. They did what I asked for three years; it made big improvements in my grammar and vocabulary although my New York accent is still around.

Franklin asked me to create a course for newcomers out of his book and then teach it. Here was another instance in which I was expected to do something I had never done before, just like Bobby Munoz expecting me to get funding for a drug program even though I had no experience there. Franklin and Bobby Munoz both just expected me to do what they asked and I did. It more or less became my function around Franklin to get things done.

Our bookstore and following were growing fast. Within a year we had thirty-five or forty students." Franklin's requirements for students were strict: they couldn't use drugs or alcohol; they had to have a job; they must become vegetarians; and they had to tithe a percentage of their income to us. We all followed those requirements strictly.

CHAPTER 31

THE GOD BUSINESS

I think it's critical here to get into why people were so intrigued with Franklin and others like him. When Franklin sat in meditation with a group, there was a tangible presence everyone could feel. He called it the Siddi, a Hindu word for spiritual power or force. It was used to initiate newcomers into "spiritual practice."

Those who give men like him their complete attention generate this power. It also tends to put an aura around their body. It's actually a very natural occurrence in the physics of things. You see it in movie stars, rock stars, politicians, and other types who are well known for one reason or another. We've all seen these types of people who draw everyone's attention when they walk into a room.

It's simply the electro-magnetic nature of attention, and it operates in and outside of space and time. The people who get that kind of attention become intensely addicted to it; they get high off it. People who are and have been involved in the god business throughout the millennium are aware of it.

The spiritual practices of the East actually work with this energy or life force as part of their practice. In yoga meditation the yogis, through breathing practices, draw this energy down through the "chakras" or nervous system.

When they breathe in they pull the life force from the head down through the seven charkas into the root chakra located at the base of the spine in the tailbone area. When they release the breath, the life force ascends back to the head and comes to rest for a moment, forming a circle. In that moment of rest, the life force dissolves into a formless silence in the heart area, the place where consciousness enters and resides prior to animating the body. It's where consciousness temporally withdraws when we sleep and the world disappears.

Jesus was a yogi before he became a religion. He described this process in allegorical terms. He described consciousness in its formless condition as resting in the region of the heart as the Father; its perfect reflection formless light as the Son, the halo residing in the head; the circle of descending and ascending light, the process of converting light into manifest existence, as the power of the Holy Ghost.

All the great spiritual teachers of the world describe this process in some form or another. In the case of Jesus, it was the "Father, the Son, and the Holy Ghost. There is nothing spiritual about it. It's the natural electro-magnetic field that animates the body and indeed all of existence. It can be used to enhance healing or well-being by directing attention or the laying on of hands.

What do you think prayer or laying on of hands is about? When you tell someone *my thoughts are with you,* what do you think you are doing? Positive thoughts are, in fact, "blessings." So, it is not alien to us at all. It's just in the context of creating a holy man that it is seen and used as mystical power.

Franklin and Rudy were acutely aware of it. Indeed, they were masters of it. For Franklin, meditation was meant to initiate and intensify the student's life. People always felt better after meditating with him. It was the "mystical" dimension of his power that drew people to him. I know what this sounds like if you've never had the experience, but it's very common in spiritual cults and practices and even in churches today.

Before long we needed more space. I found a large office space on the second floor in a building on La Brea. One day he sent someone to buy beer to have a party. Everyone was very surprised but glad to have a break from a year of strict dietary discipline.

Whenever he changed the game like this, he always gave talks or "lessons" to justify the change. He said a party was necessary because people were getting too uptight. It was the beginning of a partying practice that became a permanent part of our community culture.

At those parties, he started to have sex with two women who became his permanent mistresses. One of the women was already in a relationship with another man she had come with from New York; it didn't seem to matter. These parties would sometimes last for weeks at a time.

The group was continuing to grow, and the membership had reached about sixty members. The income was also growing. One day Franklin told me that he needed a much larger circumstance to do his "work." He asked me to find a property where we could accommodate hundreds of people and living space for a large staff.

This was to be the self-contained community we had so often talked about in New York. I got very excited and asked, "Where should I look for something like that?"

He said, "Look in Northern California, somewhere close to San Francisco so people can find jobs."

Craig Lesser was a kid from a wealthy family. He was a wiry skinny kid who always seemed nervous. I liked him a lot. He never became a formal staff member but was the go-to guy for special assignments. His father, Lou Lesser, whom I later became friends with, was a wheeler-dealer business guy who owned a few companies. Craig lived with his girlfriend on Malibu Beach in a small cabin his father built for him behind the main house.

Craig was always privy to interesting information and gossip. He came to see me one day to tell me he was going to Saudi Arabia on a business trip with his father, who was flying there with Henry Salvatori, chairman of Occidental Oil.

I asked Craig why were they going, and he said, "We are going to raise the price of oil." I laughed because everybody knew the Saudi oil cartel-controlled oil prices.

A couple of months after Craig returned from Saudi Arabia, the price of gas started to go up. I asked Craig, "How the fuck did you guys manage to do that? I thought the Saudis owned the oil."

He said, "The Saudis own the oil in the ground, not when it comes out. We made our deals with them years ago. They get 7 percent a barrel of the market price. Don't forget, they didn't have the means to drill, ship, or refine the oil at that time. We leased the property from them and did everything else ourselves."

Craig was one of the first six members in the very early days in Los Angeles and was a new/ age and guru aficionado. He knew where all the new religious movements were located and many of the people who were active in them. He and I formed a very tight bond over the years. He liked hanging out with me because it gave him a lot of access to Franklin.

I gave Craig the task of finding the property. A couple of weeks later he came into my office very excited. He had discovered that Yogi Bhajan, the founder of Transcendental Meditation, had exactly the property we were looking for in Lake County two and a half hours from San Francisco, and it was for sale.

It was the old Siegler Springs Resort, an old, sacred Indian, hot springs converted into a resort with a ten thousand-square foot hotel,

On the property were ten motel style buildings, with eight rooms in each, including an eighty by forty-foot dance hall with twenty-foot ceilings. It also had thirteen cottages, a huge hot spring swimming pool and bathhouse with eight separate baths, and a full commercial kitchen and dining room.

It came with a twenty-five hundred-square foot private residence all on forty-five acres on Cobb Mountain. It had been the last legal gambling place in California and the last stop of the pony express. The hot springs were the healing waters for the local Indian tribes.

Franklin and I flew up to the property and spent a night there. Bhajan's group was asking $250,000. The place needed millions for it to work out for us, including creating a commercial sewage system.

I spent a couple of days up there trying to get those guys to get real. They all looked very holy with their beards, robes, and beads. I offered them 150k with 25k down, but they were hard-core business types and wouldn't budge. Meanwhile, Franklin was busting my balls: "Sal, where's my property?"

So I went to the Bank of America in Lakeport which held the paper on the loan and found out that the Yogi Bhajan group had bought the property two years before for $100,000, with $5,000 down.

They had not made a payment for months and were going to lose it. The guy I was negotiating with was a major asshole. They wanted to make a $125,000 profit on something they never paid for. I don't know whether they were stupid, or they thought I was.

Finally, I offered, "I'll give you $5,000 for your moving expenses and take over the loan or I'll wait for the bank to foreclose and I'll buy it from them." He gave in.

I got the bank to agree to take $25,000 down, and we made the deal. I had, of course, one small problem. I didn't have the money.

I went to Dennis Duff, one of the wealthier members of our inner group, and asked him if he would donate the $25,000, and he did. A couple of days later he came to me and handed me a large $100,000 negotiable note as a gift to the community to pay for the property. The note looked just like U.S. currency except it was much larger. I 'd never seen anything like that before. I remember thinking, *so this is how the big boys move cash around.*

Franklin was beside himself with pure joy. Even he couldn't believe we did it. I was personally excited because this is what Franklin and I had talked for about for years in New York, the idea that we would own a large property where everyone could build his or her own home on a private. non-profit community and manage our own lives.

I thought we could get a tax-free status. It turned out when I tried to incorporate as a community like that, there was no such category; the closest thing to it was a church. So we became a church.

Now all I had to do was to move forty-five members and their families to San Francisco and the rest of us, the core group, - Franklin, Nina, Louise, Pat, Neil Panico I, and half dozen others – onto the property.

Six of us were responsible for and ran the operation. Louise was the treasurer and bookkeeper, and Nina was in charge of the education department. Neil ran the publication department, and Pat basically did design work. She made the property beautiful, sewed Franklin's clothes and transformed his house into something exquisite.

My overall responsibility seemed to be the political, legal, and financial welfare of the non-profit church and the personal safety of Franklin. I say, "seem to be," because I was never formally given those responsibilities, but anytime something came up relative to those things, it was always given to me to handle. I was also gatekeeper for Franklin, who had since changed his name to Bubba Free John.

Neil moved his print business up to Lake County and with it a small group to run it. We also moved a small group up to maintain the place, which Franklin named Persimmon.

Within six months, we opened up a bookstore and center on Polk and California Street in San Francisco and closed the one in LA. Every weekend scores of people would come up to the property and work. We had architects, engineers, tradesmen, landscapers, and many others. The project was ongoing and would last for years.

I was known as Franklin's closest confidant, which I was and the one running the show for Franklin, which I did for the first five years. Other than myself, Nina, Pat, and Louise, no one knew what Franklin was like before he became "Enlightened".

Nina, Franklin's legal wife, didn't buy into the guru stuff for years. She would say "Oh Franklin, stop it." He never reprimanded her for it. Years later, when he acquired absolute power, he married her off to one of the early members of the community. He had acquired five women for himself and had children with three of them.

He saw no point in hanging on to Nina. It was the best thing for Nina. She was a Midwestern white Anglo-Saxon Protestant. The guy Franklin hooked her up with was a New York Jewish photographer, one of the most unlikely partners for her. Even stranger, they are still together after forty, years.

CHAPTER 32

THE PARTIES

I always understood that I was part of a unique human experiment. I was completely fascinated by it. It was interesting to me what human beings would do if they were given permission.

Surprisingly, in what amounted to orgies at these parties, it was the women who were the most uninhibited and aggressive. They seemed more like men in their nature than women in that circumstance.

I was intrigued by it. These were not party type women. They were married with children, most of whom never had sex outside their marriage. Why would they do it? I wondered.

I had a lot of other questions running through my head. One of the most perplexing was about jealousy. Is it learned or in our nature? Why can Franklin and half the world live in multiple relationships and the rest of us can't? I would find out a lot more about it in twenty years, when I moved to Africa for a couple years.

There were about thirty-five senior members of the community at various levels of authority and responsibility, but I was the only one who could and would talk straight to Franklin, only in private of course. Everyone else was too intimidated, even Neil. There was still a part of Franklin that was my old friend, and I could still reach that part of him.

Franklin's following was growing by leaps and bounds. His followers were not long-haired hippie types. They were professionals: doctors, lawyers, architects, skilled craftsmen, and business owners.

The property was run like a resort/retreat; it was referred to as "The Sanctuary." Only tithing members were allowed to come to The Sanctuary on the weekends and participate in the programs we created for them. The program consisted of work, study groups, lectures, and meditation with Franklin.

Every week members were required to write meditation reports. Meditation reports documented not only what went on in meditation but also personal information about food, sex, and use of money. Money was important because Franklin wanted to know that members were working and paying their tithes.

The reports were turned over to a senior disciple who reviewed them and spoke to members about them if necessary. These reports were not unlike the Catholic Confessionals or Scientology's auditing. It was control pure and simple.

Every weekend a small group of six or eight men who were closest to Franklin were invited to his house, where we continued to party. He would get a list of all the women coming up that weekend and invite the ones he liked. It didn't matter if they were married. I don't remember any women turning down an invitation.

Franklin criticized marriage as a cultic contract that interfered with spiritual development. To that end, he announced that when people came up on the weekend, all contracts were off. You were free to have sex with anyone you wanted, but there were to be no secrets. You had to deal with whatever the fallout your sexual contacts brought. Some marriages fell apart, but most didn't. Did that mean women had no problem with their husband fucking other women as long as they could fuck anyone they wanted to?

Another big surprise to me was how natural it was for many women to have sex with other women, particularly in threesomes.

Franklin also invited a few men from the city who were not part of his entourage. Everyone wanted to be invited to the parties. The parties continued for months, even during the week after those living outside the property left.

Franklin's behavior was continuing to change. He was getting wilder. We started to experiment with psilocybin and peyote, and pot became the Blessed Sacrament. We did peyote once that I know of. I found out later he continued to do drugs out of my sight. Franklin started to distance himself from me. The more professionals who came on staff the less he needed me.

One of our members was a woman named Tanya Constantine. Her father was Eddie Constantine. a very famous French actor of the fifties. While living in Europe, Tanya had met and married Jacque Barzaghi and had two children with him. They left Paris and moved to L.A. in the late sixties. Jacque and Tanya met Jerry Brown at a party in L.A, just after they moved here from Paris. When I knew her, Tanya was a long-time member and was married to John Krieveski, one of the first people involved with our group. He knew Franklin even before I arrived in L.A. I bring up Tanya because she was asked to translate Franklin's book into French. Suddenly, out of nowhere, Tanya and John were leaving the community. I was blown away and wanted to know what happen.

When I asked her why they were leaving she said, "Franklin's teaching. It's bullshit." I was surprised since Tanya had joined the community because of a speech I had given. She explained that when she was translating what Franklin was saying into French it all fell apart, and she concluded he was full of shit. This happened at the same time Franklin decided to move the operation to Hawaii. Tanya and I are still friends after forty years.

CHAPTER 33

JERRY BROWN AND JACQUE BARZAGHI

There was something similar in the relationship between Jerry Brown and Jacque Barzaghi and the relationship between Franklin and me. Jerry, like Franklin, was very smart and well educated, but was not street smart at all. Jacque and I were street smart. I had what Franklin didn't have and needed, and he had what I didn't have and wanted. It was not surprising that Jacque became Jerry Browns "mentor." Eventually, Jerry gave Jacque a post on the California Arts Commission and a few other posts to keep him in money and to keep him close.

Jerry and Jacque were both very interested in Eastern religions but for very different reasons. Jacque, I felt, wanted to have the power of a guru and the women that seem to go along with the position. He wanted to be worshiped and served. Jerry, on the other hand, was sincere and searching for the truth. After all, you don't enter a Jesuit seminary for four years unless you're seriously looking for answers.

Jacque was researching all the gurus who were starting movements around California and would arrange meetings with them for Jerry. Jacque tried to arrange meetings with Franklin through various members of our community but was told it was not possible.

A woman named Susan Pottish had lived with Jerry for a year or so while he was running for office. She got into the film business and did a documentary on Franklin, which is how she met him. Jacque was a friend of hers and contacted her to try and arrange a meeting with Franklin. She told him she couldn't do it, but that I might be able to. I spoke to Jacque several times but kept turning him down.

Franklin didn't want to meet anyone who wasn't already pre-indoctrinated, especially the governor. Looking back, I suspect he was afraid Jerry would see through him.

Jacque was getting married with Jerry as his best man, and he invited Susan to the wedding. Susan asked Jacque if it would be okay to bring me as an escort. He said, "Oh, yes, of course. I've been wanting to meet him for a long time." I knew why he wanted to meet me.

At the community, we were having a lot of problems with oil companies, and I thought it would be a good opportunity to meet Jerry and speak to him about it. I asked Franklin what he thought, and he said, "Sure why not? Let's see what these clowns are up to." Franklin was becoming arrogant. The more power he acquired the more arrogant he became. I didn't like seeing that in him.

After Jacque's wedding ceremony, Tony Kline wanted to take the whole wedding party out to eat. Tony loved Susan and was very happy to see her at the wedding. He came over and invited all of us to go with him for dinner. We accepted, but Jerry said he had a prior commitment to have dinner with Roshi Baker and some friends. Then Jerry invited Susan and me to go with him. Tony, Jacque and the others left, and Susan and I went Jerry.

I liked Tony. The movie "The Candidate" with Robert Redford and Peter Boyle was supposedly based on the story of two friends Tony and Jerry, who decided to run one of them for Secretary of State as a joke and won. Later I spoke to Tanya about it and she told me it wasn't a joke. They were very serious.

Tanya also told me that during Jerry's campaign for Governor of California, there were a dozen people all sleeping on mattresses on the floor in Jerry's house in Laurel Canyon, L.A., including her and Susan Pottish. By coincidence Franklin was living in Laurel Canyon at the same time.

The dinner guests at Roshi Baker's place were an interesting group: Stuart Brand from Convolution Quarterly; Jerry's sister Kathleen Brown, who at the time was a member L.A. City Board of Education; Roshi Baker, of course; and four or five others whose names I can't recall.

The dinner was a very odd experience for me never having met Jerry before. We all sat at a long low table on cushions, except Jerry who sat off to the corner of the room by himself flipping through a paperback book.

When I went to the bathroom and returned, Jerry was sitting in my seat next to Susan. I took a seat next to Jerry. There was a somewhat heated discussion going on between Kathleen and Jerry about how to give parents more control over what goes on in their schools.

Jerry wanted to pay the school $25 per student, so if the parents didn't like what was going on, they could move their kids somewhere else, and the funding would go with them. What was odd to me, beside Jerry sitting in the corner, was the way he handled the discussion.

He went around the table asking the other guests what they thought. Before anyone could finish speaking, he cut them off by asking the next guest what they thought. He wasn't trying to be rude, but his mind worked at the speed of light.

While we are on the subject of Jerry, I want to tell you something about him. Jerry is not your run-of-the-mill politician. He is a moral man and a real statesman. By "statesman," I mean someone who takes his responsibilities very seriously and who puts his constituencies' interest before his own, which is the antithesis of almost every political leader in America, both then and now, save for Jimmy Carter, and we saw what happened to him.

Career politicians are interested in only three things: power, fame, and money.

Jerry's political career survived and thrived many years because of his integrity. He couldn't be bought or compromised by power, fame, or money, because he already had all of that. The people of California were very lucky to have him. I was hoping he would run for President. I ran into Tony Kline a couple of years ago and asked him why Jerry didn't run for President. He said because he was too old. I disagreed.

Tony's time with Susan at the wedding was short, so a couple of weeks later at Susan's invitation Tony came up to the property to see her. We had lunch, showed Tony around the property and took a dip in our large indoor hot spring pool.

While he was there, I told Tony about the problem we were having with several oil companies, which were exploring geothermal resources in the area. I had not gotten the opportunity to talk to Jerry about it at the dinner.

The oil companies were drilling "exploratory" wells pretty much wherever they wanted. They drilled without consulting surrounding citizens. Geothermal steam, unlike oil, cannot be transported. So where you find the steam is where you put the plant.

The emissions from those plants smell of sulfur, in other words, like rotten eggs. The entire Lake County Board of Supervisors had their own land under lease to the oil companies, so I assumed they were bought and paid for by the oil companies. The environmental impact reports were rigged and always approved.

When Tony visited, I asked him if he had any suggestions to help us stop the oil companies. He told me to go see Gene Varanini, executive assistant to state assemblyman, Charlie Warren. Gene had actually written the bill that created the State Energy Commission. It was his baby.

Bob Moretti, speaker of the House, ran for governor of California against Jerry Brown in 1974 and lost. Moretti was made the head of the Energy Commission as a political consolation prize. He stacked the commission with oil company men. I went to see Gene about the problem. We had quite a few meetings and became friends. Gene hated Moretti for turning the agency over to the oil companies.

Two weeks after the big wedding, I got a call from Jacque who said, "I'm here with Jerry and Grey Davis. We happen to be in the neighborhood, and we would like to pay a visit to the community. "Gray Davis, later Governor of California, was Jerry's chief of staff at the time.

Now, there was no way in the world they "happened to be in the neighborhood. "I thought the claim was pretty ballsy.

About twenty of us were partying at Franklin's house when they called. We were all naked and smoking dope. Motioning Franklin out of the room, I told him about the call and asked him," What do you want to do?"

He said, "Tell Jacque the protocol and have him explain it to Jerry," The protocol was that only members had access to Franklin. But Franklin added that they were welcome to tour the property without him.

I told Jacque, but it didn't fly with him.

I went back to Franklin and told him, "We got to do better than that. We don't want to offend Jerry. After all he is the Governor."

"Okay," he agreed. "Tell Jacque we are partying. Jerry is welcome to join us as long as he understands when he walks through the door, he's not the governor, but just an invited guest, and only he is invited." Franklin knew Jerry wasn't going to do it,

I went to the hotel where Jerry and the others were watching a video. I said to Jerry, "Let me show you around the property."

While we were walking around the property, I explained to him what was going on at the house. I didn't tell him we were naked and smoking pot, of course, but if he were willing to come alone, I would take him right over. He didn't answer and I didn't push him to answer.

Jerry was very impressed with the facility and asked me how much it cost to run it; I told him our budget was $80,000 a month. He was surprised and said, "I could do it for half that amount." I thought it was an odd question and the answer even more odd. Then he said, "People think I'm a fiscal conservative, but I'm not. I'm just cheap." We both laughed.

Jerry thanked me for showing him around, and as we walked to his plain white government Plymouth, he asked me out of the blue, "How do you think Moretti would feel if I appointed Gene Varanini to the empty seat on the California Energy Commission?"

Without missing a beat, I said, "Like you put an alligator in his pocket." He didn't say he was going to do it, but I thought, *why else would he ask me a question like that?* We shook hands and I said to him, "You're welcome to come to our next budget meeting."

We both laughed and said good-bye. Clearly, Tony Kline or maybe Susan had briefed him about the problem with the oil companies, because I never brought it up.

It was a Sunday when Jerry was visiting us. Monday morning at 10 a.m., I called Gene and said, "I hear you are going to be appointed to the Energy Commission."

He asked, "Where did you get this from?"

"A little voice whispered it in my ear."

"How long have you been hearing these voices, Sal?" he asked as if I had gone completely out of my mind.

Playing along I said, "Well, to tell you the truth, Gene, they just started yesterday." I didn't want to get into anything about it, because I didn't know for sure if Jerry would do it, but by noon Jerry had done it. Gene called me. He was completely blown away and elated. "How the fuck did you know it?"

"I told you. It was those voices."

"Did you have anything to do with this happening?" he asked.

I said, "No I didn't, Gene. It's just poetic justice and your turn to stick it to Moretti and take the agency back from those assholes running it. I have just the thing we can start with."

I told him that I wanted the state commission to allow for a local community board with the power to stop oil companies' applications. Gene could do it with Jerry's backing.

It only took a couple of months, and we stopped the rubber-stamping approvals of the County Board of Supervisors. We weren't interested in stopping geothermal exploration. We saw it as a good alternative energy source. We just wanted to have local say in the matter.

Because I was the visible one opposing rampant drilling, I began to get death threats. These were threats to be taken seriously. At one rally, I was told, "If you don't leave town, you'll be dead by the end of the week." Being born and raised in East Harlem I could tell an idle threat from a real one, and I knew the guy saying this to me meant what he said.

My first thought was, *not if I get to you first motherfucker.* I could feel the street and fear I grew up with in Harlem take over my entire being; it made me sick to my stomach. Being Italian with a New York accent in Lake County in those days was like being Black in Mississippi in 1950. I knew I had to do something different. I couldn't be out front anymore.

We weren't the only citizens in Lake County concerned about the way oil companies were doing business. It was also homeowners seeing the value of their homes go down, not to mention having to live with the smell.

The real estate and construction businesses were being affected as well. If the oil companies couldn't lease certain lands they wanted, they would buy or lease lands next to those lands and then slant drill into their target area, effectively stealing the resources.

The citizens and politicians of Lake County didn't know what to make of us in the community. We were not like any church they've ever seen, and yet we had the power to jam the oil companies. I decided we needed a big public relations campaign and to run one of our members for the County Board of Supervisors. I would make him the new front man to represent our interests and the interests of the whole area.

I chose Bill Strathen, a schoolteacher of twenty years. Then I sent a group of our members into town and had them volunteer their time for every worthy cause where they could be of help, just as we had done in the south Bronx with the drug program. Bill didn't win the election, but we won the acceptance of the town and the death threats stopped.

Meanwhile, Franklin's parties were getting out of hand. At one point I found him in the community kitchen on top of a fifteen-year-old girl. I pulled him off her and said, "You could go to jail for twenty years if this girl files a complaint."

I walked him back to the house and told him to stay there while I talked to the girl and her mother. They were devotees of Franklin and saw no problem with his behavior. In fact, they felt blessed by the incident. In my culture he would have been killed right then and there.

I wasn't as brainwashed as most of the other members. I had enough mental freedom to question what I was witnessing. It was probably because of my long-term prior relationship with Franklin, but I was still brainwashed. I also had status and power in the community, which I liked, and that made me overlook some of Franklin's behavior.

One day Franklin announced that, because of the size of the community, "institutions" needed to be created in order to communicate his teachings. To accomplish this end, he appointed twelve disciples and their wives to pass on his teachings to others. Picking twelve disciples was not arbitrary; Franklin was nothing if not calculating. He knew what that would play into for the "chosen ones" with its parallel to the disciples of Jesus.

Wives didn't have status. Only the men did. He asked the six hundred or so members to choose which couples they would like to be with, and half of them chose me. I didn't know it at the time, but that was the beginning of the end for me because Franklin saw that as a threat to his control.

Franklin was often taking Neil and a half a dozen of his "wives" on vacations to Hawaii. He never took me. I couldn't figure out why, and I was beginning to resent it. I always had to "stay and mind the store," in Franklin's words. Since he always left me in charge as a figurehead when he left for his frequent vacations, it should have come as no surprise to him, then, that half the members chose me. He didn't like me having that kind of influence.

I think the real reason he didn't take me on the holidays was his drinking and drugging, but I didn't know it at the time.

If you recall, I talked about the magnetic energy that comes from having a lot of attention put on you. Because of all the attention put on me while he was gone, members began to have a similar experience in my company as they had with Franklin.

They began to write about me in their meditation reports. That pretty much sealed my fate. I began to get suspicious when a staff attorney came to me and asked, "Sal, if you wanted to move money out of the country without using banks to transfer it how would you do it?"

I asked him, "Why do you want to know that?"

He said something about someone who wanted to make donations but hide it from his wife. I didn't buy it, and he was caught off guard just because I asked the question.

I told him, "It's pretty simple. You buy something in this country, like art, then ship it to another country and sell it there, which ends the paper trail."

"Great! I'll tell the donor, thanks Sal." The conversation gave me great pause. It could only mean one thing; Franklin was stashing money for himself. He knew I would never go for it and that it would end his status as guru for me. Furthermore, if I left the community and gave that as my reason, the whole game would blow up in his face. He couldn't take that chance. He wanted to get rid of me but he better have good reasons. Mind you, I didn't suspect what was going on at the time.

You have to understand, the guru is absolutely moral and infallible. His claim is that everything the guru does is to teach you a lesson; therefore, he's never to be second-guessed.

Shortly after my conversation with the attorney about transferring money to another country, Franklin had a lot of art bought up for him.

Franklin had always portrayed me as a tough New York street guy and used it to protect himself. Implicit in that characterization was that I was someone who would operate outside the law and should be feared.

To be fair, it wasn't a complete mischaracterization of me. I am an outlaw, but not a criminal. Franklin didn't know the difference. Most people don't. When outlaws disagree with the laws imposed on them, they have no problem violating those laws and profiting from them. Like prohibition in the twenties and pot laws in the sixties. These laws create victimless crimes and are politically rather than morally motivated.

For a criminal to make money, someone has to suffer a loss of some kind. In other words there's got to be a victim for there to be a crime. So, in that sense I am an outlaw, and so is everyone else in this country who ever smoked a joint or bought pot.

Franklin was the real criminal. He did irreparable damage to hundreds if not thousands of people and their families, both financially and, more importantly, emotionally.

Whatever good intention we had when we started the community, something was very wrong now. It was hard for me to tell at the time if he was conscious of what he was doing or if he had just gone psychotic. I already knew he was guilty of rape.

Franklin's use of drugs and alcohol were making him extremely paranoid. At the time, I didn't know he was doing any drugs. He took extreme caution to make sure neither the community nor I would find out, which is why he stayed away more often.

CHAPTER 34

THE GAME WAS ABOUT TO CHANGE

Franklin was taking a lot of trips to Hawaii, to the point where he rented a house there and was staying for months. Then suddenly the word came that he was moving to Hawaii permanently and wanted as many members who could to move there too.

Like many times before, I was in charge of the details necessary to translate Franklin's ideas into action. I was left with moving some forty households from San Francisco to Hawaii. After I tied up all the ends, I flew to Hawaii with my wife and two of my three children. My oldest son Carl remained in San Francisco living in one of the community houses.

When we got off the plane, some of my staff members were waiting for us. My wife and kids were taken to where they would be staying. I was taken to Franklin's house for an "important" high-level meeting that Franklin was conducting with eleven of the twelve chosen ones. It seems they wanted to buy a permanent residence for Franklin and needed money.

Franklin and the chosen ones had been assembled for a while, but they were waiting for me to arrive. They were all sitting at a long table with Franklin enthroned at the head. I hadn't even sat down when William, a man who had been jockeying for my position ever since he joined the community, said to me. "We have decided to take over the income of all the businesses and put the owners of the business on a $150 a week salary."

There were eleven profitable businesses owned by eleven members of the community. I was in charge of overseeing those businesses. I had a fiercely loyal staff working for me, including the owners of those businesses. Now I knew why they were waiting for me.

I said, "That's not going to fly." I thought taking the owners' profits would be unethical if not illegal.

Everyone froze with the look of horror on their faces. In their eyes, I had just defied god himself. They all looked at Franklin waiting to see what he was going to do.

Franklin motioned everyone to leave the room by nodding his head.

It was just he and I alone. He asked, "What's happening?"

I said, "You tell me. This isn't what I signed up for. What happen to all our plans we talked about in New York?" He didn't answer me. He just sat there pretending to go into one of his meditative trances.

I left and one of the chosen ones drove me to where I would be staying. Within an hour William showed up with messages from Franklin. I was to leave the community for a while and live in the world. Franklin had done this a few times to other close members, all of whom had returned after a few months to a year.

It would be nine years before I dealt with Franklin and his community again. In the meantime, I had to create a life for myself.

CHAPTER 35

STARTING OVER IN 1979

I was in shock. *Devastated* is a better word. I really didn't grasp the magnitude of what had just happened, nor did I know what the community was told about my absence. I did find out later more than one hundred followers left the community when they learned that I was no longer there. That meant that Franklin took a big financial hit.

I stayed with my family in Hawaii for about a year and a half then we moved to San Francisco. Louise got a job bookkeeping, and I went to work for a non-profit drug program called Reality House West, a program started by Leroy Looper originally in New York.

He opened Realty House West and took a contract as a halfway house for federal prisoners getting out of jail. Leroy had been a heroin addict for twenty years and started the first rehab programs in open cellar basements in New York. At the time he had no money and lived off what he and the other addicts could beg for in the streets. He was a remarkable man. He mentored me, and we became lifelong friends.

Leroy started sending me to a lot of political meetings representing Reality House. I was on the Mayor's Justice Department Task-force redesigning prison infrastructure and programs. I eventually got to know a lot of people in San Francisco politics. A young lawyer named Mike Hennessy, who worked for the sheriff's department, decided to run for sheriff against his boss. He came to Reality House looking for support from the Black community. I knew all the various Black program leaders so Leroy asked me to take Mike around and introduce him. Mike was the son of a doctor from a very small town, and he was not your classic politician.

The people backing him practically had to hold him down to get him into a suit and pose for pictures in front of a sheriff's car. He ran with virtually no money and won. He remained the sheriff of San Francisco for thirty-five years. No one ever ran against him. He was the first sheriff to hire ex-convicts as prison guards.

Leroy was well established in San Francisco, and I worked as a counselor for him for five years. I worked a four p.m.-to-midnight shift three days a week, and, instead of going home at midnight, I slept at the facility three nights a week, which gave me full pay and left my days free. During that time, I spent a year getting a hairdresser's license. I did the training because Franklin had encouraged me to do a service for people. I didn't really practice, and there was no money in it anyway. I didn't know what I was going to do for a living next.

One of my clients from Reality House was a lawyer named Manual Abscal. Manual had been busted for having an enormous amount of LSD and was sentenced to nine years. He was able to get himself out after four years by overturning his conviction. We became friends. He would check into Reality House at midnight and then we would talk until two in the morning.

Manual talked me into going to New College Law School. It was an advocacy law school where you could attend without the requisite college degree. I had to take an associate degree equivalency test put out by the Bar since I didn't even have a high school diploma.

I passed the test, and after a year I would have to take the "baby bar" exam and if I passed that, I could get a degree in advocacy law in three years. I was bored to tears after four or five months of studying. My studies were as interesting as reading a telephone book.

It was actually worse. The training seemed to be geared to turning human behavior into formulas, without much regard for common sense or justice. What I was interested in doing with my degree was to make sure the intent of legislation was implemented by the agencies in charge. I realized it was never going to happen.

My marriage to Louise ended around 1980. She wanted out for the same reason I had left for Las Vegas. We had been together for more than twenty years, and she had never been free. I understood completely because that's the way I felt when I left. The kids were grown by then. Carl, my oldest, had already moved out, and the other two weren't far behind. I still hadn't found a way to earn a decent living.

In 1980, I answered an ad that said "Financial investments $50,000 a year." I applied along with others who had degrees in finance or experience in the business. Two Mormons owned the company called Control Financial Group. They in turn had contracted out the sales to another company owned by two New Yorkers one Irish, the other Italian.

I was told that I didn't really have the qualifications but that they had good feelings about me. I think they liked me because I was from New York and could hold my own in the interview. Anyway, they said if I could pass the series 22-license test, they would hire me. I passed the test and got the job. A Series 22 was a limited license, which would allow me to sell non-negotiable instruments, such as Limited Partnerships.

The company was selling EKG computers as tax shelters. They put ads in the Wall Street Journal and as calls came in, they would go to the next salesman in rotation.

Buying an EKG computer required putting $8,000 down on a $32,000 computer and signing a note for the rest. All in all, the buyer got a 4-to-1 tax write- off. There were about twenty salesmen on the phones. I got a call from the lawyer of a tomato farmer who wanted to cover five million dollars in profits. I closed the deal and made $150,000 dollars in commissions.

Shortly after that, the IRS ruled against these write-offs. I was able to save my farmer by making changes in the sale/lease agreements. Maybe the law school wasn't a total loss. Then I resigned. I still had forty single unit deals on the table that would never receive the tax write-off, and the Mormons wanted me to close the deals and stay with the company. Unwilling to cheat the customers, I left.

I decided to open my own shop. I didn't see why I couldn't do the same financing they were doing, but with a real benefit to the clients. I was working on a deal with the San Francisco transit system.

A friend of mine, Jon Miller, who was the head of maintenance for the bus system in San Francisco, desperately needed new buses but couldn't afford to buy them. It was a hot issue politically because people couldn't get to work on time and the mayor was on the hot seat.

I went to see Jon and told him that I would completely renovate the buses that weren't running anymore. I told him I would buy fifty buses at a time for a dollar a piece, refurbish them and lease them back to the city for payments they could afford to pay.

It would cost $50,000 to refurbish each bus, and I would give them a five-year lease based on a $100,000 each purchase price. New buses would have cost them far more, and they didn't have the money anyway, so it was a good deal for them. Jon was sure he could get the mayor to do the deal. I told him not to pitch the deal until I could put the financing in place.

I needed five million dollars to do the bus deal. I decided to work with the Mormons. They had raised 22 million on that computer deal, and they were going to continue to sell more computers while their lawyers dealt with the IRS. The Mormons liked my proposal but wanted two thirds of the profits and complete control. They told me, "We don't do anything where we don't have complete control."

I said, "Neither do I." The deal never happened.

I named the company I started Western Investments and rented a storefront on Church Street for offices. I wanted to take the investment companies out of the expensive towers and put them on the street where the ordinary person had easy access. I also wanted to do solid deals without the large overhead. It was a simple finance/lease business.

I went to the most likely lender who had five million dollars, the San Francisco pension fund. I knew it was going to take time to negotiate with the city and the pension fund, but I had enough money to cover myself for least a year or more.

One day a man named Robert Bryce walked into my office. He had with him a miniature windmill. He asked me, "Do you remember Rumpelstiltskin who turned straw into gold?" Then he spun the blades on the windmill and said, "We are going to turn wind into cash.

I said, "Sit right down, my friend."

I liked Bryce immediately. He was from upstate New York. He was tall, blond, blue eyed, and Robert Redford good looking.

Bryce had an incredibly dry, understated sense of humor. The first successful business he started in California was called "Rent-a-Wreck." He rented old cars for very cheap prices. You got to love a guy like that.

Bryce wanted to build wind farms and sell the juice to the electric companies, which by law they had to buy. There were also very large federal and state tax incentives for investors in wind energy. Bryce owned a leasing company in San Jose, California, about forty miles south of San Francisco, with a large client base. I had a substantial client base from my time selling tax shelters.

He, along with four partners, started a corporation. The partners consisted of one manufacturer, who was going to build the windmills; one engineer, who worked for the electric company; a corporate executive, who would run the company; and a wind energy expert from UC Berkeley. The windmills were for sale at $50,000 each and would cost the company $30,000 each to build. There were special tax credits all over the place. The bottom line was a clean, 4-to-1 tax write-off.

Bryce had all the pieces to make our plan work. I did the numbers and put together a sales brochure ready to show in two weeks. I was offered a 5 percent commission. I wanted to sell the machine for $65,000 and asked Bryce if he cared. The 5 percent commission was not enough for me. He liked the idea and thought his leasing company should do the same.

I brought in a couple of my airline pilot clients and sold them two windmills each. Those two clients brought in about twenty more pilots, all wanting to buy at least one machine. Because of these sales, I decided to option fifty windmills. If the manufacturer could build that many and I sold them for $100,000 a piece, it would be a big success. The windmills had to be in place and ready for service by the end of the year for the investors to take their tax write-offs.

At the same time, I took in a partner, Ross Allen, I knew him from the community though he had since left. Ross was a very capable administrator. He could write up deals and work with attorneys and know what they were talking about. I'd known him for twelve years and trusted him. We were a good team. I could put deals together, and he could execute them.

Between Bryce, a CPA firm, and myself we sold 110 machines. It was a very successful year, so Ross, Bryce and I decided to rent a boat and sail the Caribbean. I got a call from Bryce a couple of days before we were about to leave. He told me the shaft of the windmills on which the blades spin was too short and didn't reach the propeller blades.

I said, "You got to be kidding me!"

"I wish." He explained, "The idiots welded a piece on the shaft, so it would reach the blades. That way the windmills will look ready for service so the investors can take their tax write-offs, but those blades will fly off as soon as the machines are started."

"Can't you make all new shafts and replace the others?" I asked.

"Yes, that's what we're going to do after the clients get their tax write-offs," he said.

The arrangements for our trip were already made and paid for, so we decided to go in spite of the disaster. There wasn't much we could do, and I saw no point in canceling.

When we got back on land in Florida, Bryce called his office to find out how things were going. He was on the phone while I watched his tan face turn white. He handed me the phone and said, "I'm going to call back my office, and I want you to hear what I just heard."

I got on the phone, and the secretary informed me that the president of the windmill manufacturing company, Bob Janis, had emptied the corporate account of 1.3 million dollars. He took all of the design and engineering plans and rented offices upstairs in the same building and moved his desk and files there then started his own company. He had two partners, a Japanese engineer and Richard Nixon's brother.

I kept shaking my head in disbelief.

I told the secretary to call an emergency board meeting and to let them know I was coming as head of the investment group and to make sure that asshole president was there.

Surprisingly, Mr. Janis was glad about the meeting. He intended to justify what he had done by claiming it was to protect the investors from the incompetence of the present administration, of which he was the president.

I looked at Bryce and asked, "What makes him think he can get away with something like this?"

Bryce said, "Out here in California, Sal, they steal your money then hide behind lawyers."

"Do you think he will show up?"

"Yeah, he'll show up" Bryce was seeing this guy's daughter.

We flew back to California the next day, and I made a few phone calls to surprise this jerk-off. At the meeting I asked Mr. Janis to explain why he thought he could just steal a million three and get away with it. He said, "We need that money to fix those machines, and I don't trust the gentlemen here to do it right."

"I can appreciate your concern, Mr. Janis," I said, "but taking the cash and assets of a company that doesn't belong to you is a felony. What you've taken doesn't even belong to the men in this room. It belongs to my investors, and I am responsible for their money. I'm going to adjourn this meeting and would like you to stay here with me to discuss this further."

The conversation was unreal. I could not believe the audacity of this piece of shit. I was so pissed off I really had to stop myself from putting him into a hospital for a couple of years. The only thing that stopped me was the money, which I intended to get back.

After the room emptied out, I sat next to him and pulled his chair close to mine. Then I leaned over close to his ear and said, "There is a car waiting for us downstairs. You and I are going to the bank and transferring all those funds back into the accounts. Or I'm going to take you to a big hole in the ground and put you in it."

"You're not serious," he said. I grabbed him by his arm and walked him to the elevator. When the doors opened, I pushed him into it real hard. In the elevator I said to him, "You don't really believe you're going to steal my investors' hard-earned money, and I'm going to let you live, do you?"

He didn't really believe what I was saying until we got outside, and the three Hell's Angels I had asked to come were waiting for us. He turned and looked at me in complete disbelief and fear. One of the Hell's Angels drove us to the bank, and the other two followed on their bikes. We walked into the bank conference room, Mr. Janis and I and the two bikers, who sat on either side of him until the transaction was complete.

After the money was transferred back, I had Mr. Janis taken off the accounts and fired him as president. While the transaction was going on. I couldn't help but wonder why this guy would do something that blatant and think he could get away with it. Then it dawned on me. Bryce was exactly right: they were going to steal the money and hide in the courts. Even though what Janis did was criminal, it would first be handled as a civil matter and by the time that was over the money would be gone.

When we were outside the bank, I said to him, "I want you and your two partners to understand how lucky you all are that you didn't get away with it because no lawyers or courts would save you guys from me. Make sure you tell them, Bob." I thought to myself: *There is more honor and integrity in the streets of Harlem than I've seen out here in the so-called "legitimate" business world. This is a good example of the real criminal class.*

The windmills were finally fixed, but the IRS disallowed the tax benefits anyway. As soon as the oil companies saw the potential of renewable power, they sent an army of lobbyists to state and federal legislators to take away the tax benefits and end the development of the technology.

I had bought two windmills and was assessed for $30,000 in taxes. Over the years that number grew to almost two hundred thousand with interest and penalties It kept me underground for years. I didn't know it, but the investors had gotten together and spent five years suing the IRS and won, so they got the tax benefits, but I didn't know they had done that. Years later I got a letter from my accountant stating that the IRS really owed me $8,000, but I never got the money.

CHAPTER 36

THE CRIMINAL WORLD OF LEGITIMATE BUSINESS

During the windmill deal, my company expanded to about twelve people. Even my ex-wife Louise and oldest son Carl worked for me. I was into cocaine and partying and met Penelope my future wife during that time.

My secretary introduced me to her girlfriend who was going with a man named Lou Coppage out of Denver. Lou was in the investment business big time. He had 1,500 independent financial planners nationwide that sold his investments for him. In fact, they depended on him to give them something to sell.

He had 80 million dollars under management. He invested the money in a technology that injected microbes into oil wells to recover more oil. Oil prices dropped, and he was in trouble with his investors unless he could put together a deal with a lot of tax benefits. Windmills had those benefits.

Lou was way out of my league. I met with him in San Francisco where he kept a condo. He needed a $75 million project to straighten out his problem. He wanted my company to put the project together, and he would finance it.

I found out a guy that was once in the community was also in the windmill business. He owned a factory building windmills and had land leased in Altamont Pass right next to a Merrill Lynch project. He was about to lose his lease if he didn't make a twenty-five thousand-dollar payment.

I made a deal with him to make the payment, take over the lease and to buy twelve million dollars' worth of his machines for the project. I was going to establish a wind farm with a four-megawatt facility costing us thirty-five million to build and install and Lou would sell it to his investors for 75 million. After all the expenses, the total profit would be about 30 million to be split between Lou's company and mine. My company would make 15 million.

Lou was a broker/dealer. As such, he was legally able to take only 12 percent of the money raised. Out of that he had to pay his sales force 10 percent. It was early spring when we cut the deal. Lou came to town from Denver to meet with me. He brought his limo driver and moved him into his San Francisco condo. Both his limo and driver were at our service. At the meeting he said he wanted half the profits to do the deal. It wasn't unreasonable, but it was illegal. I ran it by Ross and as usual Ross left it up to me.

Shortly after I made the deal with Lou, he took Ross to Switzerland to set up a bank account for his half of the money. In the meantime, Lou's attorneys were writing the prospectus. Their offices were in Atlanta, so Ross had to make occasional trips back there and spend time with them on the prospectus.

The first time I went to Atlanta, Lou took me to an after-hour club at 2 a.m., which was bar closing time. At 3 a.m. the place filled up with mostly beautiful women. Apparently, the club owners paid off the right people. I told Lou, "Don't ever take Ross here. He gets in trouble with beautiful women."

"Don't we all, Sal?" he responded.

"Yes, Lou, we do, but not like Ross does." Two weeks later Ross went to Atlanta. I warned him about the beautiful women and made him promises to be back in three days. He was there two weeks and came back engaged.

The project required parts that had to be ordered months in advance. Lou knew that and agreed to front the money. He was giving my company $50,000 every couple of weeks or as needed. I didn't have that kind of money. I had about $150,000 that I used to cover my own staff and expenses.

These deals were made on a handshake, as we obviously couldn't write up everything we were doing. I knew that Lou's driver was reporting back to him everything we did, and I wasn't comfortable with it. So I decided to hire my own driver. I was seeing Melvin Belli's secretary at the time and told her I was looking for a driver I could trust. She recommended her ex-boyfriend. I agreed to meet with him and picked him up in the city.

Before the interview he asked me to take him to a theater to pick up his girlfriend who was rehearsing for a show. That's how I met Penelope my future wife. No, he didn't get the job.

Penny and I saw a lot of each other, and she moved in with me within a couple of weeks. I had a beautiful place at the top of Telegraph Hill by Coit Tower. Penny was Eurasian, very beautiful, very smart, and twenty years younger than I. I was quite taken with her. At the time we were both strung out on cocaine.

We went to the Cliff House for lunch one day, and I ran into Neil Lupa and his wife Heather. I hadn't seen him in nine years since I left the community in Hawaii. He had been out of the community five years already, and he and Heather ran a little travel business taking well-off high school kids from Marin County to Europe.

He asked, "Sal, why don't you come to Europe with us. It's only fifteen hundred bucks." Penny wanted to go, but I was in the middle of problems with Lou Coppage.

I told Penny to go and paid for her trip. Then Lupa asked me to go to a dinner to raise money for a few of the kids that couldn't afford to go. I went to the dinner, had too many drinks and wound up agreeing to go on the trip too.

At the same time, I needed another fifty grand from Lou. He called me and said he wanted half my company. I said, "That's not our deal, Lou. You have half of the project, not half of my company." He was already in the deal for about $400,000. I didn't believe he would walk from it. The clock was ticking, and he had to get the deal on the streets in a matter of weeks. I was getting suspicious because the prospectus was having "delays." He was stalling to squeeze me into a corner.

Lou said, "Well, that's the deal. Take it or leave it." I was spending thousands on legal fees to make sure Ross and I didn't have any problems.

"I have to talk to Ross, Lou." I told him.

I spoke to Ross who said our lawyer thought if Lou did anything illegal we would be accountable along with him. The lawyer also informed us that the Securities and Exchange Commission (SEC) had been watching him for years. Turning down the fifteen million dollars we would make by sticking with Lou was not an easy decision to make. I was up all night. If I made that deal, Lou would be running my life.

Lou called the next day, "Well, what are going to do Sal?" he asked me.

"The answer is no, Lou."

He laughed and said, "You mean to tell me you're going to walk away from fifteen million dollars? Why would you do something like that?"

"Because you can't be trusted, Lou. Not only did you break your word, but also you're now trying to steal half my company. If you wanted half my company, Lou, why didn't you offer to buy it? Why would I trust anyone who just tried to rob me?"

"I don't believe you," Lou said.

"Yeah? Just watch me," and I hung up. I got calls from Lou's lawyers and junior partner for days trying to put the deal back together. I never responded.

I had intended to split what we made with my staff, but that deal left my company bankrupt. Sometimes, I think it was a stupid decision, and I should've taken the money.

Most businessmen would have taken it without a second thought but given what our lawyers told us about the SEC watching Lou, I didn't want to take a chance of being caught up in Lou's shit. Ross tied up the loose ends of the company, and I left for Europe with Penny the following week.

CHAPTER 37

TAKING CARE OF UNFINISHED BUSINESS

During the trip to Europe, I asked Neil Lupa to tell me what had gone on in the community after I left. He told me Franklin had lost a chunk of the community but wouldn't say much more. He did say a lot of shit happened, but because he was one of the attorneys at the time, he couldn't talk about it.

Neil rented a small bus and driver. We traveled throughout Italy and stayed at small private pensions. One day he said, "I have a surprise for you. Do you remember Kathy, the hairdresser?"

"Yes, of course. I really liked her; she was in my group in the community."

"Well she's going to meet us in Florence. She married an Italian named Ugo. He's from Florence, and they're here visiting his parents. She can tell you a lot more about Franklin than I can. She was close to Franklin's women and knew a lot.

We met Kathy in the square where Michelangelo's David is on display. When she saw me she threw her arms around me and held me tight, "God, it's so good to see you, Sal. I can't tell you how often I think about you and wonder if you're all right. When Neil told me you were coming, I got so excited."

"It's wonderful seeing you," I responded. "I haven't seen anyone from the community since I left. It seems that I'm persona non grata, which is fine with me."

"I never believed you embezzled money from the community. Most people didn't."

"Is that the reason they gave for asking me to leave the community?" My head was spinning. I couldn't think straight. I spent the whole rest of the trip wanting to get home to deal with that bastard, Franklin. I snapped. Whatever brainwash was left in me was gone. There was no way they could have said that about me without him knowing it. So that's how he had explained to the community why he had asked me to leave.

I spoke to Neil, "Why didn't you tell me what was said?'

"It's better you got it from someone else"

"Better for who, Neil?" I got pissed at him. He was being too careful, and I didn't like it. He seemed to be up to something. Neil was a cunning man, which is probably why Franklin hung on to him.

I said, "Stop fucking me around, Neil. I want to know what's going on and don't play that attorney/client lawyer shit with me."

"There's a lot going on at the moment, Sal. Beverly O'Manny and two other women left the community and are getting divorces from their husbands. Brian O'Manny, Beverly's husband, is the head of the community and is keeping the kids. Same thing happened with the other two women and their kids.

Neil went on, "I just found out about it a few days before we left. I told them I was meeting you in Italy, and they asked me to ask you if you would meet with them. I told them I would."

"Why do they want to meet with me?"

"I don't know, Sal, but if you really want to find out what's been going on since you left, these women would know everything and be glad to tell you. If you want, I will arrange a meeting with them at my house when we get back."

"Okay, Neil, do it." I was furious. I had left the community with a twenty million dollar net worth but had been given only a fifty-dollar a week stipend for all the years I was there, not to mention that I had put all the money to start the community and raised the money to buy the property. Not only that, but I never signed on the bank accounts and had no way of getting into them. Louise signed on the accounts, which meant they were calling her a thief, too.

When I got back to the U.S., I went straight to the community's offices in San Raphael. The head guy was Rod Grisso whom I knew very well. I was a legend in the community. Most of the members had heard of me but had never met me or even seen me. I heard later that Franklin had pulled everything you could read about me from the archives, as well as any photos with the two of us together, and there were many.

In Franklin's book "The Garbage and the Goddess," I appeared frequently in pictures along with quotes from me. Twenty-five hundred copies were printed. Franklin bought back all he could find for twenty-five dollars each. Then I heard he paid as much as two hundred and fifty for some of the remaining copies. That's how determined he was to erase me from the community history. I had been gone for nine years, and I had no idea he had been doing that.

I walked into the community office and told the secretary I wanted to see Rod. She asked me who I was and if I had an appointment. I told her I didn't need an appointment. Then I walked around her desk and into Rod's office. He was on the phone. I took the phone out of his hand and hung it up. He stared at me as if I was a ghost.

I said, "I want to hear your understanding of why I was asked to leave the community."

"Because the Guru said it was part of what you had to do for your spiritual progress."

"Don't lie to me, you low-life prick," I grabbed him by his shirt and said "because I'll give you the beating of your life right here and now. You never heard that I embezzled from the community? Is that what your telling me?" I was three inches from his face and ten seconds from putting him in a hospital. "Go ahead, Rod, lie to me again and see what happens."

He was scared to death, and he had a right to be that scared. I was on the edge and he knew it." He answered, "Yes, I heard it, but I never believed it, Sal."

"Okay, here's what you're going to do. You get the word to that low life cocksucker Franklin that I want to see him now"

"Sal, he lives in Fiji. He's not going to see you."

"You tell him I want to meet with him face-to-face. He's going to hear what I have to say. I'll meet him in Hawaii at McDonnell's without his entourage. He will hear what I have to say Rod. The only thing we are discussing here is the venue. We can do it in the courts, in the newspapers, or on TV news shows. Telex him what I said, and I want a copy of the telex. Do you understand me, Rodney?

"Yes, I do, Sal."

I felt so fucked over by that asshole Franklin because we had been best friends. If he wanted to end this friendship, he should have done it face-to-face the way it started and not send some lackey to give me a bullshit story. He never had any balls. This was a personal matter and had nothing to do with being in the community or not. No one understood that because no one else had a personal friendship with him.

A few days later I went to Neil's house, where five women came to meet me. I knew all of them. I sat and I listened for a couple of hours. Beverly O Manning, the wife of the current head of the community, told me that Franklin gave instructions to the men to beat their women and defecate on them. Many of the children of senior members were sent to New York to a special school run by the community. There they were indoctrinated, and some were being molested. It was difficult to believe, but I believed it.

Franklin had become a drunk and drug addict and was heavy into Viagra. I already knew he had cancer. According to the women, he was a mean, violent drunk and often beat his women. I was getting sick listening to them. I couldn't help but feel responsible in some way for what was going on. I felt strangely guilty.

I made up my mind I was going to take him down. My feeling was that I had made him, and now I was going to unmake him. He thought he might be famous some day; I was determined to make him infamous. Finally, I asked the women, "What do you want from me? What can I do?"

"We want you to help get our kids back and lead a war against the community. Something must be done about Franklin, Sal," Beverly answered.

I said, "I agree but you need lawyers and money for that, Beverly. I can help you with getting a lawyer who will take this on and help with some money. I have no legal standing to be on a lawsuit with you."

"Sal, you don't understand. Franklin and his people are deathly afraid of you. I've heard many conversations about you and how dangerous you are. Franklin fears for his life with you." It's not the first time I had heard that. I heard it from William, the guy who delivered the message to leave the community. He told me it came straight from Franklin.

Beverly said, "We just want your permission to let them know that you're behind us."

"That won't be necessary, Beverly, I've already sent word to Fiji that I want to see him. So they already know they have big problems with me. It won't take them long to figure out that I'm with you. I'm waiting to hear back now."

I took Beverly and the other two women to my attorney and gave him six thousand bucks to file the suit. Then I put together a volunteer media staff to get the story out to all media outlets that would run with it.

We couldn't just go to the press with the story. We had to file a suit first and tell the story there before the press would touch it. Fortunately, the community had a five-million-dollar insurance policy to cover damages like this.

It took three weeks before I heard back from Fiji. I went to Rod's office to read the telex from Fiji. It said, "You are not spiritually mature enough to be in the presence of the Lord." It was signed William.

I knew immediately that William didn't tell Franklin and had no intentions of telling him anything because Franklin would never deal with me so carelessly. He knew better than that. I sent word back to William strongly advising him to call me. He didn't respond.

Franklin was notorious for shooting the messenger. He never wanted to hear bad news. After all, God should never be disturbed with reality. When the suit was ready to be filed, I had twenty-two, full-time volunteer dissidents ready to hit the media with press releases telling the world what a dangerous cult the community was.

Finally I pulled the plug and told the women to file the suit. The story took off like wildfire. The *LA Times*, the *New York Times*, the *San Francisco Chronicle* - all the nationwide papers – were on it. The TV program *20-20*, TV news and all the local morning TV shows covered it.

Many of the dissidents who were seriously damaged had never had a chance to do anything about it were on TV telling their story. It was Franklin's worse nightmare and William's demise. William called me two days after it hit the news.

"Sal, we need to talk."

"I've been trying to do just that for weeks, but it's too late now, you stupid prick. I'm going to make sure the world knows what a con artist Franklin really is. You tell him that. I made him and now I'm going to unmake him. The lawsuit has nothing to do with me. This is a personal matter."

"Tell me what the matter is."

"It's none of your fuckin' business asshole. Only he can straighten this out with me, but he doesn't have the balls. He's never had any balls. Now he's surrounded himself with people like you. That's like going to war without an army."

I hung up. I found out years later that Franklin threw him out of the community for seven years.

A couple of days after the media blitz started, I got a call from Cheech Marrero, my partner in the drug program who had come out and joined the community. I wasn't talking to anyone in the community. I made an exception for him because of all the years we had known each other. They all wanted to get to me. It was after that meeting, that I was being described as Judas.

Cheech said to me, "You have become Judas."

"Yes, I have and for the same reasons. Judas found out that Jesus was full of shit and was in it for the money, and all the women he could fuck."

"Your son Vincent wants to talk to you." Vincent still lived in the community.

"Good, tell him to come here in the morning." I said. The next day Vincent came to see me. He was manifesting all of Franklin's mannerisms. It made me really pissed to see it.

I asked him, "You think Franklin gives a fuck about you? All I have to do is tell them to throw you out, and you'll be out on your ass in a heartbeat." He didn't believe me, so I called Cheech and told him to let Vincent go, or they were going to have a whole new set of problems with me, and they won't be legal ones." Cheech knew what I meant, and he knew I meant it. They cut Vincent loose the next day.

Within a week the community filed a twenty-million-dollar lawsuit against me, to which I never responded. Next, they went to the DA's office, and said I was a drug dealer. The DA they went to was named Bernard, a former monk of twenty years from another cult. He knew about me from Crane Montano who had also spent twenty years as a monk with him in the same cult, but Crane was now with Franklin as a high-ranking member of Franklin's community.

I got a call from this DA who said, "Sal, you don't know me, but I know a lot about you from Crane. We were monks together. Crane was just here making a lot of accusations about you, and I'd like you to drop by and see me."

I went to see him the next day. He told me the community was watching me and claimed that I was dealing coke out of my house.

So I asked, "What are you going to do about it?"

He said, "Nothing. We have had a cult department here ever since that Jim Jones massacre happened. I've turned the information about the community over to them. We are very interested in what your former cult is doing and would like any information you have or may learn about them and about Franklin Jones in particular.

He went on to say, "You should be very careful with these people, Sal. We consider them dangerous. I also told Crane we are opening an investigation on them as a result of his coming here. That should take some wind out of their sails. We've had a lot of reports from others about Franklin Jones and his group, but this is heating up."

"Thanks, Bernard. I appreciate the warning."

Later the community sent Craig Lesser to see me. Craig was completely bewildered and really shaken by all of it. "I don't understand it, Sal. I'm part of the community because of you."

"Yes, I know, and I apologize for that."

He asked me, "What has turned you against Franklin?"

"Lies, deceit, and breaking all the agreements we had which brought me out here in the first place. He is nothing but a con man," I said.

Craig cringed every time I spoke that way about Franklin. I could see his world falling apart right in front of me.

He said, "Look, Sal, please stop what you're doing. The lawyers have authorized me to offer you $150,000 to settle this whole thing."

I asked him, "Do I look like a hooker to you?"

"What do you mean?"

"Do I look like someone you can fuck and pay, Craig?"
Tears started running down Craig's face.

I told him, "I am not on the suit against the community. My problem is not with the community. It's with Franklin. Furthermore, I'm not interested in the money."

The community had gotten new lawyers and was told by them if they didn't get me in some sort of an agreement this would never end. So Craig asked me "What would it take for you to walk away?"

I told him, "I've been telling all of you what I want from the very beginning, a face-to-face meeting with that punk, but no one seems to believe me."

"He's never going to do that, Sal."

"Well that's too fuckin' bad isn't it because as long as I'm alive, he will never be safe. I will never sign anything that would stop me from exposing him. This is not about money."

Slowly but surely, they paid everyone else off. Neil got Heather $350,000 for Franklin injuring her with a dildo, and therein lies the reason Neil wouldn't tell me anything. He was negotiating with them separately and not telling anyone. I was pretty much disgusted with all of them.

I got married on March 1, 1986, and was busted on a drug charge by the FBI on March 27.

CHAPTER 38

ADVENTURE IN SIERRA LEONE

It was around December 1989 when I found myself traveling along the Sierra Leone coastline in an old dugout powered by an equally old outboard motor. I was on my way to meet Joseph Momoh, the President of Sierra Leone, at his "summer" home. He didn't live on an island. There were just no roads outside the city of Freetown.

Freetown was established by the British during the time of the Abolition. All slaves under the control of the British Empire were given the option to return to Africa or remain in the Empire. Those who did return went to Freetown, Sierra Leone, the port where the Portuguese merchants had bought them, hence the name Freetown.

As a result they all became citizens of the British Empire. The English pound became the country's currency until Siaka Stevens, the former President/dictator, broke from England and printed his own currency. Of course, since Sierra Leone had nothing to export, the Leone, as the currency was called, was completely worthless.

My traveling companion was Albert Metzger, a British barrister who had arranged the meeting with President Joseph Momoh. Albert was a friend and the personal attorney of the President. He was also responsible for writing a major part of the new constitution for the country.

The purpose of the meeting was to discuss a problem the president was having with the Lebanese community in

Freetown. I, too, had a problem and needed help. Albert felt the meeting would be to our mutual benefit.

The Lebanese population had been living in Sierra Leone for sixty years by the time I arrived in 1989. They owned almost all of the retail businesses that supplied the city and country with things the country didn't have, which was just about everything, especially canned tomato paste and rice, (the country's staple, refrigerators, mining equipment, marine supplies, and automobiles, but most of the money the Lebanese made was from buying and mining diamonds.

Not long before I arrived in Sierra Leone, a group of Israelis had arrived. They rented the former president's fifty-five-bedroom mansion. They brought with them a small fleet of SUV's, Mercedes Benz, mining equipment, and their best diamond experts. They then started a mining and trading company and began buying up raw diamonds.

The head of the company was an Israeli named Boaz. He had two partners. One was a very wealthy French industrialist - the moneyman. The other was the President of Sierra Leone.

A close friend of the President, who also had the tobacco concession for the country, was there at the meeting. I suspect he was the front man for President Momoh in the diamond company.

The story goes that Boaz was the youngest solider in the successful raid at the Entebbe airport that freed eighteen hostages. As a reward for his valor, he was made Menachem Begin's personal bodyguard, which gave him access to a broad network of business and political contacts.

Ironically, it was the wives who brought the men together. Momoh's wife met both the wife of Boaz and the wife of the French investor in London.

Here is where the President's problems began. Because of Boaz's political and military background, the Lebanese were convinced he was an Israeli CIA operative there to undercut them in the diamond business, and, therefore, undermined the Lebanese's ability to send cash or raw diamonds back to Lebanon to fight the Israelis. It was not an illogical speculation.

What does all this have to do with me? I'm Sicilian. I look Lebanese and was easily accepted into their community. I ate their food in their homes and restaurants. I bought supplies from them and spent a good deal of social time with them. I liked them, and they liked me even though I was an American. I listened to the problems they were having competing with the Israelis who had very deep pockets. The Israelis were bringing in metric tons of rice and selling it for Leones (the country's currency) then using the money to buy diamonds. Many of the native diamond miners lived and worked in the bush and wanted to be paid in Leones.

It was illegal to use foreign currency in the country even though everyone did it. The Leone was virtually worthless outside the country, so as a businessman you were allowed to have a dollar account to purchase goods outside the country and a Leone account to deposit the proceeds from the sales inside the county. Then you had to go to the thriving black market to buy dollars and put them in your dollar account. This system allowed you to get around the currency laws because the country literally could not survive without it. One could see how this might create a problem for Momoh. The Lebanese virtually controlled the internal commerce in the city of Freetown.

I suggested to my Lebanese friends that they put together a buying syndicate and jointly put up letters of credit, which would allow them to buy large quantities of rice and tomato paste and thereby compete. It was that suggestion that endeared me to the Lebanese and the reason why the President, at Albert's suggestion, wanted to meet with me.

My problem was that an American Black named Warner Becket and his son Billy from the states were ripping me off. I needed to go back to California to straighten out the problem. Warner was in the states. Billy was in Sierra Leone.

My wife and son were with me in Sierra Leone. They had arrived sometime after I got there. I didn't know they were coming, but they were told I sent for them. It was a ploy of Warner Becket to keep me under control.

I didn't want Billy Beckett to know I was gone until after I got to the states, which meant my wife and son had to stay in Sierra Leone for the month I would be gone. I needed to know they would be safe, and that's what I wanted from President Momoh.

The two boatmen traveling with us pulled the boat ashore, so Albert and I could disembark. There were no docks just a beach. Albert looked about sixty years old, five foot, eight and weighed about two hundred pounds and of course, as an English barrister spoke with an English accent as did most of the educated Sierra Leone natives including President Joseph Momoh. Momoh had graduated from Sandhurst military school in England and went on to become the General of the Sierra Leone Army.

I didn't then and still don't know the events that precipitated Momoh's rise to power. It was the first time a sitting civilian President voluntarily turned over the government to the military without a violent coop, which was how General Joseph Momoh became the President of Sierra Leone.

I was told that Momoh was taken by surprise by that event. He celebrated by going on a two-year bender with his Grenadian friend, who was also in attendance at the meeting the day I went to see him.

Apparently Momoh spent most of the first two years in office partying and screwing as many women as he could. His wife and the Grenadian's wife were fed up with them and left for London where they met the wife of Momoh's future French investor.

I took off my shoes, stepped into the water and climbed out of the boat. Then I helped Albert get out. When I turned around, I saw Momoh and his Grenadian friend sitting on a low covered dais to keep them off the sandy beach and out of the sun. In front of them were two bottles of Johnny Walker Black, glasses and a bucket full of ice.

"Good afternoon, Mr. President," Albert said smiling. Momoh stepped down off the dais to greet Albert warmly. He and Albert hugged one another patting each other on the back. They both started laughing.

"Hello, Albert," said the President. "It's so good to see you. Take off your jacket and shirt. Make yourself comfortable."

"Thank you, Joseph. It has been a while hasn't it?"

"Indeed it has." It was clear to me by their informality that they were very good friends.

Momoh was topless, wearing sandals and shorts. I'd say his waistline was between 48 and 52 inches. In spite of his size and weight, I heard he was an agile tennis player. He had around his neck a very large key hanging from a leather string. The key resembled something that would open a castle door. I couldn't help but wonder what it was for. I was sure it wasn't for his front door.

Albert introduced me. "Mr. President, may I present Mr. Salvatore Lucania."

It was obvious Momoh wanted this meeting informal. He squeezed and shook my hand jovially and said, "Welcome, Mr. Salvatore (he pronounced it Salvatory). It is good to meet you, and thank you for coming. We were just going to have a drink. Will you join us?" he asked graciously.

"I most certainly will, sir." He seemed quite pleased that I was willing to party with him. Albert and I stepped up onto the dais and sat down. Momoh introduced me to his friend, but for the life of me I cannot remember his name.

Momoh dismissed his houseboys and poured the drinks himself. Then he said, "I understand we have a problem." I was sure someone had briefed him on the matter, so I saw no reason to go into it again, unless he wanted me to. I knew what I needed from him, but I didn't know what I could do for him.

"Yes, sir, but it's my problem not yours." I said.

"You are wrong, Mr. Salvatory. It is our problem. You see, men like the Becketts stop legitimate investors from investing in my country. So you see it is my problem as well as yours. How can I help you?" he asked, pouring the second round.

I explained, "I must leave the country for a few weeks, sir, and I'm concerned for my family's safety."

"Quite so, I'm sure we can arrange to secure your family while you are gone. I can assign military guards at your house, or your family could be my guests at my home, whichever you prefer. Would that be satisfactory?"

Momoh's house was just down the road from mine. Freetown had intermittent electricity. Momoh always had power. So did I because of my proximity to his house. The rest of the town had to make do with generators or nothing at all.

At the time there were thirteen countries in the world below third world status. Meaning no roads, no power, and no sewerage system. Sierra Leone was eleventh on that list.

"Yes, sir, that would be most satisfactory. It's very kind of you to offer your home, but I think my wife would be more comfortable in our home, I said drinking my second shot, which really was a double at least. I was already feeling a little high. Sierra Leone is near the equator, so it doesn't take long for the body to absorb booze.

"Well, jolly good then. It is settled," he said, happily downing his drink and pouring another. There was no way I could keep up with him. He weighed at least 100 pounds more than I did.

"Sir, what is it you think I can do for you?" I asked noticing one of the bottles was almost gone.

"Well, Mr. Salvatory, I am told you have become friends with the Wanzas. They are a very prominent Lebanese family here in Sierra Leone. Mr. Wanza is a businessman and the head of the Lebanese businessmen's association, as you probably know. You, I am told, have given them a great deal of advice with regards to successfully competing with the Israelis. As a result, Albert tells me, you have earned their respect, trust, and confidence. Mr. Boaz and his group have come here to do business. They are welcome here as are many other businessmen such as yourself.

"Unfortunately, because of Mr. Boaz's nationality and his previous military background, the Lebanese community is very distrustful of him and his motives for being here. They have come to the conclusion that he is an Israeli CIA agent here to undermine them."

"Undermine them, in what way sir," I asked. "I don't understand. I don't know Mr. Boaz or his group, but I assume they are just businessmen trying to make money."

"You are absolutely correct, Mr. Salvatory. That is exactly the case, but Mr. Wanza and the Lebanese community are of the opinion that Mr. Boaz is here more for political reasons then financial ones," he said breaking into the second bottle of Johnny Walker Black.

"Political reasons, sir?" I had heard the rumors, of course, but I wanted to hear his view of it.

"Yes, it is no secret the Lebanese and the Israelis are enemies. The Lebanese believe the Israelis are here to take over the diamond business to stop them from sending diamonds and cash to Lebanon, which is being used to fight Israel. While that is not an unreasonable speculation, it's simply not true."

Albert had already told me that Momoh was one of three partners. Momoh didn't need or want to acknowledge his personal involvement.

"How can I help, sir?" I asked.

"I would like you to allay their concerns if you can. Let them know it's just a business arrangement that has nothing to do with international politics."

"Forgive me, sir, but how could I give them such assurances. How would I know if he is or isn't an Israeli operative? Surely they will ask me"

"Yes, that is true," he agreed. "There is no real way for you to prove it one way or another. Such is my dilemma. I can assure you that Sierra Leone's interest is purely economic." I believed him because, like every official in Sierra Leone, Momoh was in business for himself.

This would be big money for him. Typically, when investors show up and want to do business, they meet with one minister or another. Those ministers cut their own deals for themselves. Rarely does the President have direct contact with the money people, and I suspect gets cut out of any real money. But this deal was different.

The President told me, "I had Albert meet with Mr. Boaz and his partner to address the issue. In that meeting Mr. Boaz assured his partner and Albert that he no longer had any government affiliations and hasn't for many years."

"I believe you Mr. President and I believe Mr. Boaz, because I think it would be foolish to jeopardize this business venture and his relationship to you and his partner. I will talk with Mr. Wanza and tell him I believe his fears are unfounded. It's really all I can do, sir."

I didn't think Boaz was an Israeli CIA operative for two reasons. First, because the partners met through their wives, who were now, I was told, close friends living in London and second, given the players, this deal was worth many millions to all of them and money trumps everything.

The President said, "Yes, quite. I understand, and I thank you for your effort. Tell me, Mr. Salvatory, do you play tennis?"

"No, sir, I don't. Ping pong is the closest I got to tennis, but I understand you are very good at tennis." By this time, we were pretty smashed, at least I was. The key around his neck was still something I couldn't get out of my mind, and

I was now drunk enough to ask, pointing to the key, "Tell me sir, if you don't mind me asking, what's with the key?"

Momoh roared laughing. It took him awhile before he could answer me. He held the key up and said, "Do you see all my soldiers walking around out there with those automatic weapons? Well, I have the bullets." Then he continued to laugh hysterically.

I found the men of Sierra Leone very warm and friendly. They laughed easily and walked hand in hand, as well as arm in arm. It was part of their tribal culture, and I enjoyed it immensely.

CHAPTER 39

HOW AND WHY I WENT TO SIERRA LEONE

I met Warner Beckett in 1985. A friend in the investment business introduced me to him. Mr. Beckett ran a company called Trans-Africa Corp. located in Hayward, California.

Warner was a Black man in his sixties. He was not a specimen of good health, to say the least. He looked about five-foot, six or seven, but it was hard to tell because he was slightly bent over.

He had had a tracheotomy, so when he spoke saliva dripped from his mouth into a handkerchief he always carried with him. He tilted his head up to look up at me and had one eye looking in the wrong direction. He looked very much like a character from the movie "Planet of the Apes".

His wife was a large, light-skinned Creole woman with beautiful green eyes. It was hard not to look at her. She was warm and very friendly towards me.

Warner was an honoree Consulate for Sierra Leone. It was a business consulate that gave him the power to issue visas to anyone who wanted to do business in the country. He went to Sierra Leone seven years before with a million dollars and came back broke. It had been his dream to go back there and make a fortune.

Warner had five children. His youngest, Billy Beckett, was in Sierra Leone with him and was married to a Fula tribal chief's daughter. Billy was still living there at the time I first met Warner.

Warner wanted to buy uncut diamonds in Sierra Leone. Then cut and sell them here in the United States. I was intrigued by the idea, but at the time of the conversation I was addicted to cocaine, had just lost my business, and was fighting the Franklin Jones cult. I was living in San Francisco with my pregnant girlfriend Penney who was twenty years my junior.

I didn't have the money to invest, but I might be willing to raise the money if I thought it was a viable deal. Warner and I spent some time meeting and talking over the next few weeks. I was getting married, and I invited Warner to the wedding.

CHAPTER 40

THE BUST

I married Penelope on March 1, and three weeks later I was busted. I was set up in a coke sting by a man named Gary Latreall, who managed the law offices of David Cunningham, the attorney I had hired to fight the Franklin Jones cult. Gary had a partner name Owen Stevenson whom I met only once for five minutes in the lobby of the Saint Francis Hotel. Both these men were stock scammers, professional con artists.

Gary knew I needed money and that I was strung out on coke, so he knew I had access to coke. He lured me into a deal to get a kilo of coke for a friend of his. His friend was an FBI undercover agent, Roger Regan. It was a complicated sting operation, complicated because the feds' only interest in me was to use me as a pawn in a broader scheme to bust a Colombian.

The courts were completely politicized in the mid-eighties. There was no such thing as justice. If you were busted for drugs, you were going to jail. Many people in the justice business were making a lot of money. Defense lawyers and the government were cleaning up with the confiscation laws, not to mention all the drug money law enforcement was stealing. The prison industry budgets were growing rapidly,

It seems the FBI was after a Colombian who was operating out of a jewelry store he owned on Union Street in San Francisco. The FBI set up a young pot dealer name John Kingham to buy twenty kilos of coke from the Colombian.

John Kingham did not have any connections in the coke business, nor did he have the money to do a deal like that. Through another informant, I suspect Owen Stevenson, the FBI managed to get Kingham introduced to the Colombian. Then they were going to give Kingham the cash to make the buy.

The FBI didn't want to put an agent directly next to Kingham for fear it would look too much like entrapment in a court, which it was. Instead, they introduced me to Kingham as a buyer, and I suppose they were going to give me the cash to give to him. I didn't know any of this at the time.

It was the classic FBI entrapment. They would target someone they suspected, supply him with the money and with the connection for the drugs, and then bust him. That's what happened to DeLorean. They introduced me to Kingham and an FBI agent to Kingham, as two possible buyers. Kingham thought me suspicious and chose the FBI agent. They apparently didn't have time to find someone else and went ahead and arrested Kingham and the Colombian. I was busted six months later without any knowledge of what had happened to Kingham.

In the meantime, Regan, the undercover FBI agent, pursued me to get him a kilo of coke. I really wasn't needed anymore; I was just supposed to be a pawn. Anyway, I got it for him and was busted. Seven agents crashed the house, guns drawn, of course. They found the coke in the yard where I had stashed it just before Regan came to the house. They had watched me do it.

The FBI supervisor of the case was a man named McKennin. He took me out on my deck with a tape recorder and began to question me about my sources. Then he began to threaten me with arresting my wife if I didn't cooperate.

The rest of the agents went through the house. McKennin was the whitest guy I have ever seen in my life. He looked like he had walked straight out of Dickens novel. He wore a reddish toupee that sat on his head like a hat that didn't fit, and the color didn't match the rest of his hair.

A young wise-ass agent came out of the bedroom with a dildo. He dangled it in front of my wife with a smirk on his face and asked, "What's this?"

My wife answered without skipping a beat "What's the matter, didn't your mother teach you anything? Don't worry. It comes with a set of instructions."

His face turned red and the other agents laughed at him. They loved it, and so did I. Regan, the undercover agent, was out on the deck with me. He said to me, " That's a hell of a woman you have there." And she was. She was fearless in the face of these men.

They had a female agent with them to talk to Penny, but she got nowhere. They didn't charge her with anything. The feds don't do well prosecuting pregnant women. They usually used them to force you into pleading guilty, so they don't have to prove anything in a trial.

Growing up Sicilian in East Harlem, I was told very early on, "If you ever get in trouble with the law, never talk to cops. Say nothing at all, not even your name." While out on the balcony with McKennin, all I could hear in my head was *nothing, remember say nothing.* So I said nothing, not even my name. They already had it, of course, but I didn't want my voice on the tape recorder.

I was taken to the federal building at 450 Golden Gate Street in San Francisco to be booked and interrogated. By that time I was sure they knew I was related to Lucky Luciano but didn't know exactly how. After all, they only had to type my name into a computer and Lucky's name would come up. I was forty-three years old, and I'd never been arrested for anything in my life. I'm sure this disappointed them.

Furthermore, unbeknown to me, they were having big problems with a man named Bill Halverson. Bill owned a large deli and liquor store in Sausalito. He was taken for $400,000 by two stock scammers, who also happen to be the same two stool pigeons that set me up in the drug deal. Bill went to the feds to get them arrested, but the feds wouldn't do anything.

When Bill learned they were FBI informants he flipped out. They were also trying to lure him into a coke deal after they robbed him. Bill was street smart and had already been to prison. He knew immediately what they were up to. He began spreading their names everywhere in Marin County trying to blow their cover. McKennin sent Regan to tell Bill that he was endangering lives and obstructing justice, and if he didn't stop they would bust him, which enraged him even more.

It was found out later that the informants worked for the FBI and for McKennin specifically for eight years. The deal was that the informants were free, with the FBI's knowledge, to rip off anyone they wanted to then set up the victims in a coke deal to recoup their losses with big profits. Then the FBI would get the credit for busting them. I still didn't have any knowledge of this yet.

The feds didn't have a jail. They contracted San Francisco and Oakland jails to hold prisoners while they waited for bail or court appearances. I was cuffed to a chair when the wise ass with the dildo came over and said, "We got you on the phone with Michael Franzese, Andy Orena, and Nicky Scarfo in Jersey…" and a few other people I didn't know.

At first, I ignored him as if he weren't there, which infuriated him. I must admit I came very close to going off on him. It was a good thing I was cuffed, or I just might have slapped him for that stunt he pulled with my pregnant wife.

I finally said to him, "You know, little boy, you watch too much television." Regan, the undercover agent, fed up with the young asshole himself, finally said to him, "You have no idea who you're talking to. Just leave him the fuck alone."

I found out later that Regan really liked me and hated McKennin. It seems a lot a people hated McKennin. Regan knew this was a bullshit bust, which shouldn't have happened after the Kingham bust. McKennin made him do it because he knew with my name he could get press. He tried, but someone at the *San Francisco Examiner* who knew me didn't buy it and killed the story.

By the time I got out of prison, Regan had retired. I learned he and Bill Halverson became golf buddies. While having lunch at the Olympic Club, I ran into Bill who said, "Sal, you're out. It's good to see you. Do you have a minute?

"Sure, Bill, what's up?

You know, Sal, Regan and I became friends after he retired."

Yeah, I heard that and was a little surprised." Bill had done time before and had no use for any cops.

"Yeah, well me too. McKennin sent him to intimidate me. I was warning everyone I knew that Latreall and Stevenson were federal informants. I told Regan that he, his two stool pigeons, and McKennin could go fuck themselves. I hope someone kills those two bastards. I continued to expose them."

To my surprise, Regan apologized to me and said he didn't blame me. Then he laid out the whole game that McKennin and his two rats have been doing for years. He hated what was going on and didn't want any part of it. McKennin was his boss. He was close to retirement and was afraid McKennin would find a way to fuck up his retirement.

Bill went on to say, "Regan talked a lot about you. He felt bad because your wife was going to have a baby, and it bothered him. There was a sense of decency in him. He said if I saw you to ask you if you would let him buy you dinner or a drink. He wanted to apologize personally."

This whole affair was getting stranger the more I found out, but there is more to come. I said, "No, Bill, I'm not in the absolution business. Tell him to see a priest. They're in the forgiveness business, not me. They had forty-six years of indictments on me. They tried to make me into a Mafia figure because of my family name. Do you understand Bill?

I was in front of the judge, slamming Sam Conti, who never gave less than a ten-year sentence for drugs. I could've gotten twenty years just so they could make collar and a few headlines."

"Yeah, but, Sal, Regan was caught in the middle. There was nothing he could do."

"No, Bill. I was the one caught in the middle, not him. He could have refused to do it on the grounds it was entrapment and was illegal, then turn in McKennin. Or he could have tipped me off. So fuck him."

"Okay, Sal, I understand and I believe he will too."

After I was fingerprinted and booked, the younger agents came over and brought me coffee. They offered to go out and get me something to eat. A couple of them said to me it wasn't personal. They were just doing their job.

I couldn't believe it, but I think they really felt bad. I was being treated almost like a celebrity, probably because of my name. I didn't know what to make of these guys.

McKennin and a couple of his agents took me to the San Francisco jail to be held in custody. I was checking in my valuables - ring, watch etc. I was wearing a running suit. When I reached into a zipped up back pocket, I found five, one hundred dollar bills I didn't remember I had.

McKennin quickly grabbed them and said, "Don't worry, Sal, I'm going to turn this in." Someone had already ripped off a few grand from my house.

I said, "Why don't you keep it and buy yourself a good wig." The officer behind the gate putting my stuff in an envelope loved it. He laughed out loud in McKennin's face. The San Francisco police hated the FBI. They hated them being in their city and interfering in their business.

A day later I was transferred to the Oakland jail because of overcrowding. I was put into a large room with fifty other men, all Black. My first thought was, *I might have some trouble here, and I don't like the odds.* I wanted to be moved somewhere else. I grew up in Harlem and was very comfortable with my Black friends. I had a lot of them because I used to sing with them in Harlem.

I was surprised to find out that because I was a federal prisoner in for drugs and Italian I had status and was treated respectfully. It seems there is a class system in the criminal world too.

I was there for ten days. Finally, my bail was set at the high figure of $100,000. I thought to myself, *who do they think they have here?*

The second day I was there, I was watching the news. There was a rape trial going on in San Francisco. The father of the girl walked into the courtroom and open fired on the guy who raped his daughter. He got out on $25,000 bail before I did.

Tony Serra's office arranged the bail and wanted $75,000 to handle the case. My sister in New York put up her house to secure the bail. I was broke, and a friend of mine told me to stay away from high profile drug lawyers and get a public defender, so I did.

Here is the way the system works. It's the luck of the draw. The next lawyer up gets the case. I got Barry Portman, the head of the Public Defender's Office, for my attorney. The prosecutor was a Puerto Rican who failed the bar eight times. But the judge was slamming Sam Conti, notorious for giving over the top sentences.

Barry was from Boston and had been with the Defender's Office for fourteen years. I told him the whole story. He said, "Look, Sal, I want you to tell me anything that could come back at me in court. I don't want to be blindsided."

I said, "Lucky Luciano is my cousin. I never met him. He went to jail six years before I was born and was deported when I was 3 years old. My father once told me my name would create problems for me all my life."

At the time I had asked my father, "Are telling me I'm guilty by birth?"

He said, "That's exactly what I'm telling you."

Barry told me, "Okay, good. Don't worry about the Luciano thing. They can't get anywhere with that. You are not guilty by birth."

I pleaded not guilty and a trial date was set for September. As soon as I got out, I went to the office of the attorney David Cunningham in Sausalito looking for that rat Gary Latreall who works for Cunningham as his office manager.

"David, where's Gary?" I asked him. "I want to know everything you know about him, and you can start with his address."

"He's gone, Sal. He doesn't really have an address. He used to sleep here."

David's office was on a large houseboat. I didn't like what I was hearing and started to get suspicious of him. It was a Sunday morning, and David's phone rang in the middle of our conversation.

David handed me the phone and said, "It's a private detective named David Fetchheimer, and he wants to talk to you." I wondered how he knew I was there but figured Penny had told him since she was the only one who knew.

On the phone he said, "I'd like to come and talk to you about John Kingham." I told him I didn't know the name, but if he wanted I could meet him the next day. He said that was too late and asked me if he could come then. He could be there in fifteen minutes. I said okay.

He came to David's office and showed me a picture of Kingham, which I recognized. Fetchheimer asked me to call him Fetch, then proceeded to layout Kingham's case to me. He told me that the informants in my case were the same informants in Kingham's case and that McKennin was the FBI supervisor in both cases.

I asked, "So, why is that significant?"

"McKennin has committed perjury. He signed a sworn affidavit stating he didn't know Gary Latreall or Owen Stevenson when in fact they were paid informants and have been working with the FBI and with McKennin for years."

Now I was really pissed off. I don't like rats. I don't think anybody does. "If you can't do the time, don't do the crime," was a saying everyone knew in my neighborhood. I can even understand someone rolling on his partners to save his own ass, but these rats fucked up my life for money. To me that was unforgivable.

"What can I do?" I asked.

"John Kingham's trial starts tomorrow morning in judge Lynch's court on the 17th floor of the Federal Building. We want you to testify to the fact that McKennin and both informants were the players in your case."

Just then, Cunningham said, "You can't do that, Sal, without jeopardizing your own case. If you're going to claim entrapment, how are you going to explain having prior deals?" He was right, of course.

"I'm sorry, Fetch, I would love to hang that fuckin prick McKennin, but that's too dangerous for me. You know I'm going in front of Judge Conti facing forty-six years of indictments. I'm also the cousin of Lucky Luciano. I could get buried by Conti, especially if he's looking for headlines."

I walked Fetch outside onto the dock. He said to me, "I know who you are, Sal, and I understand the problem."

I said, "You know that rat Gary Lateral works for Cunningham. I came here looking for him, and he told me Gary lived here on his boat. I think Cunningham knows a lot more than he's saying."

I found out in prison that Cunningham worked with State prosecutors and would give up privileged information about his clients that didn't have money, so they would get a conviction in exchange for letting other clients of his go, those with big money. What a fuckin' cesspool the justice system was and still is.

Fetch said, "He's full of shit. Gary doesn't live on the boat. I already found the both of those stool pigeons and served them with a subpoena to appear in court tomorrow morning, so if you want to find them, that's where they will be at 9 a.m."

"How the fuck did you do that?"

"I contacted them on their business phone and told them I had $500,000 in cash and wanted to buy the stock they were selling. They came to meet me, and I served them."

"They bought that?"

"The easiest people to con, Sal, are con men, especially greedy ones."

I really admired Fetch's balls. He thanked me and asked me where he could reach me in an hour. I gave him my home number and told him I would be home or still here, and then he left.

An hour and a half later he called me at home. He asked, "Do you know Bill Bonanno?"

I said, "No, but I know who he is and who his father is." I remember being introduced to him once at an airport in New York. We just shook hands and that was it. I didn't want to admit to even that on the phone.

I said, "Why don't we meet in fifteen minutes at Capps Corner, a bar in North Beach." I lived in North Beach, and so did Fetch.

Now I was getting confused, if not concerned. I wondered, *What the hell does Bill Bonanno have to do with anything?*

Fetch was written up in G.Q. as one of the best private detectives in the U.S. He was instrumental in breaking the DeLorean entrapment case, which explains why he was hired for Kingham's case. He was also hired by the government to gather evidence against eighteen prison guards after the Attica prison riots in New York.

It turned out that Kingham's father sold jets to the military and was very wealthy. He hired Charles Gary who in turn hired Fetch. Charles Gary was a take-no-prisoners civil rights attorney. He hated the feds and their illegal tactics. He defended Bobby Seal, one of the Chicago 7, as well as Huey Newton

Fetch said, "Sal, Bill Bonanno would like you to do him a favor and show up at Judge Lynch's court tomorrow morning. I work for Charles Garry, Kingham's attorney. He understands why you can't testify, but we want McKennin to think you're going to testify.

"McKennin testified in written affidavits that he doesn't know Latreall or Stevenson. When he shows up and sees you there, he'll know he's fucked. Will you do it?"

I said, "It will be my pleasure, Fetch, but first I need to know how and why Bill Bonanno is involved with this. What's the connection? I don't get it."

"Well, not many people know this but Charles Garry and Bill's father, Joe, are very close friends. In fact, Garry has been handling the old man's legal work for many years and never sends him a bill. When I told Garry who you were, he called Joe and asked him if there was anything he could do to get your help. You do know your cousin Charlie and Joe came up together and were very close.

"Yes, I do know that," I said.

"So the old man called Bill to see if he would talk to you about helping Garry with the case. Bill wanted to meet you and ask you personally, but since both of you are under indictment (Bill had a state case) he didn't think it would be a good idea to be seen together."

"I agree and I'll see you in the morning."

"Thanks, Sal, we appreciate what you are doing and won't forget it. I'll let Bill know." I had no idea what was going to happen. I went home and told my wife what I was going do.

She said, "You know, Sal, McKennin is going to have a real hard-on for you."

"He already does, Penny. You should have seen him after I told him to buy a good wig."

"Oh, Sal, I wish I was there."

The trial was scheduled to start at 10 a.m. I got there at 8:30 a.m. John Kingham and his wife showed up at nine when the doors opened.

Next, Charles Garry and Fetch showed up. Fetch introduced me to Garry who smiled warmly and thanked me for coming. Garry was wearing a burgundy polyester suit, burgundy patent leather shoes, a dull yellow shirt with a large seventies collar, a dark green tie with white polka dots the size of silver dollars. I thought, *Where the he hell did he find this stuff?* I was sure he dressed that way to offend the court. I couldn't imagine him doing it for any other reason.

He seemed to be in his sixties, bald, on top with very long side hair. I would call it the Ben Franklin look. I didn't know what I expected him to look like, but I wasn't expecting this.

We were all standing in the hallway talking when the elevator door opened and out walked Gary Latreall and his partner Owen Stevenson. I was the last person they expected to see. Gary turned and ran straight for the bathroom. I went right after him.

Fetch called out to me in a loud whisper. "Sal, where are you going? There's cameras all over this place."

"Not in the bathroom" I grabbed Latreall and shoved him into one of the stalls and locked my hands around his neck.

"Sal, I swear I didn't know Roger was an agent…" My hands were so tight around his throat he could barely talk.

Fetch came into the bathroom right behind me. "Sal, let him go. This is not the time or place to deal with him." Then pulled me off him.

I went back and joined the others. My adrenalin was pumping, and my hands were shaking. I was standing between Fetch and Charles Garry when the elevator door opened and out walked McKennin and four of his agents. He was carrying some of the evidence, a box with five kilos of coke in it. When he saw me, he stopped dead in his tracts, turned and handed the coke to one of his agents and walked straight toward me.

Fetch leaned over and said, "This asshole is going to try and intimidate you." McKennin came up to my face smiling with his fangs hanging out of his mouth. I could feel the hate and venom oozing out of him.

He said, "Hi Sal. Aren't you going to say hello?"

My response surprised everyone there, including me. I spit right in his face and said, "I'll say hello to you when I get in there, you fuckin' pussy."

I could hear Fetch say under his breath, "Perfect." Charles Garry quickly stepped between me and McKennin moving him back. McKennin wiped his face with his suit sleeve.

Charles Garry turned around, faced me, grabbed my head with both hands, pulled it toward him, and kissed me on the forehead, then said, like a proud father, "They don't make them like you anymore, Sal."

Pointing at the small glass window on the courtroom door he said, "I want you to look through the glass when I have him on the stand. I'm going to skewer him." I wanted to go in, but Garry said I couldn't because witnesses were not allowed to be in the courtroom before they testified.

I am sure there wasn't any doubt in McKennin's mind that I was going to testify against him. Unfortunately, I wasn't able to hear what Garry did to him on the stand, but I did see him squirming in the witness chair.

Later I found out what happened in court when Garry asked him if he knew Gary Latreall and Owen Stevenson. Because I was just outside the courtroom, he had to admit that he did. Then Garry asked him, "Are you telling the truth?" and of course he was in that instance.

Then Garry handed McKennin his own sworn testimony denying that he knew them. "Can you explain to me and the court how your testimony here this morning is the truth and how your sworn testimony saying you do not know them is also true?"

McKennin started to back pedal and stutter. He was completely caught off guard. Garry pressed on. "Have you

always had a problem understanding what the truth is?"
Garry was merciless.

I was pacing the hallways, and I was scared. I knew I
wasn't making a lot of friends here. Spiting on a federal
agent was not the smartest thing to do. It was a knee jerk
response. I didn't think. I just did it. Now I was worried
about it.

I decided to leave. My job was done. I needed a cigarette
and a drink. When I entered the elevator to leave, a tall guy
jumped in with me just before the door closed. It was just
the two of us and I felt cornered. He asked, looking at me
intensely, "Are you going to testify?"

"Who the fuck are you?" I fired back

"I'm the head of the federal district attorneys' office." I
looked him straight in the eye without so much as a blink
and wondered, *Does he really expect me to answer him?* I
said nothing for the whole seventeen-floor ride down to the
street. I looked at him with the contempt he deserved and
walked outside to find the nearest bar.

When Kingham's case was finished, he was found guilty.
The judge had the nerve to say that McKennin was the only
credible witness in the case then sentenced Kingham to five
years. That was justice in the eighties at the start of The War
on Drugs.

I remained friends with Fetch over the years. I would
bring him Cuban cigars from Costa Rica, where my son
was living, when they weren't easy to get. I exchanged
information with him whenever we could help each other.
We were both traveling a lot. I often ran into him in the
airport on my way to see my son, The last time I ran into
him, he was going to see the Bonanno family in Arizona for
a celebration.

I asked him, "What's the occasion?

He said, "It's the first time in twenty years no one in the
family is under indictment." Such is the glamorous life of
"gangsters." In one of Bill Bonanno's cases, while on the

stand he was asked what he did for a living? He said, "I'm a professional defendant."

CHAPTER 41

BACK TO MY CASE

My attorney, Barry Portman, called me into his office the next day. Barry was an East Coast guy from Boston. We got along very well, and I trusted him. He knew I was getting fucked over and really wanted to help.

"Well, Sal, you're famous here."

"You heard?"

"An hour after you spit on McKennin, everyone in this building heard."

"Including, Judge Conti, no doubt." I said

"Yes, including Judge Conti. This building is like a small town. There's a lot of gossip and rivalries between departments. Many of the employees have known one another for years. You might keep that in mind the next time you get pissed off." Barry was chuckling while saying this to me. He seemed quite amused. He was about my height, five foot eight, inches tall, with blue eyes, very preppy looking and very smart.

"Listen Sal, what if I could get you a three-year sentence and you do twenty months, would you take a plea?

I didn't need any time to think about it. "In a heartbeat, Barry. Put it in writing and I'll sign it right now."

He said, "I can't get it from Conti in writing. I've been here for fourteen years and Conti became a judge right out of this office. I know him very well and for many years. He has always kept his word."

I said, "I like you Barry and I trust you, but why would Conti want to give me a break? I wouldn't cooperate, I spit on a federal agent, I exposed federal informants, and my cousin is Lucky Luciano. So tell me, why would Conti make a deal like this with me?"

"I can't tell you, but it's for real. I know this sounds strange, Sal, but as much as defendants get pressured to turn on their friends, the moment they do, these feds look down on them. They have the same feelings of contempt for rats as you do. It's probably the reason why all those agents treated you so well after you wouldn't talk. It's not something they typically see around here."

"Sorry, Barry, I can't accept the offer because it just doesn't make any sense.

A month later Barry took another run at me. Again, I turned him down.

Six weeks before my trial he met with me again and said, "We are getting close to trial, Sal. If you lose in front of a jury, you're going to get slammed. I don't want to see that happen and neither does Conti"

"So tell me why he would do this?"

Just when I thought this case couldn't get any more bizarre, he said, "Okay, I will. First of all, Conti hates McKennin and has handled enough of his cases to know he's dirty. Second, he loved it when he heard you spit in McKennin's face. He told me, 'Find out what is the least amount of time I can give him and offer it to him."

I said, "That's it? This is what you couldn't tell me?"

"Well no. Here's what I was reluctant to tell you. Conti is a big fan of your cousin Lucky and all things about the Mafia. After the Godfather movie he became fascinated with the Mafia culture.

He went on, "You're like a celebrity in his court. It's the closest he'll ever come to any Mafia figure." I stood there with my mouth open. I was truly speechless.

"Now do you see why I was so reluctant tell you? Who would believe a story like that?"

"You know, Barry, this story is so outrageous I'm beginning to believe you. No one could or would make something like that up."

"Wait, it gets better. He also wanted to know if it was true that Lucky wore a diamond in his navel."

"How the fuck would I know something like that. Okay, Barry I've heard enough. You got yourself a deal. It's just too far out there to be bullshit. Tell Conti, I have no idea if he had a diamond in his navel, but I seriously doubt it. I can tell him he was a true patriot. He did a lot for the war effort and was rewarded with his freedom.

On my father's visit to see Charlie in 1957, Charlie amusingly told my father that he had made a good deal for himself because he would have done it for nothing had they just asked. He wanted more than anything else to be back in America.

Conti was very cool. He allowed me to stay out of prison until a month after my son Alex was born, which was months away. He also arranged for me to report to the prison on my own, rather than being cuffed and driven by the federal marshals.

Typically before a person is sentenced, friends, family, and business associates are asked to write the judge to tell him how wonderful you are and why he should be lenient. Warner Beckett wrote Conti on formal Sierra Leone stationary telling him how I was going to help Sierra Leone develop their natural resources. Warner was hanging on to me.

CHAPTER 42

PRISON AND AFRICA

I arrived at Boron Federal Prison Camp on October 20, 1985, the day after my 43rd birthday. Boron was a former Air Force base now used as a prison camp. It is located in Death Valley, about 120 miles east of L.A.

There were no fences or walls when I got there, and it housed about 350 prisoners. You could walk away if you wanted to, but no one did because they had less than two years to serve. There were 650 inmates there when I left and fences were built. Business was good.

There was a mix of inmates: drug dealers mostly, Hell's Angels, bank embezzlers, insurance scammers, and tax evaders. The one thing they all had in common was that they were big time players. I learned about a lot of insurance fraud cases. I was told similar stories by a few of the inmates who were there for insurance fraud.

According to them, the FBI worked closely with insurance companies, and when the claims were too high, and they didn't want to pay, the FBI would be called in, and they filed criminal charges against the insured. It was a good source of cases for the FBI, and the insurance companies didn't have to pay the claims.

On my first day, I met Jimmy Caci, Mafia boss of Palm Springs. My name was being announced over the PA system to report to the administration office to complete some paperwork.

Jimmy was in his sixties at the time. He called me over and asked me my first name and where I came from. Jimmy knew Lucky Luciano's real name was Lucania. He said, "Come over and see me after you're through. I'm in barracks seven, room four. It turned out I was assigned to the same barracks just above him on the second floor.

We became very close friends. It was Jimmy who put me together with Eric Weiss after I got out. Eric put up all the money for me to go to Africa. The next major surprise was when I saw John Kingham. He had gotten there a few months before me. Later John was able to get his sentenced reduced because of McKennin's perjury.

He also began an affair with the woman who was teaching pottery at the camp. She, through various connections, got him an early release. John seemed to know how to take care of himself.

Jimmy introduced me to all the "boys" who were doing time there. Many were coming down from longer sentences, ten years or more. They could finish their sentences in camps when they were no longer at risk of escaping. Most of them were at least ten years older than I was.

Again I was surprised with the way I was treated. Because of my cousin Charlie I was treated with respect that bordered on reverence. Even the guards treated me that way. I had no idea why my cousin was such a celebrity and still carried so much weight. After all he had been dead for more than twenty ears. Over the years the press had made him into some kind of hero or movie star.

I've always felt burdened by my name, but this time the name worked in my favor. It got me off the hook with Conti, and now my life in jail was made easier. It was usually in the ordinary citizen's world that it worked against me, but this was the outlaw world. I met very few people I didn't like while in prison. It was not what I expected at all.

There were times I'd be walking around the grounds and hear some inmate call out "Hey Lucky!" to which I would reply looking at where we were, "You call this lucky?"

My room was next to the TV room. In all the time I was there I never watched TV. Every once in a while, I would go and ask them to turn it down. "Miami Vice" was a big show. Half the inmates on the floor watched it religiously.

I walked in one night when they were all cheering the cops on "Miami Vice" about something, and I said, "Do you guys have any idea where you are? Why are you rooting for the cops?"

H. R. Haldeman, Nixon's henchmen did his time there. His job was to manage the sewer system. Given his experience in Washington, I thought it was a job for which he was eminently well qualified.

It took me about three months to adjust to my situation. I was concerned about my wife and newborn son. I felt helpless, I had always been in control of my life, and now I had no control. The real punishment of jail is that they take your life away while you're still alive. You can't do anything. You can't even go buy an ice cream cone.

Everyone has a job in jail. Mine was to keep the education department clean. The law library was located there, and when I was finished working, which took only about two hours, I spent the rest of my time in the law library teaching myself how to draw. Time magazine always had a headshot of some celebrity on the cover, and each week I would draw that celebrity. Even today I sometimes do it.

To draw or paint, you must shift from the left to the right hemisphere of the brain. It's a timeless place where the chattering of the left hemisphere does not exist. I could draw for hours and think it was minutes. It's the same state you go into when you are on a long drive or practicing meditation. It's a hypnotic state, like when you're sleeping but conscious at the same time. You lose your sense of time. I learned how to do time by stepping out of time.

At night I would lie in my bunk and read everything I could get my hands on. I started to relax, and then realized it was the first time in my life I lived without the stress of trying to survive. I had lots of things to worry about, but because there was absolutely nothing I could do about them, I just had to let them go. I had the freedom of my attention, which was a luxury, so I could read without the interruption of my concerns.

I also never had to go to the military, so I looked at my two years in prison, as the two years I supposedly owed the feds. *Better here than Vietnam,* I thought. I made up my mind to meet and find out what the men did that got them in prison and in that process explore the minds and the tactics of the people who put them there, as well as the justice system itself.

I met Cactus Sam, a 75-year-old man who was doing a two-year sentence for stealing cactus from federal land. *How strange,* I thought. I asked Sam why he was stealing cactus and what he did with it.

He said, "Some cactus take hundreds of years to grow to a certain size. That's what makes them so valuable."

"How valuable?"

"It depends on the age, but I was getting $20,000 to $30,000 for something over 150 years old."

"Really, who bought them?"

"Bank of America, Wells Fargo. Companies like that."

"What happen to the banks? That's receiving stolen property."

"Nothing. You can't put a bank in jail. They get fined and keep the cactus."

The camp was a wonderful source of amusement. I walked into the pottery room one day, and the teacher had managed to lock herself out of her file cabinet. She had three guys there trying to open it. She was saying, "What kind of criminals are you guys. You can't even break into a file cabinet. No wonder you're in jail."

One of the guys told her to shut off the light. "I'm used to working in the dark." She did and he opened it.

In prison you are counted every four hours. The afternoon count was at four, and everyone had to be in their rooms. There was a Black staffer named Frank that was always a little drunk and not very bright. There were 400 prisoners in the camp in twelve buildings. Each building was counted and reported. The numbers had to be right before we could go to eat. It usually took twenty minutes, but one afternoon we were waiting an hour and a half. We all thought maybe somebody had escaped.

If you were not in your bunk at the count it meant you were probably in the bathroom. Frank kept going into the bathroom and counting himself when he saw his reflection in the mirror. We weren't one person short. We were one over.

There were about twenty guys from Vegas there. One of them, Ruby Goldstein, was a friend and business associate of Lefty Rosenthal. Rosenthal was the man Robert De Niro played in the movie "Casino." Goldstein and Rosenthal came out of Miami together and wound up in Vegas.

Ruby Goldstein looked and spoke like an actor named Huntz Hall who played a character named Glimpy in the *Dead End Kids* movies that were popular in the forties. After I got out, Jimmy introduced me to the actor Huntz Hall.

Ruby was in his late fifties; six feet, four inches, slender and was doing a two-year sentence for a gambling offense. He had done time twice before on gambling charges.

At dinner one night I asked him, "What are you in for?"

He said, "Gambling"

I laughed out loud and said, "Ruby, how do you get busted for gambling in Las Vegas?"

"It's complicated, but I got lucky. I should have gotten ten years. I was a three-time loser."

"How'd you manage to get away with two years?"

"My lawyer's ability to state the obvious. You see, both times I got arrested and convicted I had the same judge and the same lawyer. The judge was handing out the sentences one at a time to a dozen of my co-defendants.

"My lawyer says to the judge, 'Your Honor, as you know, Mr. Goldstein is at the peak of a mediocre career.' The judge almost fell off his chair. He couldn't stop laughing. That's how I got off light."

One of the best stories I heard was from a Hungarian man named Coco. Coco was in his sixties. He had a slight build, was a little bald, and had a great sense of humor. Coco came from Beverly Hills and apparently had always made a lot of money.

I noticed him for the first time when I saw him push Dutch Shultz, the President of the San Diego chapter of the Hell's Angels, out of the chow line and take his place in the front of the line. It was so outrageously funny that Dutch, who weighed at least twice as much as Coco, started laughing so hard he could hardly breath.

Well, that got my attention. I wanted to know who this guy was and what he was doing here. I caught up to him on one of my walks. "Hi, Coco, my name is..." He interrupted me, I know who you are, Sal. I asked Jimmy about you." Then he shook my hand.

I asked him, "Coco, I'm very curious. What did you get busted for?"

"For selling Paper Mate pens and making more money than Paper Mate could."

"What do you mean?"

"Well, Paper Mate decided it was going to compete with Bic's 19-cent pens. Bic was kicking the shit out of them in the market. Paper Mate pens usually started at a $1.69 and went up from there. They manufactured five million cheap pens and tried to sell them for 29 cents each, but they wouldn't sell, and they couldn't figure out why. Anyway, I bought their entire inventory for two cents a pen and sold them wholesale for 25 cents each. Later the people who bought them from me retailed them for 69 cents each.

Paper Mate couldn't sell them because 29 cents was too cheap for a Paper Mate, so I raised the price. I set up a phone room and sold them by the gross over the phone nationwide."

"You mean nobody got pissed off that they weren't getting what they thought was the traditional Paper Mate?"

"Surprisingly, not that many, but if anybody did, I fully refunded every dime, so there were no complaints."

"So what happened?"

"Paper Mate accused me of fraud. Their problem was they couldn't find anyone to file a complaint because no one lost any money. They were really upset because the reason the pens wouldn't sell was because they were priced too cheap for a Paper Mate, and they were too stupid to figure that out."

"I got convicted on some tax thing, and I got five years. The three executives of Paper Mate were all fired."

CHAPTER 43

VISITS

Boron was 126 miles from L.A. My mother and father had moved there. They spent most of their married life living apart until I brought them out to California. It was a very interesting time for me. My father, who was not around much when I was growing up, came to see me almost every weekend.

He was very upset that I was in prison and blamed himself. Jimmy would time his visits with my father's visits so we could all hang together. Jimmy got out before me, and he and my father started hanging out together. My father got Jimmy signed up for Social Security.

I really loved Jimmy. He was the real thing. Jimmy was about five foot, six inches tall, but from the waist up he could have been six feet, four inches. His hands were huge with thick wrists and fingers. His chest and shoulders were wide and strong. His eyes were blue like my father's. He seemed always to be in good spirits and was always a little mischievous.

Everyone seemed to love Jimmy, even the hacks (prison guards). He was sort of a legend. One day a young biker type stepped in front of Jimmy in the dinner line. Jimmy waited until they got into the dining room and then let him have it. He beat him from one end of the dining room to the other. The security guards took them to the captain's office.

The captain asked the kid, "Why are you picking on this old man?"

The kid objected, "Old man? He damned near killed me." Typically when there was a fight between inmates they would ship both men out to higher security prisons. They shipped the kid out, but not Jimmy.

My wife drove down with my son Alex once a month from San Francisco. She stayed with my parents in L.A., and then drove out to Boron and got a motel so, she could visit both days. I watched my son learn to crawl in a prison visiting room, not my finest hour.

One visit she was breast-feeding, and the hack made her sit in the bathroom alone to feed him for fear someone might see her commit this shameful act. I felt like I was living in the Victorian era.

The place was full of jailhouse religious conversions, thanks to Chuck Colson's Jesus vendors. Colson had initiated an organization of evangelicals with the specific purpose of visiting prisons around the country looking to convert prisoners, a captive audience. Colson was one of Nixon's boys who went to jail for Nixon. I think more people have found God in jail than in any church. It's too bad they couldn't find any morality to go along with it. You got a little better play with the evangelical parole board if you had found Jesus.

Colson and his gang of Jesus vendors were given cart blanche access to the prisons and would corner the inmates at lunch and dinner and lay on their evangelical bullshit sales pitch. They always implied that if you took Jesus into your heart the parole board would look favorably upon you. I truly hated those hucksters.

I started a routine of walking every day. There was a steep hill in the camp, at the top of which sat a huge white golf ball about ten feet in diameter. It housed the radar for Edwards Air Force base thirty-five miles away. The hill was four tenths of a mile up and another four tenths down the other side. I walked up and down and around for ten laps a day every day the entire time I was there. It kept me reasonably sane and made me thirty-five pounds lighter.

One day while on my walk I found myself being trailed by two of Jesus's chosen ones. They were comparing themselves to Jesus's disciples. I couldn't help myself and said, "Jesus and his disciples were all fagots. Why do you think that never had women with them?"

I thought they would kick the shit out of me on the hill. No one would have seen them do it, but no, they were going to tell the warden and get me transferred to another prison. They did tell him, but he did nothing, I was told the warden informed them of the free speech amendment and that ended it.

The prison had a deal with Edwards Air Force and would send forty to fifty inmates to work there every day. The inmates got to leave the prison and would also be paid a few bucks for the day. One day after they got back from work, they were talking about what they saw at the base.

It was budget time, and the way that works in government is that if you didn't spend everything in the budget, the following year you would get less. So the base took dozens of brand new Selectric typewriters still in the box, along with new motorcycles still in the crates and other equipment, and buried them.

They dug a large hole with a bulldozer, dumped the stuff into it, and covered it up. I remember one of the guys commenting, "They call us criminals! They weren't even smart enough to sell the stuff. That's the real crime."

The head of the kitchen was a Black guy they called "Too Tall." I never knew his real name. He was about five feet, seven inches tall. When the tractor-trailers pulled up to unload the food supplies, it went in the front, and the good stuff went right out the back: steaks, pork chops, and more. There was no way to get away with that unless the higher ups were getting their share.

I was going through big changes. I hated the rat Gary Latreall until one day I made up my mind to kill him when I got out. Suddenly, I felt a tremendous relief I didn't understand. It was like the deed was done, and Gary was already dead.

I felt completely different as a man, almost like I had just become a man. My mind became clear and focused. Even my gate was different. That night I had dinner with Jimmy and a couple of other "made men." They were saying things in front of me as if I were one of them even though I wasn't.

Jimmy was telling one of them, "If you've got to take care of him, you owe him the respect of letting him see it's coming. Do you understand?" I wasn't used to conversations like that but given what I had decided to do that day, it didn't seem that out of bounds. During dinner Jimmy asked me a few times, "Are you all right?"

"Yeah, why?

"Oh nothing, just asking."

The next day, coming down from my last lap, I saw Jimmy sitting on the wooden bench at the bottom of the hill. He waived at me to come and sit with him. I was always pleased to be around him. When I was with him, I always walked away knowing more about life and the world around me.

He called me Sally, a name I didn't care for, but he said it so affectionately, I couldn't correct him. Today's conversation was eerie and yet profound in a perverse way.

"Sally, you're going to kill the rat, aren't you?" Jimmy knew something about my case but not much detail. He knew there was a rat I hated, but I couldn't understand how he would know what I had just decided to do.

"What are you talking about, what makes you say that?" I'm smart enough to know, if you are going to do something like that, you tell no one. Ever.

"It's in your eyes Sally. I can see it in your eyes. The look in your eyes is what makes me say what I'm saying. I've seen it before, and I've been there before - a few times."

Here's what sounded perverse to me. "You know Sally, you can't really understand what your life means until you are capable of taking someone else's life. If you're going to take someone's life you must also be willing to give up yours." Jimmy had his own views on killing.

He continued, "The government doesn't have a moral problem with killing anyone. If it did you wouldn't have capital punishment. The problem is they think they're the only ones who get to decide who lives and who dies. They think because it's legal it's also moral?"

I asked him, "Do you think it's wrong to kill?"

"Of course not. Right and wrong has nothing to do with it. Death is part of life no matter how it happens. When you decided to kill him, did you ask yourself if it was right or wrong to kill?"

"No I didn't, I only felt he didn't deserve to be alive anymore"

"So right or wrong, you've made that decision and now there is nothing stopping you from doing it. Except I'm asking you not to do it."

"Why?"

"Because you have a young wife and son, that's why. Just because he has it coming, it doesn't mean you get a pass. If you get caught, what happens to your wife and your boy? Besides, it's not justice. He didn't kill anyone."

"Justice!!! You've got to be kidding me. Are you saying I'm wrong to kill him?"

"No, I'm not. I told you right and wrong has nothing to do with it. I'm talking about justice. Killing someone like him is an act of mercy. Are you feeling merciful?"

"What?!!!!

"You don't want him dead, Sally. You want him wishing he was dead every day of his miserable fuckin' life. In a wheelchair, his tongue hanging out of the side of his mouth, with no one to care for him or about him. That's justice. What your talking about is giving him a pass for the pain and misery he caused you and many others. Do you get what I'm telling you?"

"Yes, I do and you're right, Jimmy. I just never looked at it that way." I was so touched by his warmth and concern I almost started to cry.

He said, "I want you to do something for me. I want you to forego this matter and leave it to me. Will you do that for me?"

"Yes, of course." I gave Jimmy all the information I had on Gary. Jimmy got out eight months before me and sent word back to me that he found out that Gary was working at the Palm Springs airport near where Jimmy lived. It was the last I heard about the matter. As much as I wanted to know what happen to Gary, I knew better than to ask. I just assumed Jimmy took care of it.

I found out much later on that Owen Stevenson bilked some woman for a few hundred thousand, then set her up and got her busted. Instead of calling her lawyer, she picked up the phone and called Edwin Meese, the Attorney General of the United States, and was immediately put through to him. I never heard what happened to Stevenson, but I'm sure his career was over.

Those three years, the bust, prison, and everything that went along with it changed my whole life forever. I knew without any doubt that I was capable of taking another's life, if I had to. It gave me an odd sense of power and fear.

My fear was that I never wanted to find myself in a position where I had to kill anyone because I knew I could and would if I had to. Jimmy made me realize what a real man was about. I no longer felt a need to prove anything to anyone.

Men like Jimmy with real power over life and death never show it. Jimmy was kind, gentle, caring, and just. He had a high regard for women, loved to have fun and play with kids. He could draw all the Disney characters perfectly from his head. In many ways he was a kid himself. I loved him, and I still miss him.

A couple of days before I was released, my wife told me McKennin had called her. He told her there was no way I was going to walk with a two-year sentence and that he was coming after me. He also wanted her to pick up my stuff that was left over from the bust.

I told her not to go there and tell him to mail whatever he had. A couple of days later an envelope arrived with a rolled up five-dollar bill. You know, the kind you use to snort coke with. I knew McKennin was going to go for me big time.

Penny was living with her mother, which was my new address. I still had six months to do in a halfway house. My first day home, the IRS showed up. They certainly didn't waste any time. The agent was a Black man. He spent about three hours with me and was surprisingly nice to me.

Two and half of those hours he spent asking me what it was like in federal prison. I said to him at the end of the meeting, "You know this wasn't what I expected."

He said something to me, I think only a Black man could have said, "Sal, if I had found a new Benz in the driveway in front of a million dollar home that you owned, we would have had a different conversation. You have nothing but your dignity, and I have no interest in taking that from you." I'm sure, as a Black man, he understood that.

"Well happens now?" I asked him.

"I'm going to put you into my computer, and the first time you make more than eighteen thousand a year, I'll come back and set up a payment plan."

"That's it?"

"Yeah that's it." He shook my hand and wished me the best of luck and meant it.

Given what my life looked like at that moment, Warner Beckett's offer of Africa was looking like a good idea. I knew the only way to beat McKennin was to be completely out of his reach. I thought moving to the other side of the world would do the trick.

I couldn't leave the country for another year. I still had a year of parole to do. I spent a lot of time with Warner Beckett going through the possible African investments. In the end I had only one question for Beckett, and I wasn't going anywhere until he could answer me, and it made sense to me.

I asked him, "Warner, with all those opportunities there, why isn't money pouring into that country?"

"It is," He said. "The Koreans are there in the shrimp industry and so are the Chinese, Japanese, Germans, and Nigerians."

"Yes, but why aren't the American companies there? I'm not going for the deal, Warner, unless I know why." I had a check from Eric Weiss for a $150,000 in my pocket. We were down to the wire. I was prepared to close the deal at that meeting, but my question still wasn't answered.

I pulled the check out of my pocket, showed it to him and said, "I'm here to make this deal, Warner. The check is made out to your company as you can see, but you still haven't answered my question. I'm not going to give it to you and go to Africa unless you tell me why the Americans haven't jumped on this."

Warner went into a small safe and pulled out a couple of documents and said, "I'm going to show you why. I won't give you copies or ever admit I have them" Then handed them to me. They were official looking CIA reports written to the White House during the Carter administration.

According to the reports, the CIA did not want Sierra Leone and other African countries to have strong economies. They feared if those countries had strong economies they would fund Black political power groups in the United States. I found it hard to believe, but it did answer my question.

CHAPTER 44

WELCOME TO A DIFFERENT WORLD

Sierra Leone was a trip back in time in many ways. I found the people very warm and friendly. There was no violent crime. Most crimes were petty crimes: stealing food, shoes, clothes, VCR tapes. Those crimes were handled by the citizens themselves, usually by slapping (not punching) the criminal publicly and humiliating him.

I got to know a lot of officials, and when I would walk with them, they would hold my hand like girlfriends sometimes do. I walked that way with ministers and bank presidents. Apologies are made by lying flat on the ground face down with one hand placed on the foot of the offended party. It was hard for me to get used to those customs.

When I arrived, Warner's son Billy Beckett, Jamal Kunzi, and Solo Thomas came to pick me up. They were all wearing sweaters or jackets, which I thought was strange since we were six degrees from the equator.

Jamal said, "Wait until you acclimatize. You'll be wearing sweaters too, and he was right. They drove me to the house I rented, three floors, forty-five hundred square feet, made of concrete. Inside, the ceilings, doors, and trim were all done in dark hardwood. The main floor walls were also done in beautiful wood.

The rent was $15,000 year. Warner said no one would do business with us unless we had a permanent residence. I had a bobo (house boy), cook, and driver, which cost me $120 a month. It came to three times that amount because I fed everyone and was taking care of their medicine, shoes, family needs, and more.

It was truly a different part of the world, and I could literally feel it. The air smelled different, and the water in the toilet whirlpooled down in the opposite direction.

None of the natives really made any money. People were hungry and living day to day. Natives typically ate once a day, usually fish, rice in a cassava leaf stew or soup with tomato paste. It cost about $13 for a 100-kilo sack of rice, which could feed a family of four for a month. The cop on the beat there made $9 a month and hadn't been paid in seven months.

Government employees made little more than the police. As a consequence, you had to pay for all their services. Jamal, my right-hand guy, whose job it was to watch my back, got me an international driver's license for $2.75, and I didn't even have to show up. On weekends the police blocked the only road to the beach. They would stop anyone they thought had a little money. I typically gave them a few Leones (25 cents) and they were happy to get it.

My house was high enough on the mountain to see the ocean, which was less than a half a mile away. "Sierra Leone" is Portuguese for Mountain of Lions. Viewed from the bay the mountain looks like two lions lying next to one another. Every night the sun would go down at 7 p.m. The fishermen used large nets to pull in their catch by hand. They didn't sell their catch by weight. I could buy three large fish weighing five or six pounds for $2.

The beaches were beautiful white sand that went on for fifteen miles. The waters were pristine. There was no industry to pollute them. I noticed I had gotten incredibly calm. All the stress I usually carried in my head and heart stopped. The psychological stuff just disappeared. Then I realized what was going on. I wrote to my wife, "I can't tell you what a relief it is to be free from the electronic psyche of America.

There were few phones in the country and no broadcast TV. The ones that could afford TV watched DVD's. To call outside the country, most people had to go to the phone company and wait in lines for hours to use a phone for fifteen minutes, and it cost $20. There were only two lines going to the states.

Solo Thomas, one of my new partners, had a complete inventory of natural resources to explore: forestry, fishing, gold and diamond mining. The Japanese and Koreans had large industrial fishing ships. They had floating factories that fished illegally a few miles offshore. The government lacked the resources to buy boats to police them.

We lacked the kind of money to get involved with timber or fishing fleets. Solo suggested we mine diamonds to build up capital. I said, "Even that will take large amounts of capital for mining equipment, and it would be labor intensive, not to mention we have no I idea what we are doing."

In the meantime, Billy Beckett was getting my money sent to him by his father and buying raw diamond stones. They looked like the bottom of a broken Coca-Cola bottle. He was marketing the stones by motorcycling through the jungles into Liberia and then to Belgium. I knew what he was doing but could do nothing about it. I had to stop the money at the source, in the states.

One way to get the stones was with boats and vacuum equipment, and Solo suggested we do that. He explained, "If we mine the river, we'll need a boat, which we can rent and commercial vacuum equipment. We'll need a place and about ten men to sift through the dirt and sort out the stones."

To get manpower, Solo took me to a small tribal village of about 300 or 400 people. When we got there the chief was marrying a 14-year-old girl. He was 64. To celebrate the marriage, they were killing a cow and distributing its parts.

The village survived by fishing shrimp. They had about six dugout boats and drop nets. None of the fishermen could swim. To help them out and to make an arrangement for manpower from the village, I got word back to my partner in Phoenix to send me three small outboard motors, fish finder scopes to see where the shrimp were, and half dozen life jackets. With this equipment, the village shrimp catch went up seven hundred percent.

But before we could start mining diamonds, I had to get back to the states to straighten out Beckett because my money was going around me rather than through me.

I made my reservation and was going to leave in a couple of days. Wanza, my Lebanese business friend, had a few sons I became friends with. They believed in voodoo magic, as did my wife. On the day I was supposed to leave, they insisted I visit a shaman to put a spell on Warner before I left. We traveled a couple of hours on what you might call a road. I didn't believe in voodoo, but I liked the idea of ceremony before you go to war.

We got to a little village where the houses were made of mud and the floors were made of cow dung. Inside, a little man was wearing only a short leather skirt. He had beads and various neckpieces around his neck and a band around his head with feathers hanging from it. Through interpreters, he asked me to write on a piece of paper the name of my adversary and the name of the town where he lived, He then asked me to pay him to twenty dollars for the spell he would cast.

He then proceeded to dance around pointing a decorated stick toward the United States. He even had gun power, which he lit at the end of the ceremony. He guaranteed me that Warner would be dead. He told me it would take two days before the voodoo would kill him, because he was so far away.

The deed was done, and I still had a ferry and plane to catch. It was getting late, and I was worried I was going to miss the flight. There were two ways to get to the airport, ferry or helicopter. The Wanzas said I could take the helicopter if I was worried about missing the flight. The helicopters were notorious for having problems. They were badly maintained even when parts were available.

I was going to take the helicopter because time was getting very short. I didn't want to miss the flight, which was going to take twenty-five hours with the various layovers. I was about to board the helicopter when I got this sinking feeling in my stomach. I turned around and took the ferry instead. The helicopter went down shortly after it took off.

I had made arrangements to have Warner meet my partner Ron from Phoenix at Erick's house in Palace Verde, California. Ron was supposedly coming with $500,000 to buy the entire inventory from Warner. I landed in L.A., so before the meeting with Warner, which was the following day, I called Jimmy Caci and met with him in Palm Springs. I told him that Erik was double-crossing us and was making money around me with Warner and I was out of the loop.

Jimmy called Erik and had him come to a cocktail lounge in Palm Springs. Erik had no idea I would be there. When he walked over to Jimmy's table, he didn't recognize me.

I had contracted Draunculiasis, better known as Guinea Worm, a parasite that takes weeks if not months to work its way through the body exiting through the calves of the leg. I had already gotten malaria twice and had lost a lot of weight. With the guinea worm, I had lost even more weight. When Erick saw me he said, "Holy shit! What happen to you?"

Jimmy said, "Never mind that right now. What the fuck are you up to? You and that nigger have been fucking us; you sent Sal's wife and kid there without telling him?"

"No, Jimmy I swear. Warner told me Sal wanted them to go." One thing Jimmy knew for sure, I would never lie to him. So he knew on the spot that Erick was lying. Without another word, Jimmy backhanded him right off the chair.

"Jimmy, I swear this is all a misunderstanding," said Erick.

Jimmy responded, "You better do whatever Sal says to straighten this out or so help me God, I'll put you in a hole in the ground in that desert." Erick knew Jimmy meant it, and he was scared shitless.

"Sal, please tell me what I need to do to make this right. Warner told me you were going your own way. I had no way of reaching you. God, you look terrible. Let me get you some antibiotics before we do anything else.

Erick was a pharmacist, so we drove to a pharmacy he knew. Erick once had seven pharmacies and lost them all when he got busted. He got me five of the strongest antibiotics he could give me without putting me on an IV.

"This should do it," he assured me. "You're lucky you're alive."

So are you, Erick," I returned. He couldn't look at me.

"What do you want me to do, Sal? I'll do anything to make this right with you and Jimmy."

"I want fifty grand, and I want it now."

We went straight to his bank, and I had it in an hour. Then I told him my plan to get Beckett to come to his house to meet my partner Ron, who was supposed to have $500,000 in cash with him to buy all the stones Beckett had.

Erick asked, "Then what?"

"Then he's out," I said.

"Sal, I've got a ton of money in this deal. What's going to happen if you cut him out of it?"

"Nothing. I don't need him. I have all the contacts I need over there. What I don't have is the $150,000 I gave him when we cut the deal. The $50,000 you just gave me will kick start what I want to do, but I will probably need another couple of hundred grand."

"Okay, but what about Billy? Aren't you worried about him?"

"Billy is finished in that country." I didn't want to tell Erick about my contacts in the government. I didn't trust him anymore.

I slept at Erick's house in Pacific Palisades that night. Beckett was coming the next morning. Erick's house had three floors facing the ocean. He and I were downstairs when the front doorbell rang. Erick ran up to answer it then came down to tell me that Beckett had sent his two kids. By "kids" I mean 40-year-olds who were running his company.

I hobbled upstairs, barely able to walk. The antibiotics were draining the life out of me. When I got on the main floor, his kids were sitting at a table. I walked over to them, but they didn't recognize me until I spoke to them. I sat down and said, "What's the matter? Don't you recognize me, or didn't you think you would ever see me again?"

Beckett's daughter kept her cool, but her brother was a nervous wreck.

I said, "Where's your father?"

"He wasn't feeling well, so he sent us."

"To do what? What are you doing here? Did you bring the inventory your father has been stealing?"

"I don't know anything about any inventory," his daughter said.

"Then, why are you're here?" She was straight up lying to me.

"To meet someone named Ron, a possible investor."

I didn't see any point in dancing around with her. "You know, if your father was here and instead of you and came empty handed, like you just did, he'd be in a dumpster. What did you think was going to happen? Did you expect me to crawl under a rock somewhere and die?"

"I don't know what you're talking about, Sal?"

"You know damned well what I'm talking about. Don't play stupid with me."

Her brother was freaking out. He kept saying, "I want to go right now."

I saw no point in continuing the conversation. "You tell your father I'm coming to get my inventory tomorrow, and he better have it. Then I said to Erick, "Get them the fuck out of here." I was furious.

When Becket's kids told him what they walked into, he had a massive heart attack. He wound up in a wheelchair paralyzed, unable to speak for the rest of his life. I thought maybe there was something to this voodoo stuff.

I went to see my partner Ron, in Tempe, Arizona, where he lived. He took me to meet some Vietnam veterans who were diamond cutters he trusted. I made arrangements with them to do the cutting for us, in anticipation of sending back stones when I got back to Sierra Leone.

I also made arrangements for Ron to send the $50,000 I got from Erick to my account at Barclays Bank in London. It was a backup plan in case the things got really fucked up with Beckett. I told Solo to set up a deal to buy diamonds for when I got back.

I stopped in London, for a couple of days. I wanted to pick up the cash Ron transferred to my account. I went to Barclay's Bank on Fleet Street to arrange for the cash. First of all, I went to the wrong offices. I went to Barclays' headquarters.

I was staying at Freddie Shears' London residence. Freddie was the treasurer of the only political party in Sierra Leone. He was the one lamenting that his first wife left him.

London, of course, was cold, and I was freezing. Freddie's son loaned me his black leather jacket, black sweater, and a black knitted hat. I met with two officers of the bank. London bankers are nothing like American bankers. They wore pin striped suits and had a condescending attitude. I assume they didn't like my banking attire. They asked me who I was and what business I had in Sierra Leone. Mind you, I had an account at Barclays in Sierra Leone.

They asked me, "Why do you want $50,000 in cash?"

After all the shit I just went through, I was in no mood for these assholes. I said, "In America when someone deposits $50,000 in a bank, they are welcomed, not interrogated."

"Yes, but you are not in America. Asking for $50,000 in cash is not a typical request. We would like to understand your request."

"Okay, if you transfer the cash to Sierra Leone, I will lose 50 percent of its value when it's changed to Leones, a worthless currency as I'm sure you know. You've already charged me to convert my dollars in to pounds."

Then I asked them, "Are you telling me you will not give me my money if you don't approve of my answer? You know, where I come from, they call that stealing."

They bristled at my comment.

I continued, "I want my money, or I'll have my barrister Albert Metzger deal with you guys."

"You have a barrister?"

"Yes, his name is Albert Metzger. He represents my company in Sierra Leone. Albert's son is also a barrister and is located just down the street. Albert told me if I had any problems to call his son. Shall I call him and let him explain why you should give me what belongs to me?"

Their attitude changed. They told me it would take three days to arrange the transaction and it would cost me 8 percent.

I said, "Eight percent? Not a chance in hell. That's stealing, and I'm not paying it. You can send the fucking money back. I'll have Metzger deal with your superiors. It's no wonder you guys lost your empire. You're just a bunch of thieves." They were the perfect example of the criminal class.

That did it. They changed their mind, but instead of giving me my money they gave me the name of women at one of their branches and said she would handle the transaction.

They were charging me for converting my dollars to pounds, then pounds back to dollars and again for giving me cash. I finally got it done for 2 percent.

When I got back to Sierra Leone, I wrote to the bank President and told him how I was treated. His response was to close all my accounts without explanation.

Later, close to New Years, I was in Palm Springs with Jimmy. He asked me what I was doing for the holidays. I had no plans. I didn't even realize it was close to any holidays.

Jimmy said, "Why don't you stay with me? My brother Bobby and Keely Smith are playing in town. Jimmy's brother was a musician. He called himself Bobby Milanno after Peter Milanno his godfather and the Las Vegas Mafia boss.

Bobby and Keely Smith had become a team. They traveled all over the country in one of those customized coaches they owned. Keely had been with Louie Prima for years. Together they became a very well known singing team in the fifties. Keely was still well-known so they were able to make a pretty good living playing the clubs around the country and the lounges in Vegas.

I told Jimmy, "I want to get back to Sierra Leone and straighten out that prick Billy Beckett."

"Forget it, Sal, by the time you get back there he'll be gone. Take a break. You need to get better. You don't look too good." He was right. I didn't feel well at all. The antibiotics were kicking my ass. Erick had told me I would start to feel better in four or five days, so I decided to stay. It had been a year since I had been in civilization, and I felt very disoriented.

Jimmy had been separated from his wife for eighteen years. Neither believed in divorce, so they never got one. Jimmy was dating Connie Stevens for a long time. Women loved him. He was a legend in his own time. I felt bad for Jimmy. He was never going to make the money he used to make. His time had passed. His era was gone forever.

I had dinner with Jimmy, his wife, Keely Smith, and Bobby Milanno at Keely's house that night. I gave Jimmy five grand out of the money Erick had given me. He didn't want to take it, but I knew he needed it. I certainly knew he deserved it after all he had done for me.

I accepted Jimmy's invitation and went to the supper club. There was a table set for ten. A couple of Jimmy's friends were there and brought their daughters with them. Jimmy's son and his wife were there along with Jimmy and me. About an hour after we arrived, Liza Minnelli joined us. She sat next to me. She was a little bit of a thing, I don't think she was five foot tall. She was very friendly and asked me to dance.

She said, "Jimmy told me you just got back from Africa. What were you doing there, or shouldn't I ask?

"No, not at all," I said. "I'm starting a mining business. I came home to take care of some business and to visit Jimmy for the holidays."

"That's great. He was very excited you were here. He called me and told me he wanted me to meet you."

"Really! Well, I'm honored. I had no idea." I guess Jimmy thought I would feel uncomfortable without a "date." I wish he had told me.

We sat together and had a really nice time. She wanted to know all about Sierra Leone, the weather, the people, and more. She was her mother's daughter in many ways, but she identified with being Italian.

"How do you know Jimmy?" I asked her.

"I've known Jimmy since I was a little girl. He was a friend of my family. You know, I saw the picture you did of Frank Sinatra. it's very good and Jimmy is very proud of it. Are you an artist?"

"No, I'm not."

"Where did you learn to draw like that?" I was reluctant to tell her, but then I thought, *Why not?* It's not likely I would ever see her again.

"I learned to draw in prison, which is where I met Jimmy. I drew the picture of Frank that you saw, and he loved it. He got out months before me, but the prison wouldn't let him take it with him. So I mailed it to him. A couple of months later he wanted me to draw another one for Jilly."

One day Jilly, Frank Sinatra's right-hand man, stopped by Jimmy's house where he saw the picture and wanted it to give to Frank, but Jimmy wouldn't give it to him. Jilly kept busting Jimmy's balls about it, so Jimmy said he would ask me to do another one for him, and he would give his to Jilly. I couldn't figure out why Jilly thought Frank would want a picture of himself, but it was probably Jilly that wanted it.

I told Jimmy I would do another one and then asked him if he could arrange for my father to meet Frank over a drink or something, and my father could give Frank the picture personally as a gift. I knew my father would be thrilled to meet Frank. Who wouldn't be? It took Jilly months to arrange it. About ten days before they were to meet, my father died in his sleep.

When I explained all this to Liza she said, "Oh, Sal, that's so sad."

"Yeah I know, but life seems to have its own agenda doesn't it? I wanted so much to do that for him."

I stayed at Jimmy's house for another week. I was feeling a lot better. I got up one morning and Jimmy said to me, "Come on we're going to L.A. I have a surprise for you."

"What's the surprise?"

"If I tell you it won't be a surprise, right?"

He took me to the Ivy, one of my favorite restaurants in L.A. There was an old man waiting at a table for us. Then Jimmy introduced me, "Sal, I'd like you to meet Huntz Hall of the *Dead End Kids.*"

I couldn't believe it. I didn't think he was even alive anymore. It was a wonderful day, and it pulled me out of all the shit I was dealing with. I told Huntz the story about Ruby Goldstein. He got a big kick out of it. I didn't learn what he was doing for a living, but he said he said he hadn't made a movie in thirty years.

"Thanks Jimmy, it was a great surprise, and I'll never forget it. Inviting Liza was a big surprise too it made my night. Listen, Jimmy, it's time for me to head back. There's nothing more I can do here, and Penny wasn't feeling well when I left. Who knows what I'll find when I get back. Now it's time to make us some money. Hang on to Erick in case we need more money."

"Don't worry about him. He belongs to us now. Sally, are you sure you'll be okay?" Jimmy looked a little worried.

"I'll be fine, Jimmy, after all I made it out of Harlem." Jimmy laughed. He drove me to the L.A airport a couple of days later.

Before I had left for the States, I had asked Solo Thomas to arrange a meeting with Boaz for me if he could. I wanted to see if his cutters would cut some of my stones there, so I could take them straight to Belgium for fast cash. I also wanted to tell him about my meeting with President Momoh.

Solo and my wife Penny picked me up at the airport. "How did it go, Sal?" I told her what happen to Warner Becket and then said, "Remind me to send the shaman a couple of extra bucks.

"You see, I told you juju works," she said.

I asked her, "How are you feeling?"

"I'm pregnant, that's why I've been sick." I thought, *Great, I wonder what other surprises I have in store for me?*

"You can't stay here, Penny," I told her. "It's too dangerous."

"Yes, I know, I want to leave as soon as possible. How do you feel about it?

"About the baby or about you leaving?"

"Both"

"I'm fine about the baby, but I'll miss you. You've been great, Penny. You have more guts than any of the clowns I've been dealing with. Don't waste any time, Honey, make the reservations and go."

Our son Alex, had gotten Malaria the month before. It would not be good if Penny got it while she was pregnant.

I turned to Solo and asked, "What's going on here? Have you seen or heard from Billy?

"No, but Jamal is contacting his mother-in-law and the rest of the guys that work for him. We should know something soon."

I gave Solo the cash and had him make the diamond buy. The next day, I got a hold of Ron and told him to come in and pick up the parcel of diamonds that Solo had bought and take to the United States. I wanted Penny to wait for Ron, so they could go back to the states together. Ron arrived a few days later.

I was feeling uneasy about a lot of things, especially Ron's quick turnaround. The States were cracking down on drugs, and I didn't want the feds falling on the stones. Even though they were not illegal, they could still be seized. I felt certain Ron would be searched.

Penny said, "Why don't you give me the stones, and I will land in Chicago, then take a flight to L.A. They won't know I was in Africa."

"That's a great idea, Baby."

Ron was searched in L.A. but Penney put the stones in a rubber and stuffed them up her vagina. It's not illegal to bring diamonds into the United States and there are no tariffs for uncut stones should they find them, so I knew she'd be all right. Penny would make a perfect outlaw. She was a cool partner to have.

After Penny and Ron left, Solo and I went to the office of Boaz, the Israeli. He was out of town, but the Frenchman agreed to meet with me. I started to pitch him when he interrupted me and said, "Mr. Boaz is no longer part of this company. I have diversified my interest, and am no longer in the diamond business."

I don't know if that was true or not, but the Frenchman seemed really pissed about something. It could have just been a way of solving the Lebanese concern about Boaz. Whatever it was it didn't concern me. I had enough on my plate.

Back at my house I asked Jamal, "Where's Billy?

He said, "He's back in the States. Interpol has been looking for him all over Freetown, and his father had heart attack."

"Yeah I heard," I later told Jamal what had happened to Beckett. Next I met with the Wanzas. I told them that, according to his French partner, Boaz was no longer in the deal or in the country. They would know very quickly if that were true or not. Then I met with Albert Metzger and told him what Boaz's partner had told me.

"He's out, Albert," I said. "I don't have any details, but you'll probably know soon enough. As you know, I've been out of the country. I told the Wanzas that Boaz is out, and he should no longer be a concern for them.

"Tell the President I relayed all of this to the Wanzas, and they seemed satisfied. Please thank Momoh for protecting my family."

"I will, Sal, and thank you very much for your help. If there is anything we can do for you don't hesitate to call me."

"I won't Albert. It's been an adventure knowing you." That night I had dinner with Solo and Jamal. I said good-bye to them and promised Jamal I would try to get him into the U.S. I did get him letters for employment but then lost contact with him.

CHAPTER 45

COMING HOME

I got back to the States broke. I went to see my old partner Ross from the windmill business to see what he was up to and borrow a few thousand dollars. He gave me $3,000 in cash. I told him I wanted to get into the pot business, which I had decided to do when I was in prison and asked him if he had any connections.

Ross asked, "Why the pot business?"

"Because I think there is a lot of money to be made and not a lot of legal risk connected with it. The government's war on drugs is focused on cocaine, heroin, and meth because they are harmful."

Pot falls into the category of victimless crimes, like prostitution and gambling. My cousin Charlie "Lucky" really understood that. In his day, it was alcohol prohibition. He was the pot dealer of his day. He gave people what they wanted and made them complicit.

All criminal laws are based on the idea of protecting the victims, but who is the victim if a person wants to place a bet or wants to get laid or have a drink?

You'll notice that it's the prostitute who gets busted, not the John; likewise, it's the bookie who gets busted, not the person who places the bet. It's the same with pot. You don't usually get busted for smoking pot, only for selling it. These so-called crimes are very hard to get the public behind them because people want the freedom to enjoy them. In time all those "crimes" will be legal. In the meantime, there's a lot of money to be made.

Ross said, "Well, you're in luck because I'm already in the pot business."

"No shit!"

"Yeah I'm a grower," he said.

In prison I had made connections with buyers but not sources, so this was a perfect fit. Ross and I became partners. He taught me how to grow pot indoors, which was not a common way to do it at the time. I spent the next twenty years in the business. Those years could easily make another book, but the thought of writing another book immediately puts me into a complete depression.

Many years ago I asked my father why he went to see his cousin Charlie Lucky Luciano in 1957. During my conversation with my father, he told me if I ever had the opportunity to clear up a lot of things that have been said about Charlie and about our family to do it. I said I would, but at the time I couldn't imagine having such an opportunity, but here I am. This next chapter covers what my father told me. Please bear with me for some of the redundancies you have read in previous chapters. This is the last chapter.

CHAPTER 46

THE KENNEDY CONNECTION AND WORLD WAR II

Sal's father,
Carl Lucania

Sal's cousin
Lucky Luciano

In 1957, my father made a trip Italy to see his cousin Charlie (Lucky) Luciano. He went at the request of Frank Costello because of an assassination attempt on Frank's life. Frank wanted to retire and live in peace. As Charlie's prime minister he oversaw all of Charlie's business affairs in the United States. I was fourteen at the time and knew nothing about the nature of the trip, or who sent him.

I did know that because of a rift between my father and Big John, my father's boss and cousin by marriage, he no longer worked for the "number" business. He always felt

Charlie could straighten out the problem if he could talk to him in person.

Vito Genovese was Big John's boss and Charlie's underboss or CEO, if you will. Frank Costello oversaw the "Family" for Charlie in his absence. As Charlie's "Prime Minister" he also functioned as "Chairmen of Board" for all the Families in the U.S. My father agreed to make the trip and use the opportunity to talk to Charlie on his own behalf.

My father was called Carl for Carmelo within the family, but he was known as Charlie in the neighborhood for some reason. I suspect it was some form of acknowledgement of his relationship to Charlie Luciano

He was not, as far as I know, a formal "member" of the so-called Mafia and even if he were, he would never tell me. Then again those were the days when there was no such thing as a Mafia or "organized crime" although that was about to change.

I personally believe he wasn't a "member" for a number of reasons. I felt he was too gentle of a man and lacked the kind of make-up that would allow him to hurt anyone. He was a kind, conciliatory man by nature. He was well liked and trusted, so much so that whenever there were problems in the neighborhood, people went to him to help resolve them.

He was known for giving unbiased advice. He never accepted or received any compensation. It drove my mother crazy. She would berate him for not charging or accepting money for his services even when it was offered.

She never understood that not accepting money was the very reason he was so trusted. Why did he do it? He enjoyed helping people. It made him feel good about himself. It gave him a sense of importance, and for the many people he did help, he was important.

The year 1957 also gave way to a series of events that resulted in a profound change in the political landscape of America. It began when Frank Costello, known as the Prime

Minister because he ran things for Charlie Lucky after he was deported in 1946, Frank became the victim of an attempted assassination ordered by Vito Genovese. The seeds for this event were planted in the twenties, thirties and forties.

Genovese had been one of Charlie's lieutenants since the twenties. Charlie had long ago made the drug business off limits to his nationwide organization, or "The Combination" as Charlie liked to call it. The penalty for anyone caught dealing drugs was death.

Around 1936, New York District Attorney Thomas Dewey wanted to run for governor, so he went after the Jewish gangster, Dutch Shultz, whose real name was Arthur Flegenheimer. Dutch was a bootlegger and was involved in a violent attempt to take over of the numbers business in Black West Harlem.

Dewey was going after Dutch not so much for the illegal numbers business but for the violence Dutch was using to take over. It was hurting Dewey's reputation as a crime fighter, so putting Dutch away was good for his political career.

Charlie found out Dutch was planning to kill Dewey and warned him against it. One of Charlie's most important rules was never to hurt citizens, meaning anyone who was not a "Member." In those days the so-called Mafia in large part was involved in victimless crimes, namely gambling, booze, and loan sharking. That's where they made most of their money. They were the pot dealers of their day. Almost everything those big-time gangsters did back then is legal today.

Shultz warned Charlie, "If we don't stop him, you'll be next, Charlie. Mark my words."

Charlie had Shultz killed before he could kill Dewey, effectively saving Dewey's life. Dewey then went after Charlie just as Shultz had predicted,

In 1937 Charlie started serving a fifty-year sentence for what was essentially "pimping," of all things, a crime that would have gotten a real pimp a fine or a couple of months in jail. However, Charlie spent only about nine years in prison before he was released and deported after World War II because of his contribution to America's war effort. At about the same time, Vito Genovese was indicted for murder but fled to Italy rather than stand trial.

By 1956 Vito and his lieutenant Big John Ormento were already in the heroin business. Their base of operation was the now famous Rao's restaurant on 114th Street in East Harlem. The infamous "French Connection" was just one of their suppliers.

Vito wanted to lift the ban on the heroin business that Charlie had imposed. He wanted to expand the business nationwide and control the entire importation. To do that Vito would have to take over the "Luciano" family and declare himself the head of the family and the new "Chairman of the Board," which necessarily meant the elimination of Frank Costello, Charlie's acting boss.

According to Charlie's own memoir, he told Vito, "I don't want you in that junk (heroin) business." Charlie always saw the drug business as very dangerous. He made his money in the booze business with Joe Kennedy and in the gambling business with Meyer Lansky, Frank Costello, and Benny (Bugsy) Segal.

Vito sent Chin Gigante to kill Frank Costello. Chin shot Frank outside of Frank's hotel but only grazed his head.

After the failed hit Frank decided to retire rather than have an all-out war with Vito. Frank needed to talk to Charlie first but could not leave the country to see Charlie, himself, nor could he just retire without talking to Charlie. It was this situation I later found out that led to my father's trip to Italy in 1957.

Occasionally, my father and I would meet at Rao's for dinner and a few drinks. It was a summer night in the early 1960's, I believe, that we had this remarkable conversation.

After dinner, my father who rarely got drunk started slamming down shots of scotch and was getting pretty bombed. Oddly enough he rarely spoke to me about things connected to his world; it was almost as if he didn't want me to know they existed.

Of course by that time he knew about my bootleg perfume business and that I had knocked off Big John's crap game. I was 22 or 23 years old then and had three children of my own, hardly an innocent boy anymore.

We spent hours talking that night, which had never happened before. I was always curious about his trip to see Charlie (Lucky) but would never ask him about it. I was also interested in knowing what Charlie was like.

So, when we were both drunk enough, I said, "Dad, tell me about the trip you made to see Charlie. I know you wanted to see him for personal reasons, but I remember you were asked to go. Who sent you? Why you and what happened?"

My father was a little surprised by my directness; he didn't answer me right away. Then, he looked at me with his soft blue eyes and said, "Do you remember when someone tried to kill Frank (Costello) and missed?"

"Yeah, the bullet grazed his head, and the shooter was close enough to hit him with the barrel of the gun." I laughed

"Yeah, that's because he was supposed to miss."

"What do you mean he was supposed to miss?"

"It was a message to Frank from Vito. Vito wanted Frank out of the way, so he could take over Charlie's operations, so he sent Chin (Gigante) to deliver the message. Believe me Chin wouldn't have missed. If Frank was supposed to die, he'd be dead."

"That doesn't make sense. If Vito wanted Frank out of the way, why would he let Frank live?"

"Because he really had no choice. Vito knew the rules about killing any "made man" without permission, let alone a boss. To kill the boss of a family is an automatic death sentence.

"When Charlie created The Commission, the first order of business was the rule about killing a boss: If you kill a boss you can't be a boss.

"Vito would need an okay from all the bosses nationwide to kill Frank. Without it he would be a dead man, but he didn't have the authority to call a meeting like that. Only a boss could do that.

"He also knew he would never get permission. Charlie had a lot of loyal friends that he made rich. So if Frank stepped aside, Vito, as underboss of Charlie's New York Family, would be next in line, at least temporally. Then he'd have the authority to call a nationwide meeting of all the bosses, but to get himself confirmed as the new head of the Family he had to have something to offer the other families. That was going to be opening up the drug business. He, then, would supply all the heroin, which would put him in control."

"You mean that's why Vito called the infamous the Appalachian meeting?"

"Yeah"

"Dad, I will never believe some hick motorcycle traffic cop saw suspicious traffic and got that meeting busted. Do you believe that story?" My father looked at me and smiled knowingly.

"You're very smart Butch; it's too bad you didn't stay in school."

"It's too late for that now, Dad, so, tell me what happened."

"Right after Frank was shot, he called Cousin Carl, my mentor. He asked Carl to talk to Uncle Joe, (Carl's father and Charlie's brother) and ask him if he would go to see Charlie for him. After Carl spoke to Uncle Joe, he told Frank that he didn't feel Joe was up to the task."

"Why didn't Frank ask Carl to go?"

"Because Carl was with Gambino," (meaning a made man in the Gambino Family) "and Frank didn't want anyone to know about the meeting with Charlie. If Carl went, Gambino would know."

"So, how did it come to be you?"

"Carl knew I wanted to see Charlie for personal reasons, and I could handle the matter, but he didn't know how Frank would feel about sending me, since Frank didn't know me that well.

"Frank also wanted Charlie to know who was coming and if it was okay with him. So Carl set up a meeting between Frank and me at Carl's house. That's how it came to be me."

"Why are you so sure Vito wanted Frank alive? I mean, what you said makes sense, but how do you know Chin didn't just blow it?"

"Because it was Frank who told me. A couple of days after the shooting, Vito sent word to Frank that if he stepped aside, he would let him retire in peace. Frank had plenty of money, and he didn't want any part of a war or the drug business."

"Why would Frank believe Vito would let him live in peace?"

"He didn't, which was one of the reasons I was going to Italy,"

"Boy, this gets better all the time." My head was spinning with excitement.

"There is a lot more to this Butch, but no one is to know about this conversation while any of these people are alive, including me." It was the same conditions Charlie put on publishing his memoirs. I was a little surprised by his concern because it would never have occurred to me to repeat anything he told me. I was sure he knew that, or he wouldn't be telling me in the first place.

I suddenly realized he wasn't that drunk. Knowing my father's silent and secretive personality, I had to wonder why is he telling me all this.

"Dad, you know I would never tell anyone what you and I talk about. Where are you going with all this?"

"Okay, I'll tell you where I'm going. I've been identified with Charlie my entire life, and it's been a double edge sword. You get respect from the neighborhood and the people who know our world, but in the world of "citizens" (that's everyone but "us"), you'll be seen as someone shady. It will bring you the kind of attention and reputation you don't want or need."

I laughed, "I know exactly what you mean."

"I know you do. I also know how it has affected my life, and I can see how it has affected yours," he said apologetically. Meaning, the illegal bootleg perfume and robbing my cousin John's crap game.

"You're acting like you're responsible for things I do, and that's ridiculous."

"No, it's not. You're a father now with three sons. If they ever got into trouble, you'd feel the same way. It comes with the turf."

"Well, I don't feel you're responsible for the things I do."

"I know you don't, and it's nice you feel that way, but it doesn't change my responsibility, and it won't change yours. There's no free pass on this one, Butch, not for me or you. Do you understand?"

"Yes, I do." And I did.

"I love you. You know that don't you?" he said warmly.

"Sure I do. I always know that."

Then he tried to explain his long absences. "I wanted to be there for you, but your mother and I just didn't get along," he said sadly.

"I understand, Dad. I don't get along with her either," I laughed trying to lighten the load for him. The truth is he was there for me in many ways. He didn't always live at home, but he was still in the neighborhood. I always had access to him.

"Someday you may find yourself in a position where you could and should straighten out a few things about Charlie and this family. To do that you must know the real story behind a lot of the bullshit that's out there." I couldn't imagine any circumstance where I would be in a position to straighten out anything, but like many predictions my father made, here I am.

"Who would I be clearing things up for?"

"I don't know, Butch, but I made a big mistake when I gave you Charles for a middle name. That left you with Charlie's first, middle and last name. People who know Charlie's real name is Lucania and not Luciano are going to know who you are." He seemed really concerned.

"It hasn't been a problem," I assured him.

"No, not yet, but it will be."

"But, I'm not Charlie; are you telling me I'm guilty by birth?"

"Yes, that's exactly what I'm telling you." Unfortunately, he turned out to be right about that too.

"Then why did you do it?"

"Out of respect for Charlie. We didn't have much money in those days. Occasionally, Charlie would ask me to drive him to the track, and then he'd slip me a hundred bucks. That was a lot of money in 1929. I admired and looked up to him." My father was about seventeen years younger than Charlie and the only boy of seven children. That money helped a lot.

"Anyway, I just think it's important for you to know about Charlie, about the things he did and didn't do. It's our family, and I'm tired of reading bullshit stories by bullshit press people. There is a saying: 'Those who talk don't know and those who know don't talk.'"

I found out forty years later how true that was. One day, after my sons dragged me kicking and screaming into the twentieth century by buying me a computer, I typed my name into my computer. There, to my amazement, were hundreds of sites on my cousin Charlie. I was stunned; I kept silent for forty years while every wanna-be journalist made names and careers for themselves telling stories about Charlie based on things they knew absolutely nothing about.

I questioned my father some more. "Okay, but first tell me what happened in Italy. What did you talk about, was he glad to see you, where did you meet?" I had wanted to know about this for a long time, but I didn't know if he would ever tell me.

"Charlie was very glad to see me. I hadn't seen or talked to him in years. I brought him fifty grand from Frank and the lox and bagels he loved so much. He hugged me and tears were coming down his face.

"Kidding, I asked him, 'Is it me you're glad to see Charlie or the lox and bagels?' He laughed and hugged me again. We met at his apartment in Naples and had lunch. I had antipasta and wine. He had the lox and bagels. Then we got down to business."

My father had a great memory. In the gambling business for years, he would memorize hundreds of bets because he never wanted to be caught with betting slips.

My father continued, "Charlie, I have a few things to go over."

" 'Okay, Carmelo,' he agreed, 'What's first?' "

"Dad," I interrupted, "Charlie called you Carmelo? I never heard anyone call you that."

"Yeah, he knew me as Carmelo. Don't forget, this was a long time ago."

That's when I realized how Sicilian we were.

My father told the rest of the story:

"I told Charlie, Frank wants to retire."

" 'How is Frank doing, Carmelo?' he asked me."

"He's okay, but very concerned about Vito."

"Yeah, he should be." said Charlie

"Vito sent word to Frank he could retire peacefully. If he stepped aside now."

"Charlie laughed and said, 'Frank will be dead an hour after Vito takes over.'

"Frank knows that, Charlie. That's one of the reasons why I'm here. He wants to know how you want this handled. Frank would love to get rid of him but doesn't have the stomach for a war."

'I understand. It wouldn't do any good. Big John would only take his place and he'd kill Frank anyway. It's that fuckin' junk (heroin) business and that greedy prick, Vito.

'I should have killed that greedy little cocksucker in Cuba when he tried to talk me into retiring back then. Instead, I just gave him a fucking beating. I knew I would regret not killing that bastard. That junk business is going to tear apart our whole thing, everything we worked for all these years,' said Charlie."

"I said, Frank hasn't gotten back to Vito yet. He wanted to get your input first. In the meantime, Vito has put the word out that Frank has retired. Also Vito has called a meeting of all the bosses from around the country."

"Charlie said, 'That little prick always had more balls than brains.' Then he lit a cigarette and walked out onto the balcony of the apartment and back to the table. He did that for a while without saying anything.

"Then he says to me, 'Tell Frank, it's okay with me for him to retire. He's earned it. Tell him I want him to accept Vito's offer to retire and to make sure the Bosses around the country know it.'

"Then he started walking back and forth again and he says, 'Tell Frank I want that meeting to take place and I want it to be raided.'

"What?"

'I know what you're thinking, Carmelo, but the truth of the matter is that once Frank and me are out of the picture, the other families won't be able to turn down the money in that junk business.

'It will be the beginning of the end anyway. Mark my words, Carmelo, Vito and Big John are going to wind up in the can for the rest of their lives. They're going to die in the can. *(And they did)* This way, Frank and I will be off the government's hit list, out of the newspapers and Vito will inherit the pile of shit he's creating.'

"I said, but Charlie, what about the rest of the guys. They're all going to get bagged too?"

'For what? Having lunch. There's no law against that.'

My father paused.

I knew Charlie was right about that too. No one went to jail for attending that infamous Appalachian meeting. Big John got busted with them, but instead of going to trial like the others, he took his lawyer's advice to go on the lamb.

Also there were no conspiracy or organized crime laws on the books yet. Up to that time, J. Edgar Hoover denied there was any such thing as organized crime or the Mafia. I don't think Hoover saw victimless crimes, like gambling, prostitution, or drinking, as a danger to the public. He went after major crimes like bank robbery, arson, and extortion. All the laws on conspiracy and organized crime were instituted by Attorney General Bobby Kennedy in the sixties.

I said, "I knew that cop story was bullshit, but I never would've thought in a million years it came from Charlie."

My father said, "The irony is a lot of those guys stayed out of the drug business and out of jail as a result of being exposed like that, but Charlie had other reasons for doing what he did."

"What other reasons?"

"Charlie never gave up hope of getting back into the United States. America was his home. He hated Italy. The U.S. government knew Vito and Big John Ormento were in the heroin business. They also knew Charlie was Vito's boss, so no matter what Vito and Big John did it was always seen as the Luciano family. As long as they stayed in the heroin business, Charlie would never have a chance to come back to the States.

"Getting rid of Vito the way he did was very smart. He knew the bosses would blame Vito for exposing them. As a result, Vito lost face, his power, and any chance of taking over the national syndicate and expanding the heroin business."

I said, "What irony. Charlie has always been blamed for the heroin business in this country. Even after he was deported there were stories about him setting up heroin pipelines to the States, when nothing could've been further from the truth."

"Yeah, I know," my father replied. "It's just another bullshit story, but it's one of the reasons he hated Vito. More important to Charlie, he would no longer be seen as the head of the "Luciano family." Instead, it would become the "Genovese family" or as Charlie put it, 'Vito's pile of shit'."

"Jesus Christ, Charlie didn't really believe he had a chance to get back into the country, did he?' I asked

"Yes, he did. As far as he was concerned it was a political and public relations problem. He believed if the public knew what he really did for the country and enough time passed he'd be able to come back. He also believed we might have lost the war if he hadn't stepped in. I don't believe that, but it's what he thought."

"Did he tell you what he did for the U.S. military?"

"Yeah, that's all he wanted to talk about. He told me a lot of things I didn't know about, but it all made sense."

I said, "You have to tell me everything, but first finish telling me about your meeting with Charlie."

My father continued the story of their meeting: "Charlie asked me, 'What's next, Carmelo:'"

"I explained, 'It's about Frank's retirement. He has a chunk of cash and he wants your okay to approach Joe Kennedy to have him front some real estate for him.'

"Joe Kennedy! That Nazi loving prick. Did you know before we got into the war he supported that fuckin lunatic Jew?"

"What lunatic Jew?"

"Hitler, that's what lunatic Jew."

"Charlie, are telling me Hitler was a Jew?"

"That's right, I know for a fact he had Jewish blood in him, which tells you just how really twisted that fuckin' idiot was."

"Charlie, I knew that Kennedy was in the booze business with you and the boys, but why would Frank think Kennedy would front real estate for him?"

"Because, we were in the real estate business with Joe. You're going to love this story, Carmelo. During the depression, City Hall couldn't afford to pay themselves salaries. Those big buildings on Wall Street that everyone was jumping out of, couldn't pay their taxes, so the city auctioned the buildings off for taxes. It was a steal.

"Anyway, I get a call from Joe at six o'clock one morning, which was about the time I usually got to bed. He knew I never got up before two in the afternoon, so I thought the sky was falling.

"He says to me, 'Charlie, how'd you like to buy Wall Street?'

"I laughed and said, 'Joe, don't you think it's a little early to be in a bag?' To make a long story short, me, Meyer (Lansky), Benny (Segal), Frank (Costello), and Joe chipped in two million bucks and bought some of Wall Street; not all of it of course, but enough to legitimize that donkey (*as the Irish were called in those days*) and keep City Hall off the soup lines."

I said, "I had no idea."

"Yeah, no one did."

"What should I tell Frank?"

"Tell him it's OK with me, but unless Joe asks, keep my name out of it."

"Okay, I'll tell him."

"What else, Carmelo?"

"Frank wanted to know if Tommy "Ryan" (Eboli) could bring your cut from
now on?"

"Yeah, that's okay, what else?"

"That's it for the Frank and Vito business. I do have some things I need some help with, Charlie, but after hearing all this, I don't think there is much you can do to help me."

"What is it, Carmelo?"

"Well, I don't know whether you know this or not, but I've been working for Big John in the number office."

"Yeah, I know, Bartolla (*Charlie's other brother*) mentioned that to me the last time he was here. Are you still working for him?"

"No, that's what I wanted to talk to you about. I was gambling Charlie, and every once in a while, I would tap the bank for a few grand to cover some bets. I always repaid the bank, but one time John found out the bank was short four grand before I could replace it. He asked me about it, and I told him the truth. He fired me and never talked to me about it again."

"That was a mistake, Carmelo. Why didn't you just ask John to loan you the money?"

"Looking back, I should have, but as you know, John is married to my wife's first cousin, Millie. I was afraid if John told Millie, she might say something to my wife. I didn't want my wife to know I was gambling again. We broke up twice over it."

"I see. When did this happen?"

"About two years ago."

"How much was John paying you?"

"Two hundred bucks a week."

"That's all! What was the take from the business?"

"It varied, somewhere between forty and sixty grand a week."

"Gross?"

"No, net," Charlie hit the ceiling.

"Those dirty thieving, greedy, cock suckers (meaning Vito and Big John). They've been telling Frank that the take had fallen to 40 to 60k a month and passing up the remaining 20k to Frank, who took his third and past the rest to me. No wonder my take started getting so thin a couple of years ago.

"First of all, Carmelo, Big John wouldn't get rid of you over a stinking four grand. He and Vito wanted to start skimming and didn't want to take a chance I might find out from you."

"But, I haven't talked to you since you left the country."

"Yeah, but how would they know that? You could have told my brother Joe. They couldn't take that chance."

"I was hoping you would give me a letter, telling John to put me back to work, but if you're right it won't do any good."

"You're right, but I'm giving you that letter anyway."

"Why?"

"Because we have to assume he knows you're here. I don't want him wondering why. It could be dangerous for you. How often do you see or talk to John since you stopped working for him?"

"I see him at weddings, birthdays, and funerals, otherwise never."

"Okay, if John contacts you when you get back, that means he knows you were here. The letter will give you some cover."

When my father paused, I told him, "I remember you came back with that letter. Did John ever contact you?"

"Yeah, two days after I got back."

"Boy, he was right on it, wasn't he?" I said.

"Charlie had a gift for putting himself in anybody's shoes and know what they were thinking. Like I said, he was very smart."

"What happened when you talked with Big John, and what did the letter say?" I asked.

"The letter was very short. It just said, 'I want you to give my cousin a living,' and it was signed Charlie." My father explained what happened when he met with Big John. "When I got to the house, Millie had coffee ready for us. John and I sat outside by the pool. Remember, aside from family gatherings, I never saw John. When I did, it was like nothing ever happened.

"After some small talk, John said, 'I hear you went to Italy and saw Charlie, how is he?'

"I told him Charlie was fine.

"Then he asked, 'Was there any particular reason for making the Trip?' "

Instead of answering him, I handed him the letter.

He read the letter and says, 'Is this the only reason for the trip?' I could tell he was worried. I'm sure one of the things he was worried about was the money he and Vito were skimming.

"I told him, 'No, I hadn't seen my family in years, and I had never been to my mother and father's hometown in Sicily, and I wanted to do that.'

"John didn't dig any further. He knew I wouldn't tell him anything anyway. He just wanted to see my reaction to the questions."

I asked my father, "Then what happened?"

He told me, "John became warm and friendly. He looked at the letter again, then said, 'Okay, give me a week and I'll put something together for you.' "

I asked my father, "Did he do something for you?"

"Yeah, I made three deliveries for him, at $1,500 each, and he never paid me."

"You're shittin' me! That fuckin' asshole."

"Yeah that's a good way of putting it. You know, Butch, when I heard you took his crap game down and why, I was glad. It really infuriated him that you had the balls to fuck with him like that. Even worse, you got away with it."

"Well, I almost got away with it," I said.

"From John's point of view, you guys should've never gotten out of that basement."

"Oh, I see," I said and went on, "Tell me what Charlie said about the war. I know he helped the early war efforts by locating submarines off the New York coast, but I doubt we would have lost the war over that."

"In fact, there was a story going around that it was Charlie who had that ship at the New York docks sabotaged, so the government would run to him for help."

This story also appeared in Charlie's own memoirs, which were published ten years after his death. It confirms my belief the ghostwriter lied about that story, here's why:

My father explained, "See, that's the kind of bullshit I'm talking about. First of all, Charlie was a true patriot. He loved this country, and he'd never do anything like that. Think about it Butch, why would Charlie risk being implicated in sabotage or worse, treason, on a million to one shot the government was going to run to him for help, would you?

"That story doesn't even make sense. The government didn't go to him because that ship went down or for locating submarines off the coast."

I asked, "Did he tell you how he got involved and what he did?"

My father said, "The whole time I was there that's all he wanted to talk about. After we got finished with our business, we went for a walk and ended up at the California Cafe, his hang out in Naples. We sat outside and had coffee.

"After the waiter left he says to me out of nowhere, 'What kind of a fuckin' world is this, Carmelo? That fuckin' Kennedy made his money the same way I did. I stopped the violence in New York, I keep the lid on drugs in the country, and when the war breaks out, I make sure we win in Europe. Kennedy, who supported that lunatic Hitler before we got into the war, becomes a rich respectable aristocrat, and I become public enemy number one and get thrown out of the country I saved."

"It was a raw deal, Charlie, I know…."

"You don't know how raw, Carmelo. You remember that story about me helping the Navy locate those German submarines off the coast?"

"Yeah, I remember that,"

"It never happened."

"It never happened?"

"No, I didn't help the Navy locate those subs. The Navy already knew about those subs. The first time they came to me, this nice young Navy officer tells me they have spotted German submarines off the coast of Long Island, and they could use my help.

"I laugh at the kid and ask him what they want me to do about it. 'If you know where they are just blow them out of the water. Are you guys short on guns or something?' I said kibitzing with him."

"The kid had a sense of humor and started laughing. I really liked that about him. Then he says to me, real straight like. 'Yes, sir, we know we have that option, but that's not our problem. It's what they are doing here that interest us.'

"I asked him what they were doing here."

"Well, that's what we want to find out. We believe those subs are off loading well-trained American speaking German and Italian spies somewhere off Long Island. We know your organization offloaded imported liquor off the coast of Long Island and then brought it into the New York harbor.

"We figured you would know all the best spots to offload and that the German's would find the same ones. We were hoping you could help us with that information.'

"Is that all?" I asked him.

"He said, 'No sir, if we are right, we would like your people to watch those spots for us.'

" 'Why my people?' I asked."

"He said, 'Because your people already know where the best spots are, including any peculiarities about the terrain. It would take us time to learn all that and time is something we don't have a lot of.'

'I gotcha, you're right. What do you want us to do exactly?' I asked."

My father told me, "Charlie was a great planner, Butch, and understood the importance of detail. The Navy couldn't have found a better man to work with."

"The kid answered, 'If we are right, we want your people to watch them twenty-four hours a day. See where they go, who they contact and any other information you can gather.'

"And that's what I we did. We tracked thirteen of those spies for months. We gave the military names, addresses, and even pictures when we could get them. That's the first job I did for them, Carmelo."

I asked "What kind of deal did Charlie make with government?"

"Charlie wanted a full pardon after the war. Dewey wouldn't go for it. He wanted Charlie deported. Charlie made the deal believing it was politics, and he could deal with that after he got out of jail.

Later, when Dewey was making a run to be President, he made another deal with Charlie. If Charlie would deliver the New York delegates in his election, he promised not to block his efforts to return, but then he did.

"No wonder he was so pissed off," I said.

"Yeah, Charlie knew everything about how the war was going. He followed it like he followed the horses. He wanted it over as fast as possible.

"The next thing he talked about was our plan to invade Sicily, and the problems we were having getting Rommel out of North Africa. It's the Rommel story that the government kept and still keeps secret."

"Why?"

"Who knows all the reasons? I think they didn't want to admit that, without Charlie, it might take too long to defeat Rommel in North Africa."

"What was so important about North Africa?"

"We needed North Africa to stage the invasion of Sicily, and we needed Sicily to stage the invasion of Italy and the rest of Europe. And Dewey was concerned that, if the public knew what Charlie did, it would make Charlie a, hero and the public wouldn't stand for a hero being treated that way. Politically, it would hurt Dewey's chance to be President.

"Wow, this is heavy stuff, what the fuck did Charlie do?"

"He cut off Rommel's fuel supply?"

"You're shittin' me, how the fuck did he do that?"

"It's a great story. Here's what he told me."

'The next time the Navy came to me, the kid brings his boss with him, a sweetheart of a guy. Respectful, smart, good manners, and sharp. I was impressed.

"The first words out of his mouth, after the kid introduced him was, "Sir, my name is Steve. May I call you Charlie?"

"Yeah, sure, Steve."

"Thank you. Charlie, what I'm about to discuss with you is Top Secret. There are only five people in the world who know what I'm about to tell you. You will be the sixth."

"I know how to keep a secret, Steve."

"He laughed and says, "I know you do, Charlie. I wouldn't presume to give you, of all people, advice on the importance of secrecy.' "We both start Laughing."

"But the nature of this mission is going to involve a lot of your friends, both here and in Italy."

"I understand, Steve. Let me assure you my guys will do anything for this country. They know what being a soldier is about. You'll be proud of them. I made a deal to do everything I can to win this war. For that, I will win my freedom."

"Then I say to him, 'Can you keep a secret, Steve?' He nods his head yes, and I tell him, 'I would have done this for nothing.' We both start laughing. He starts shaking my hand and patting me on the shoulder. Then, with tears in his eyes, he says to me, 'Charlie that's what I hoped, but I never expected you to say it, and I know you mean it. It's too bad I have to keep that a secret.' We became close friends during the time we worked together."

"Charlie, we have two objectives: beat Rommel in North Africa and the successful invasion of Sicily."

"Is that all, Steve?"

He starts laughing and says. "Yep, that's all Charlie."

"I hear we're getting our ass kicked in North Africa. What's wrong over there?"

"Everything Charlie, Rommel's tanks have better armor, better fire power and more experienced men. The only chance we have of defeating him quickly is to interrupt his supply lines."

"You mean food, fuel, ammunition, spare parts, things like that?"

"Yes exactly, but if we could cut his fuel supply first, we wouldn't have to worry about the rest."

"I told Steve, 'I understand. Now what can I do for you in Sicily?'"

"He said, 'we need coordinates. The Germans and Italians are guarding the shores around the island. They can't be everywhere, but where are they exactly? Where are their ground troops stationed? How many troops are in Sicily? Where are the fuel and ammunition dumps? It will take an awful lot of co-operation and coordinated manpower to pull this off, Charlie. Do you think you can do it?'"

"Yeah, I think I can do it."

"Charlie, I must ask you, why do you think the Italians would help us? After all, we are at war with Italy. Even if they agreed to help, why should we trust them? You understand our concerns?"

"Yeah I do, I would ask the same questions, if I was you. The answer is we're not dealing with the Italians in Italy. We're dealing with the Sicilians in Sicily. In the eyes of Sicilians, Italy is another country. Sicilians, Sicilians can't even speak Italian."

"Are you serious, Charlie? We had no idea."

"Most people don't, Steve. The point is, Sicilian's don't give a fuck about Italy or that degenerate cocksucker, Mussolini. The Sicilian's want Mussolini dead more than you do."

"Washington is going to want to know why, Charlie?"

"Tell Washington, Mussolini declared war on the Sicilian clans because they were a threat to his power, and he is a threat to theirs. He's been sending death squads into the villages and executing anyone he thinks is a member of the Mafia."

"The kid stood there speechless for a minute, looking straight into my eyes. His eyes got watery and he says, with so much emotion, I thought I was going to cry, 'God is watching over our country, Charlie.' "

"So I say, kidding him, 'So am I, Steve.' "

"He smiled and said real soldier-like, 'Indeed Sir, so you are.' "

"Charlie said, "I won't ever forget that day, Carmelo. That kid was so proud of me; he made me feel proud of myself. I wish my father were there to see it.' "

"So, don't worry Steve, the Sicilians will be completely reliable. Even if they hated us, and they don't, I know how they think, 'The enemy of my enemy is my friend.' The last thing we have to worry about is their reliability."

"Okay, Charlie, I'll pass that on to Washington. I'm sure they will be very happy to hear this. When will we hear from you?"

"I'll send word to you through my attorney when I have things lined up."

When my father stopped the story for a moment, I asked, "Okay, Dad, now how was Charlie able to cut Rommel's fuel?"

He explained, "War is big business, Butch. The Mafia controlled the black market in Sicily, which is one of the reasons why Mussolini wanted to get rid of them.

"You're going to love this: in 1937 Vito Genovese was indicted for murder in New York, instead of standing trial, he goes to Italy as a fugitive at the same time Charlie goes to jail. Vito was not from Sicily. He was from Italy.

"According to Charlie, he went to Italy with three million bucks and got heavily involved in the black market. This was four years before America got into the war, don't forget. By the time we got into the war, Vito was well established with the aristocratic Italian families and the Vatican, who were all making fortunes, supplying Mussolini's and Hitler's war machine."

"Why doesn't that surprise me?" I said sarcastically.

"They were Mussolini's supporters, of course, so they cut Mussolini in for a sizable chunk of the dough. Vito socialized with the royal families and attended dinner parties for Mussolini."

I said, "Cousin Carl told me that Charlie wanted Vito to kill Hitler, so the war would end quickly. Is that true?"

My father laughed and said, "Yeah, it's true, but Vito didn't have access to Hitler."

"So, Vito was the connection to the supply line?"

"Yeah, Vito had the access, the way Charlie explained it. The Italian financiers bought diesel and sold it to the Germans and Italians at huge profits. They took delivery in Sicily and then shipped it to Rommel in North Africa.

"Vito sent all the information on the shipments to his contacts in Sicily: the size, arrival dates, and locations. Vito sent word to the Sicilian Mafia that Charlie Lucky wants the shipments blown up or stolen and that they would be paid the black-market value of the fuel, which was a lot more than market value."

I said, "I'll bet Vito took a big whack of that dough."

"I said the same thing to Charlie, but Charlie said 'No, I have to give Vito that. He was on board like the rest of us.' "

"What about the invasion of Sicily itself, how did he handle that?"

"That was a different thing, a lot more complicated and dangerous. The allies needed accurate and continuously updated information. The boys in Sicily needed a lot of manpower and the ability to communicate around the island and then to us.

"The military got Charlie moved to a prison much closer to New York and Washington. Charlie was able to have more visitors, and the military had better access to him. For this part of the mission, Charlie needed to talk to Carlo Gambino who still had relatives in Sicily. Carlo assigned Tommy Eboli as his point man. Charlie arranged a secret meeting with Steve, Tommy Eboli and himself."

"Jesus, Dad! Where the hell do you hold a "secret" meeting in a prison?"

"In the Warden's office."

"Of course. How stupid of me. Did Charlie tell you about that meeting?" I asked, enjoying this incredible journey into American history from the inside.

"Yes, he did. It was the only time I ever asked him for any details. Up until then, I just let him tell me anything he wanted, but this was something I wanted to know about. So I asked him, 'Charlie, what did it take to put that together?' "

"This is what he told me:"

"It took a lot. Steve laid out where in Sicily he needed guys placed. Carlo's man Tommy had to recruit 150 men from different parts of Sicily, which meant different families. Many of those families had vendettas going on among them for years.

"I asked Tommy how much it would take to get those guys to call a truce long enough to help us.

"He said, 'I spoke to my cousin a few weeks ago, Charlie. I told him what we were doing. I asked him to meet with the different factions and tell them that Charlie Lucania needed their help and that Charlie wanted to know what he and his friends in the American government could do for them after the war. Then I asked them how much money they wanted to do this for us.' "

"The message I got back was that they did, indeed, money because people were starving in Sicily. But more important than money, they wanted assurances that when the war was over all of their relatives would be released from the prisons where Mussolini had put them for political reasons. They also wanted all of their relatives' criminal records to be destroyed and the leaders in their provinces given official positions like mayors and magistrates. They also said they would do whatever Charlie needed them to do."

"I'm proud to say, Carmelo, they didn't think it would be right to accept money from friends who were risking their lives to help us get rid of our enemies."

"When Steve heard they would do it for me, he looked at me like I was God. He was beyond impressed and to tell you the truth, Carmelo, so was I. I had no idea I carried that kind of weight over there.

"So, I say to Steve, 'Well, Steve, can you deliver?' "

"He looked at Tommy and says, 'Tommy, please tell our new friends in Sicily they have a deal.' "

"So, I say to Steve, 'Steve, do you have the authority to make that deal?' "

"No, Charlie, but I'll have it an hour after I leave here, and I'll call Tommy to confirm it. Is that okay with you, Tommy?"

"Okay, Steve, I'll wait to hear from you."

"One more thing, Charlie. They are going to need communication equipment: two-way radios, transmitters, batteries, antennas, whatever it's going to take to pull this off."

"Steve, if you give Tommy a list of what they will need to do the job, I'll have my guy, Vito, in Italy get it down to them in Sicily."

"Vito sent the equipment to Tommy's point man who was coordinating the mission. I heard that guy became the mayor of his town. When our guys drove through the towns after they secured Sicily, the people came out waving flags with the letter L for Lucky on them, so the Americans would know who had helped them."

"Can you believe that, Carmelo? There was even a move by those crazy Sicilians to make Sicily part of the U.S."

"I remember that, Charlie, but not many people knew about it."

"Yeah, I know. It was a crazy idea."

"Jesus Dad that's an incredible story. Why did Dewey agree to let Charlie out in the first place?" I asked.

"Dewey was appointed Special Prosecutor for a grand jury investigation. He had framed Charlie by paying the hookers to lie and testify against him and then sent them out of the country.

"The women ran out money a year or so later and came back to New York. Charlie found out they were back in town and broke. He sent his attorney and Meyer Lansky see them.

"They paid the girls to recant their testimony under oath and tell the truth about Dewey's case against Charlie. Charlie filed an appeal based on the new testimony, but Dewey had political control of the courts, so the court refused to hear the case.

"But Dewey also knew he couldn't keep the case out of court forever, and if it became public that he had tampered with the witnesses, his political career was over.

"His plan was to run for Governor and then for President. He had to make a deal with Charlie sooner or later. So you see, it turns out that public enemy number one was a real hero and not a drug supplier to the U.S. The government already knew that. They were just covering their asses like they always do."

"Dad what happen to Vito Genovese?"

"Vito was brought back to New York to stand trial on the murder case. At the same time Charlie was deported to Italy. Vito beat the case because the only witness had been killed."

My father's explanation was a real lesson on how the criminal class works and specifically the "justice system." I was more restless than ever after that conversation. I didn't want to spend my life as a "Citizen" in no man's land doing nothing and affecting nothing.

THE END

For More News About Salvatore Lucania,
Signup For Our Newsletter:

http://wbp.bz/newsletter

Word-of-mouth is critical to an author's long-term success. If you appreciated this book please leave a review on the Amazon sales page:

http://wbp.bz/tgca

INTRODUCTION

My name is Joseph Silvestri. My mother called me Joseph, but to most everybody else I was Joe or Joey. I was born in Astoria, Queens, on May 1, 1932, and had five brothers and two sisters. When I was six, we moved to Jackson Heights, also in Queens. We were about the only Italian family there at the time. I'd say I had a normal childhood and was an average or above student.

If I had to name my biggest fault as a kid and young adult, I'd say it was my penchant for using my fists. I was quick to fight and was pretty good at it. I wasn't particularly big, but I packed a wallop that broke some jaws and noses over the years. That talent—if that's the right word—came in handy on some occasions and caused problems other times.

After an abbreviated stint in the US Air Force in 1949, I spent several years working as a bartender or bouncer at various clubs in New York City, including three years at the world-famous Copacabana. I also worked some of the biggest illegal blackjack and poker games in the city. In that capacity, I met and became friends with many of the greats in the entertainment industry, as well as famous sports figures. I had contact with a number of people from the other side of the law too—organized crime. In this book I'll refer to them as "very important people" or "VIPs."

The stories I'll share with you are all true, and in most cases, this may very well be the first time you've heard of them. In those you may have heard of before, such as the 1957 brawl at the Copa involving several New York Yankees players, I'll provide inside details from my position as an eyewitness and participant.

You may find some of my accounts to be serious, humorous, or simply informative. My hope is you will find them all entertaining.

1 : Fisticuffs

One of my early memories is when I graduated from grade school to high school. I was excited because I was in the chorus and we were going to sing on stage during the ceremony. I wasn't much of a cut-up, but I had two friends who were. Before we went on stage, the three of us were talking. Our music teacher told us to quiet down or we'd be excluded from singing. I became very quiet, but not my buddies.

The teacher said to me, "You're out of the exercise."

"Why? I didn't do anything."

"Okay, tell me who did."

I wouldn't give up my friends, and when the chorus was called on stage, I had to stay in my seat. *I was crushed.*

My mother and aunt were in the audience. When the diplomas were handed out and my name was called, they saw me walk up from the student section all by myself and join my classmates. On the way home, my mother asked me about it. I said, "Mama, I got a very special award and they wanted me to walk up there by myself, so I'd get full recognition."

She accepted that explanation and was proud of me.

I went on to Newtown High School in Elmhurst, Queens, where I met the girl who would become my wife a few years later. But my first day there started out with a problem. A kid I didn't know came up to me and said, "Are you Joe Silvestri?"

"Yeah, I am."

"When your older brother went to school here, he beat up my brother. Now I'm gonna kick your ass."

We went to an empty lot across the street from the school to duke it out. There was a big crowd of students around and most of them were rooting for me. I gave that kid a real whipping.

Teaching a bully a lesson was one thing, but I had trouble controlling when and on whom I used my fists. It was an issue that stayed with me most of my life.

When I turned seventeen in 1949, I quit school and joined the air force. It had just separated from the army and become its own branch. That was one of the biggest blunders I ever made in my life. I didn't know what real racial prejudice was until then.

I went for basic training in Texas, and then on to an assignment in Biloxi, Mississippi. My first problem in Biloxi came when I loaned a black kid in my outfit a civilian sweater I had. He told somebody where he got the sweater and about six guys converged on me in the barracks. They kept saying, "Where is that nigger lover?" They beat the hell out of me with their hands and feet. I sustained some injuries and still have stomach issues after all these years. Following that incident, I became rebellious—the air force wasn't for me and I wanted out.

One day when I was assigned to the company headquarters (HQ), the first sergeant gave me a letter to deliver to another HQ. On my way, I stopped by the field where the football team was practicing and didn't get the letter delivered until about an hour later. When I got back, my first sergeant was pissed off. "Where in the fuck have you been?"

"I got lost. I'd never been there before and couldn't find the right building."

"You lying guinea bastard!"

That was it. I hit him in the face so hard that his eyeglasses became embedded in the bridge of his nose. A bunch of guys grabbed me and took me to my barracks, and then to the stockade. I asked to see a priest and explained the situation to him. He was sympathetic and when I went to my court martial, I was given a general discharge under honorable conditions. I was out of the air force!

They gave me a ride into Biloxi in a Jeep. I was in the back with two MPs, and the first sergeant I'd hit was in the front. He turned to me and said, "If you ever come back on this base, I'll kill you!"

I said, "And if you ever come into town, *I'll* kill *you*."

We never saw each other again.

* * *

I liked Biloxi and stayed there for a while. I got involved with a woman several years older than me named Blossom. She taught me a lot about many things, including sex.

Next, I got a job at the Ballerina Club, which was no small thing being only seventeen. It was kind of like hitting the lottery would be today. What I didn't know at the time was that Blossom was related to the blackjack dealer there—a guy named Murphy. He'd taken a liking to me and she put in a good word for me, so he took me on.

After I was hired, Murphy started training me to deal blackjack. The first thing he did was take the ring off his pinky finger and hand it to me. "If you're going to deal blackjack, you can't have a naked hand. Wearing a ring will make you look more professional," he said. Murphy taught me a lot and he did it in a hurry. Before long, I was ready to go on my own. I broke in on quiet nights and afternoons.

One afternoon when it was really slow, I was playing solitaire when I heard a voice say, "Hey there, Joe Silvestri." I looked up and there was a kid in an air force uniform I knew from Corona. His name was Anthony. I got up from the table and we shook hands and embraced. He said he couldn't wait to get home on leave and tell all the guys that he'd seen me dealing blackjack in a big club. That gave me a real good feeling.

In addition to gambling, the Ballerina had a restaurant and dance hall with live music. They had a quartet with drums, bass, piano, and sax. They were all black and boy, could they wail. Sometimes, when it wasn't busy, I'd listen to them and dance with some of the beautiful women that hung around the club.

One night I met two gorgeous southern belles who looked like twins but weren't even related. I hooked up with one of them and we started seeing each other. It was great for a while, but then Blossom found out. I never knew what a southern temper was like until she went off on me. It was a living hell for a few days, but we got over it and I didn't stray any more.

http://wbp.bz/afba

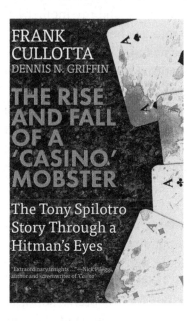
1

A Rocky Start

I'll never forget the first time I met Tony Spilotro. I was just a kid, twelve or thirteen, and I hated school. I was always in trouble with the teachers, and my mother had her hands full trying to get me into a school that could handle me. I loved to fight, too, which caused her even more grief.

Anyway, to hustle up some pocket money I started shining shoes up and down Grand Avenue. One day I noticed a kid about my age shining shoes on the opposite side of the street. He saw me at the same time, and we glared at each other for several seconds.

The other kid hollered to me, "What the fuck are you lookin' at?"

"I'm looking at you. What about it?"

We started walking toward each other, met in the middle of the street, and put down our shine boxes.

He said, "This is my fuckin' territory, and I don't want you on this street. Understand?"

He was short but looked pretty solid, and I figured he could probably take care of himself. That didn't bother me, though, because, like I said, I was a scrapper myself. "I don't see your name on any street signs, and I'm not leaving."

We shoved each other a little bit, but no punches were thrown. Then he said, "I'm coming back here tomorrow, and if I see you, we'll have to fight."

"Then that's what we'll have to do."

I went to that location the next day, but the other kid wasn't there. In fact, it was about a week later when we met again on the street. This time his attitude was different—he wasn't combative. He said, "I've been asking around about you. What's your last name?"

"Cullotta."

"Was your father Joe Cullotta?"

"Yeah. So what?"

"Your father and my father were friends. Your old man helped my old man out of a bad spot one time." He told me his name was Tony Spilotro and his father ran a well-known Italian restaurant on the east side called Patsy's.

I remembered hearing about the incident Tony was talking about. My father (who had been a gangster) liked Patsy and was a regular customer at the restaurant. Back then there was a gang called the Black Hand. It consisted of Sicilian and Italian gangsters who extorted money from their own kind, and my father hated them with a passion. Their method was to shake down business owners by demanding money in return for letting the business stay open. They were making Patsy pay dues every week. When my father heard about it, he and his crew hid in the back room of the restaurant until the Black Handers came in for their payoff. Then they burst out and killed them. After that Patsy wasn't bothered anymore.

From that day Tony and I became friends and started hanging around together. I found out he was a few months older than me, and we had some other things in common besides age and being short. We both hated school and would fight at the drop of a hat.

On weekends I'd see Tony at Riis Park, where he hung out. The first time I went there this guy, who was probably in his twenties, dressed in a shirt and tie and looking like a wiseguy, walked up to me and said, "I'll give you five dollars if you fight my brother."

"Who's your brother?"

He pointed to Tony. "Tony, he's right there."

I laughed. "No, I already had a beef with him. We're friends now."

"Oh, you must be Cullotta. Tony told me about you. I'm Vic Spilotro."

I went over with Tony. A little later Vic came over and said he'd found a kid for Tony to fight. Tony beat the hell out of the kid, and then Vic paid him the five bucks. Tony said, "Hey, what about me? I did all the work. Don't I get anything?"

Vic laughed. "Not you, you're not getting shit. I'm doing this to toughen you up, not so you can make money."

We messed around for a while longer, and then Tony said, "Come with me, and I'll show you where I live. It's right off Grand Avenue."

On the way to his house Tony told me he had five brothers. Vince was the oldest, followed by Vic and Patrick. And then came Tony and his two younger brothers, Johnny and Michael.

Tony showed me through the house. All the boys slept in one bedroom with three sets of bunk beds. While we were in the bedroom Tony's mother walked in. She was a very tiny lady, and I had the impression she wasn't very happy about me being there. She asked who I was, and I told her. If she knew about my father and the Black Hand thing, it didn't seem to make any difference. I still sensed she didn't like me. She said to Tony, "Hurry up and get out of here, the both of you."

After she left I said to Tony, "I don't think your mother likes me and probably doesn't want me around."

He laughed. "Don't worry about it. She doesn't like any of my friends. If she had her way I'd only hang around with altar boys."

As we walked out of the house Tony's mother and father were in the kitchen. Tony said something to them, but neither of them spoke to me. My name wasn't mentioned, and I don't think the father even looked at me as I passed by. Over time I got to know Tony's parents better. They were hard working, nice people. I never knew either of them to be involved in anything illegal.

After that initial meeting I didn't see much of Tony during the week because of school. But on weekends I'd catch up with him at Riis Park. I saw Vic quite a bit, too, at Riis or on the streets. I became convinced he was a gangster because of the way he dressed and that he always had a big wad of money with him. At the time I didn't really understand what it meant to be a bookie, but I'd see Vic getting slips of paper and money from people. I found out later that he was taking sports bets and his operation was backed by the Outfit. He used to run crap (dice) games, too, in the alleys behind the houses in the neighborhood. Although Tony and I were just kids, sometimes Vic let us in the games. Even then, it was obvious to me that Tony was in his element when he could bet on something.

Another guy I met hanging around with Tony was Joey Hansen. Next to me, he probably came to know Tony as well as anybody. He was jealous of my relationship with Tony, and we had a couple of fights over it. I mention him here because he played a role in some of the incidents I'll tell you about later.

Did I know then what the future held for Tony? No, I didn't. But looking back, it's my opinion that Vic Spilotro was the person most instrumental in Tony taking to the criminal life and becoming an Outfit guy. Tony idolized Vic and his lifestyle. Vic introduced Tony to a lot of his associates as he was growing up—more guys with nice clothes, women, and money. And what may have been even more important: power.

* * *

About a year after first meeting Tony we started spending more time together. The reason for that was we both got placed in the same facility—Montefiore School. It was a place that provided educational services for troublemakers—kids who couldn't get along anywhere else. I was sent there first, and Tony showed up about a week later. I don't think he was into criminal stuff then. But like me, he was a kid that most teachers couldn't control.

The student body of Montefiore was primarily black. (We called them "colored" at that time.) Tony and I were two of the half-dozen or so white kids in the place and were constantly in physical confrontations with the blacks. Another thing we didn't like was having to use public transportation to get to and from the school. We couldn't do much about the blacks, but I figured out how to take care of the other.

I'd already learned how to hotwire my mother's car. I started using that knowledge to steal cars from around my neighborhood. I drove the hot car to school and parked it a couple of blocks away. After school I'd drop Tony off at his father's restaurant, where he worked every day, and then I'd drive it back to my neighborhood. Having our own transportation was nice, but it didn't stop the fighting inside the school.

One day when I came out of wood shop I found Tony in the hallway surrounded by four or five blacks. One of them wanted to fight him alone. "Come on, white boy," he said, "just you and me."

Tony agreed. The black kid picked him up and flung him over his head to the floor. Tony got up and put a beating on the guy. Then one of the other blacks said, "Let's kill that white motherfucker," and they started to attack.

I grabbed one of the long poles with a hook on the end that was used to open and close the upper windows. I swung it at the blacks and caught a couple of them in the head, and then Tony and I ran out of the building.

When Tony told Vic what was going on with the blacks, Vic said it was time we taught them a lesson by going after their leader—a kid named Jackson—and he'd go with us.

A few days later Tony and I didn't go to classes, and Vic drove us to the school in his four-door Mercury. We got there at lunch time when we knew all the students would be in the cafeteria. Vic brought along a .45-caliber pistol.

Vic crashed the car through the gates of the fenced-in playground and parked it near the cafeteria. Tony took the gun, and he and I ran inside and grabbed Jackson out of his seat at the lunch table. As we dragged him outside to the car he was scared to death, crying, and screaming. The other blacks were shocked. They followed us outside but didn't do anything. We drove away, pistol-whipped Jackson, and then drove back to the school and dumped him off.

Tony said he wasn't going to go back to school. His father didn't want him to and said he needed him at the restaurant. I did go in the next day, and the juvenile officers were waiting for me—they wanted to throw me in jail for the Jackson thing. They wrote me up and told me I couldn't come back to Montefiore. And then they contacted my mother and said we had to appear before a juvenile court judge.

Tony got charged, too, but his lawyer told the judge that Tony worked at his father's restaurant and any action against him would cause a hardship on his family. It worked, and Tony was released to work at the restaurant. I wasn't as lucky and got placed in a reformatory for six months.

After I got out, I got into more trouble and drew nine months in another reformatory called St. Charles. So I didn't see much of Tony again until we were seventeen or so. We would run into one another from time to time and catch up on the latest happenings in the neighborhood. By that time he was making quite a name for himself as a tough guy and a thief. People already respected and feared him.

Just before Tony turned eighteen we talked about the Outfit. I'll never forget his words to me at that time: "Frankie, I'm going to become one of them. Someday I'm going to be a boss, and I'll take you with me."

At that time I didn't want anyone to run my life for me. I said, "I'm not interested in becoming a gangster."

After that we kind of went our separate ways. I was content with being a thief and running my own crew. Tony was pursuing his ambitions of becoming a member of the Outfit, and I heard he was hooked up with some big time gangsters out of Cicero.

And then one day, about a year and a half later, Tony stopped in to see me. He said he and some other guys had a big job coming up with a lot of money to be made. They were short a man, and he offered me the spot. I immediately said I was in. It was then I learned we were going to take down a bank.

2

Some Early Scores and Capers

The bank job Tony invited me on was in a small town in Indiana, a couple of hours out of Chicago. There were a total of six guys on the job—me, Tony, my friend Dicky Gorman, two who I didn't know and don't remember their names, and Joey Lombardo, who later became known as "Joey the Clown."

Lombardo was an Outfit guy, and at the time he was known as a thief and juice collector (collecting payments for loan sharks). The word on the street was that he was considered a rising star. That's when I realized Tony was hooking up with the right people for the Outfit career he wanted and would probably go places with them.

We took a scouting trip to Indiana to plan the burglary. Tony, Dicky, and I were in one car, and Lombardo and the other two guys were in another. During the ride Tony explained the job. "You know, these old farmers around here don't trust the banks. They won't deposit their money in the bank, but they will stash it in there in a safety deposit box. A lot of 'em have cash in this particular bank, and the guys in the other car know exactly where the boxes are located. All we have to do is figure the best way to get in and out."

After looking the place over we decided to go through the basement of an empty adjoining building, then up through the floor of the bank, and right into the room containing the safety deposit boxes. We thought it would take us a couple of days to get inside and clean out the boxes so we planned the score for a weekend. It was a lot of time and work because each of the boxes was like an individual safe that had to be opened. But we ended up with over $700,000 in cash plus some jewelry. Tony was nineteen and I soon would be, and we were looking at a payday of around $120,000 each.

Joey Lombardo gave us a dose of reality, though. He said we'd have to pay a tribute to the Outfit. On a score of that size they'd want a lot. Even as young as I was, I knew that's the way business was done in Chicago. If you wanted to operate as an independent thief, you had to pay those guys a street tax if you did something big. As long as you took care of the Outfit like you were supposed to they'd leave you alone. But if you held back on them and got caught you'd get a beating or worse. None of us liked it, not even Tony, but we wanted to stay healthy and be able to do more robberies in the future. Five of us (including Lombardo) agreed and kicked in twenty percent off the top for Joey to give the Outfit. The other guy wouldn't go along and refused to pay his share. That pissed the Outfit bosses off, and they ended up demanding an additional forty percent from everybody. It was either that or they'd take it all. We all paid, including the guy who held out to begin with, and they gave him a good beating besides. It could have been worse, though, because sometimes guys died for less.

When all was said and done, Tony and I each ended up with around fifty grand in cash and got more later when we sold the jewelry we stole. Although it could have been better; it wasn't a bad score for kids our age.

* * *

On another occasion Tony asked me to help him settle a personal matter. He stopped by my house and said, "Frankie, there's a guy trying to give me a fuckin', and I want to teach him a lesson. I figure you, me, and maybe one other guy ought to scoop this bastard up and give him a beating. What do you say?"

"Who is this guy? What did he do?"

"His name is Robin Dragon. He was supposed to arrange to have some legal work done for me. He told me the lawyers wanted three grand, but I found out they were only charging half that. This prick Dragon was planning to pocket the extra $1,500. We'll pick him up, take him to your garage, and work him over."

"Sure, I'll help you out. Who have you got in mind for the third guy?"

"Dicky Gorman, is that okay with you?"

"Let's do it."

Tony contacted Dragon and told him they needed to meet. Tony, Dicky, and I picked Dragon up. I was driving. Dragon got in the car without realizing what was coming. As soon as I pulled away Tony and Dicky went to work on him, tying him up and taping his mouth shut. Then they beat on him during the ride to my place and took him into the garage, where the beating continued.

Tony snarled at Dragon, "You think you're going to rob me, you rotten prick? Who do you think you're fuckin' with, you cocksucker?" He then hit Dragon so hard with his .38 that it bent the trigger guard. Dragon went into convulsions and soiled his pants. When the beating was over, Dragon got down on his knees and thanked Tony for not killing him.

We took him back to his neighborhood and dumped him down a sewer. The following day the newspapers reported that a passerby heard somebody hollering for help from the sewer. The police came and found Dragon all beat up. To his credit, he told them he'd been mugged by unknown assailants.

Tony was well on his way to earning a reputation as a fearsome enforcer—a guy capable of using extreme violence against anyone who crossed him. It was that reputation that brought him to the attention of the Outfit bosses, including

Paul "The Waiter" Ricca, and got him a position as an enforcer for an Outfit-connected bookie and loan shark. Tony was on his way up the Outfit's career ladder.

* * *

http://wbp.bz/mobstera

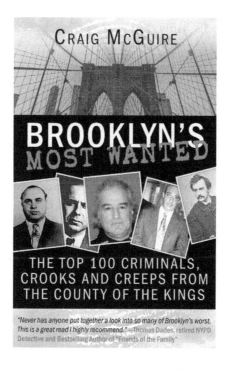

Take this guide tour through gangland that rips open the underbelly of Brooklyn, the broken land, to see what spills, from the South Brooklyn Boys to the Soviet thugs of Brighton Beach's Little Odessa.

Want to know what Billy the Kid, John Wilkes Booth and the Son of Sam all have in common?

Brooklyn.

Anthony "Gaspipe" Casso, Al Capone, Frankie Yale, Paul Vario, Roy DeMeo and so many more malicious malcontents and maniacs stalk these pages, as author Craig McGuire rank a rogues' gallery of the best of the worst from Brooklyn's crime-ridden past and present.

This includes more than a century of screaming crime blotter headlines, spotlighting epic cases, like The Brooklyn Godmother, The Sex Killer of Brooklyn, The Nurse Girl Murder, The Long Island Railroad Massacre, The Thrill Kills Gang, and many more. From "Son of Sam" to "Son of Sal," "Little Lepke" to "Big Paulie," "The Butcher of Brooklyn," "The Vampire of Brooklyn," "The Gang Who Couldn't Shoot Straight," even "The Man Who Murdered Brooklyn Baseball," they're all here.

Much more than Murder Incorporated, this book features kingpins and lone wolves alike, with a line-up featuring many of the multi-ethnic mobs mimicking the original La Cosa Nostra – the Russian Mafia, the Albanian Mafia, the Polish Mafia, the Greek Mafia – in fact, this book contains more Mafias than you can shake a bloody blackjack at. The author's proprietary Notorious Brooklyn Index analyzes criminal activity, socio-economic type, notoriety, relation to Brooklyn and more for a final score that's far from conjecture—though it will undoubtedly spark debate.

Welcome to Gangland, U.S.A. – A.K.A. the bloody, brutal killing grounds of Brooklyn, New York.

Watch your back!

http://wbp.bz/brooklynsmostwanteda

See even more at:
http://wbp.bz/tc

More True Crime You'll Love From WildBlue Press

A MURDER IN MY HOMETOWN by Rebecca Morris

Nearly 50 years after the murder of seventeen year old Dick Kitchel, Rebecca Morris returned to her hometown to write about how the murder changed a town, a school, and the lives of his friends.

wbp.bz/hometowna

BETRAYAL IN BLUE by Burl Barer & Frank C. Girardot Jr.

Adapted from Ken Eurell's shocking personal memoir, plus hundreds of hours of exclusive interviews with the major players, including former international drug lord, Adam Diaz, and Dori Eurell, revealing the truth behind what you won't see in the hit documentary THE SEVEN FIVE.

wbp.bz/biba

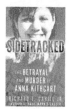

SIDETRACKED by Richard Cahill

A murder investigation is complicated by the entrance of the Reverend Al Sharpton who insists that a racist killer is responsible. Amid a growing media circus, investigators must overcome the outside forces that repeatedly sidetrack their best efforts.

wbp.bz/sidetrackeda

BETTER OFF DEAD by Michael Fleeman

A frustrated, unhappy wife. Her much younger, attentive lover. A husband who degrades and ignores her. The stage is set for a love-triangle murder that shatters family illusions and lays bare a quiet family community's secret world of sex, sin and swinging.

wbp.bz/boda